THE
SUDAN
HANDBOOK

THE
SUDAN
HANDBOOK

Edited by
JOHN RYLE
JUSTIN WILLIS
SULIMAN BALDO
& JOK MADUT JOK

JC JAMES CURREY

James Currey
www.jamescurrey.com
an imprint of
Boydell & Brewer Ltd
PO Box 9
Woodbridge
Suffolk
IP12 3DF
and of
Boydell & Brewer Inc.
668 Mt Hope Avenue
Rochester
NY 14620 USA
www.boydellandbrewer.com

The Rift Valley Institute
1 St Luke's Mews
London W11 1DF
United Kingdom
www.riftvalley.net

1 2 3 4 5 14 13 12 11 10

British Library Cataloguing in Publication Data
The Sudan handbook.
1. Sudan.
I. Ryle, John.
962.4-dc22

ISBN 978-1-84701-030-8 (James Currey paper)

Papers used by Boydell & Brewer are natural, recyclable products
made from wood grown in sustainable forests.

Typeset in 10/11pt Photina with Castellar display
by Kate Kirkwood
Printed and bound in the United States of America

Contents

1

Introduction: Many Sudans
JOHN RYLE & JUSTIN WILLIS

2

Land & Water
JUSTIN WILLIS, OMER EGEMI
& PHILIP WINTER

3

Early States on the Nile
ABDELRAHMAN ALI MOHAMMED
& DEREK WELSBY

4

Peoples & Cultures of Two Sudans
JOHN RYLE

5

Religious Practice & Belief
WENDY JAMES

List of Maps, Figures & Tables

Maps

Figures & Tables

Notes on Contributors

Abdelrahman Ali Mohamed is Director of the Sudan National Museum and co-editor of its Catalogue. He has twenty years experience conducting archaeological fieldwork in Sudan. He is author and co-author of numerous articles about Sudan's archaeology, cultural heritage and museums. He obtained his PhD in 2006 from the University of Lille III in France.

Abdel Salam Sidahmed is Associate Professor, Political Science Department, University of Windsor, Canada. He teaches international human rights, Islamic and Middle Eastern politics, and politics of the developing world. His research interests include contemporary Islamism, Sudanese affairs, and contemporary application of *sharia* laws in Muslim countries. Before joining the University of Windsor, he worked as a researcher and Middle East Programme Director at the International Secretariat of Amnesty International. His publications include: *Sudan* (2005), *Politics and Islam in Contemporary Sudan* (1997) and *Islamic Fundamentalism* (1996).

Ahmad Sikainga is a Professor in the Department of History and the Department of African and African American Studies at Ohio State University, specializing in African economic social history with a focus on slavery, emancipation, labour, and urban history. His current research examines the role of slavery, ethnicity, and identity in the development of popular culture in contemporary Sudan. His publications include: *Slaves into Workers: Emancipation and Labor in Colonial Sudan* (1996), and *City of Steel and Fire: A Social History of Atbara, Sudan's Railway Town, 1906-1984* (2002).

Cherry Leonardi is a Lecturer in African History at Durham University. Her research and publications since 2001 have focused on the historical and contemporary role of chiefs in southern Sudan, and related issues of governance, state-society relations and political and judicial cultures. She was lead researcher and author of *Local Justice in Southern Sudan*, a report for the Rift Valley Institute and the US Institute of Peace (2010). She was Director of Studies of the RVI Sudan Course 2009-2010.

Daniel Large is Research Director of the Africa Asia Centre at the School of Oriental and African Studies in London. He was the founding Director of the Sudan Open Archive (www.sudanarchive.net), a digital library established by the Rift Valley Institute in 2005 to provide open access to contemporary and historical knowledge about Sudan, and Deputy Director of the RVI Sudan Course 2005-2010.

Derek Welsby has been directing archaeological excavations in central and northern Sudan since 1982. In 1991 he joined the Department of Egyptian Antiquities – now the Department of Ancient Egypt and Sudan – at the British Museum, with special responsibility for the Sudanese and Nubian collections. He is Honorary Secretary of the Sudan Archaeological Research Society and until recently was President of the International Society for Nubian Studies.

Douglas H. Johnson is a specialist in the history of North East Africa. He has served as Assistant Director for archives in the Southern Regional Government (1980-3), as a resource person in the negotiations over the Three Areas (Abyei, the Nuba Mountains and Blue Nile) during the IGAD-sponsored peace talks (2003), as a member of the Abyei Boundary Commission (2005), and as adviser to GoSS on the north-south boundary (2007). His works include *Nuer Prophets* (1994) and *The Root Causes of Sudan's Civil Wars* (2003; revised edition 2011). His *Where Boundaries Become Borders*, a report on the north-south borderlands and the international boundaries of southern Sudan, was published by the Rift Valley Institute in 2010.

Edward Thomas worked in Sudan and Egypt for twelve years as a teacher, human rights worker and researcher. He completed a PhD at Edinburgh University in 1998 on the history of the Republican movement, a Sufi-inspired group that called for the reform of Islamic law and civil rights for all Sudanese. He is the author of *Islam's Perfect Stranger: The Life of Mahmud Muhammad Taha* (2010). He was Director of the RVI Sudan Course 2009-2010.

Gérard Prunier is a former researcher at the Centre Nationale de la Recherche Scientifique (CNRS) and has worked on East African modern history and politics for the past 20 years. He is the author of *The Rwanda Crisis (1959–1994): History of a Genocide* (1995), *Darfur: The Ambiguous Genocide* (2005) and *Africa's World War: Congo, the Rwandan Genocide, and the Making of a Continental Catastrophe* (2009). He is currently an independent consultant on African affairs.

Jérôme Tubiana is a researcher specializing on Darfur and Chad. He has travelled extensively in both countries as a consultant for the US Agency for International Development (USAID), the AU–UN Joint Mediation Support Team (JMST) for the Darfur peace process, and various NGOs. He is the author of the book *Chroniques du Darfour* (Glénat, 2010), a number of reports on Darfur and Chad for the Small Arms Survey and 'Darfur: a war for land?' in Alex de Waal (ed.), *War in Darfur and the Search for Peace* (2007). He holds a PhD in African Studies from the Institut National des Langues et Civilisations Orientales, Paris.

John Ryle is Legrand Ramsey Professor of Anthropology at Bard College, New York, and Director of the Rift Valley Institute. He has worked in Sudan as an anthropologist, writer, film-maker and human rights researcher and is the author of *Warriors of the White Nile* (1984), a book about the Agar Dinka of Lakes State. In 2002 he was a member of the International Eminent Persons Group reporting on abduction and slavery in Sudan. He was Co-Director of the RVI Sudan Course in 2004 and Director 2005-2008.

Jok Madut Jok was born and raised in southern Sudan. He is Associate Professor of History at Loyola Marymount University, Los Angeles, and author of *War and Slavery in Sudan* (2001) and *Sudan: Race, Religion, and Violence* (2007). He is the Executive Director of the Marol Academy and founder of the Marol School in Warrap state (www.marolacademysudan.org). He was recently appointed Under-secretary in the Ministry of Culture and Heritage in the Government of Southern Sudan.

Justin Willis is Professor in History at the University of Durham and former Director of the British Institute in Eastern Africa in Nairobi. He specializes in the modern history of Sudan and eastern Africa. He is the author of *Mombasa, the Swahili and the Making of the Mijikenda* (1993), *Potent Brews: A Social History of Alcohol in East Africa* (2002) and a recent Rift Valley Institute report, *Elections in Sudan: Learning from Experience* (2009). He was Director of Studies of the RVI Sudan Course 2005-2008.

Laura James is a Middle East analyst specializing in the interface between political and economic issues. She has worked as an advisor on the Sudanese economy for the Assessment and Evaluation Commission monitoring the north-south peace agreement and for the UK Government Department for International Development and the Economist Intelligence Unit. She completed her PhD at the University of Oxford, where she was a College Lecturer, and is the author of *Nasser at War: Arab Images of the Enemy* (2006).

Munzoul Assal is Associate Professor of Social Anthropology and Director of Graduate Affairs Administration at the University of Khartoum. He is the Chairman of the Sudan Chapter of the Organization for Social Science Research in Eastern and Southern Africa (OSSREA). His research focuses on refugees, migration, IDPs and development, in Darfur, Khartoum, eastern Sudan and Norway. He is the author of *Beyond Labelling: Somalis and Sudanese in Norway and the Challenge of Homemaking* (2003), and co-editor of *Diasporas Within and Without Africa: Dynamism, Heterogeneity, Variation* (2006).

Musa Adam Abdul-Jalil is Associate Professor and Head of the Department of Sociology and Social Anthropology, University of Khartoum. His research and publications have focused on the areas of ethnicity, migration, customary law, customary land tenure and traditional mechanisms for conflict management. His recently published works include: 'Intertribal Conflicts in Darfur: Scarcity of Resources or Crises of Governance?' in *Environment and Conflict in Africa: Reflections from Darfur*, edited by Marcel Leroy (2009 and 'Power-Sharing and Ethnic Mobilization: The Role of Schoolteachers in Conflict Management in North Darfur', in *Darfur and the Crisis of Governance in Sudan*, edited by Salah M. Hassan and Carina E. Ray (2009).

Omer Egemi is an Assistant Professor in the Department of Geography at the University of Khartoum. He received his PhD from the University of Bergen, Norway, in 1995; his thesis examined the political ecology of subsistence crises among the Hadendowa pastoralists of the Rea Sea Hills, Sudan. He was Project Manager for a UNDP project to reduce natural resource-based conflict between pastoralists and farmers in North Darfur, North Kordofan and the Sobat Basin.

Peter Woodward is Professor Emeritus, University of Reading. He taught in Sudan with Voluntary Service Overseas before lecturing at the University of Khartoum. He is author of many books and articles on North East Africa, most recently *US Foreign Policy and the Horn of Africa* (2006), and was Editor of *African Affairs*, the Journal of the Royal African Society from 1986 to 1997.

Philip Winter OBE is the representative for Independent Diplomat in Juba, Southern Sudan. He was a Senior Advisor in MONUC 2008–2010 and Chief of Staff for the Facilitator of the Inter-Congolese Dialogue 2000–2003. He has worked as Programme Director for Save the Children UK in the DRC, Rwanda, Burundi and southern Sudan, and, earlier, as Manager of Juba Boatyard (1976-1981). He was Co-Director of the 2004 Rift Valley Institute Sudan Course and Director of the 2010 Great Lakes Course.

Suliman Baldo is Africa Director at the International Center for Transitional Justice. He has also worked for Human Rights Watch and the International Crisis Group. He was a Lecturer at the University of Khartoum, Field Director for Oxfam America (covering Sudan and the Horn of Africa), and was the founder and Director of Al-Fanar Center for Development Services in Khartoum.

Wendy James is Professor Emeritus of Social Anthropology at the University of Oxford. Her most recent books include *The Ceremonial Animal: A New Portrait of Anthropology* (2004) and *War and Survival in Sudan's Frontierlands: Voices From the Blue Nile* (2007). She has acted as a consultant for UNHCR and other humanitarian bodies, in southern Sudan and in Ethiopia, and is Vice-President of the British Institute in Eastern Africa.

Acknowledgements

The editors thank Christopher Kidner, Programme Director of the Rift Valley Institute, for his indispensable assistance in the preparation of this book. Thanks also to other RVI staff – Jin-ho Chung, Peggy Katende, Jacob Todd and Hisham Bilal – for their support to the editorial team, to Kate Kirkwood for the maps, to Rohan Bolton for the index, to Isabel Jarrett for translation from French, to Benson Kimeu, Mohaned Kaddam, Sara Pantuliano, Magdi el-Gizouli, Emily Walmsley, Joanna Oyediran, Gill Lusk and Douglas Johnson for advice and assistance, and to the expert reviewers for their comments on chapters in the book.

Every attempt has been made to apply a consistent spelling for Sudanese group and place names, but for personal names we have adopted the versions most commonly used by the persons concerned. Southern Sudan has been formally recognised as a political and administrative entity for two periods in Sudanese history, first as the Southern Region, following the Addis Ababa Agreement, between 1972 and 1983, then from 2005 to 2011 under the Comprehensive Peace Agreement. In this book, the initial 'S' in Southern Sudan has been capitalised when referring to those periods in the history of the south. Northern Sudan, being a geographical rather than a political unit, is spelled with a lower-case 'n'.

The Sudan Handbook has grown out of the seven-year development of the Rift Valley Institute Sudan Course, which is hosted annually at the Senior Secondary School in Rumbek, in southern Sudan. The editors thank the authorities in Lakes State and the staff of the School, the many scholars and specialists who have given their time to teach on the course, and the staff who have run it, in particular, Philip Winter, Co-Director of the first course in 2004, Edward Thomas (Director 2009-2010), Cherry Leonardi (Director of Studies 2009-2010) and Daniel Large (Deputy Director 2005 onwards). The preparation of the Handbook has been funded by generous grants from the Open Society Foundations and from Eric Reeves' Sudan Aid Fund, expedited by the Office of Program Development at Bard College, NY.

Glossary

ada	(Ar.) custom, tradition or habit
AACC	All Africa Council of Churches
Abbala	(Ar.) ethnic category: Arabic-speaking camel herders in northern and western Sudan, derived from *ibl*, camel
ABCE	Abyei Boundaries Commission
ajawid	(Ar.) mediators, traditionally elderly people versed in customary law and communal customs
Almanac	Pocket-sized reference book produced for officials of the Anglo-Egyptian government
amir (emir)	(Ar.) tribal leader in northern Sudan, between an omda or sheikh and a nazir
Ansar	(Ar.) supporters of the Mahdi and his descendants
Anyanya	(Madi) snake poison; a term used for the southern guerrillas in the first civil war in the south (Anyanya I); and for a pro-government militia in the second civil war (Anyanya II)
Ashiqqa	(Ar.) 'blood brothers'; the name of a political group of pro-Egyptian nationalists that emerged in the Graduates' Congress in the 1940s and was assimilated into the NUP in 1952
AU	African Union (formerly Organization of African Unity (OAU))
Baggara	Ar.) ethnic category: Arabic-speaking, cattle-keeping peoples of northern and western Sudan
baraka	(Ar.) blessing; religious charisma
Bilad al-Sudan	(Ar.) 'The land of the blacks', the name given by medieval Muslim geographers to the lands south of Egypt, from the Red Sea to the Atlantic
boma	administrative unit in Southern Sudan, subdivision of a payam
CAR	Central African Republic
cataract	a stretch of waterfalls and rapids in a river, one of six in Sudan and Upper Egypt

CNPC	China National Petroleum Corporation
co-domini	Britain and Egypt during period of Condominium
Condominium	period of joint British and Egyptian rule in Sudan, 1899–1956
county	administrative unit in Southern Sudan, subdivision of a state
CPA	Comprehensive Peace Agreement
daluka	(Ar.) type of drum (musical instrument), normally made of clay and covered with animal skin – and type of music
dar	(Ar.) homeland; territory
dhikr	(Ar.) 'Remembrance', Sufi practice of repeating or chanting name of God to become more conscious of divine presence
diyya	blood money; compensation paid to victim's heirs by those responsible for their death.
DPA	Darfur Peace Agreement
DRC	Democratic Republic of the Congo
DUP	Democratic Unionist Party (formerly National Unionist Party)
dura	(Ar.) sorghum
ECOS	European Coalition on Oil in Sudan
EF	Eastern Front
effendiya	(Turk.) educated bureaucrats; term used by British officials during the condominium for the new class of educated Sudanese civil servants
ESPA	Eastern Sudan Peace Agreement
feddan	(Ar.) a measurement of land, 1.039 acres, 0.420 hectares
feki	(Ar.) a holy man
Funj	Sultanate in region round Sennar 16th–19th century; ethnic category in Blue Nile and Ethiopia
GDP	Gross Domestic Product
gizzu	(Ar.) desert grazing that grows in parts of northwest Darfur and Chad several months after the tiny amount of seasonal rain that falls there
GNPOC	Greater Nile Petroleum Operating Company
GoNU	Government of National Unity (from 2005)
GoS	Government of Sudan (before 2005)
GoSS	Government of Southern Sudan (from 2005)
goz	(Ar.) stabilized sand dune
hakuma	(Ar.) government or state, from *hakm*, to rule or govern
hakura	estate of land in Darfur, historically administered on behalf of a Sultan
ICC	International Criminal Court
ICF	Islamic Charter Front
ICRC	International Committee of the Red Cross

idara ahliya	See Native Administration
IDP	Internally Displaced Person
IM	Islamic Movement
IGAD	Inter-Governmental Authority on Development (formerly IGADD, Inter-Governmental Authority on Drought and Desertification)
Imam	religious leader or official of a mosque
IMF	International Monetary Fund
Ingaz	(Ar.) name for NIF/NCP government that came to power in 1989, literally 'Salvation'
jallaba	(Ar.) merchant; used by southern Sudanese to refer to northern Sudanese generally
janjawid	(Ar.) bandits; more recently, pro-government militias in Darfur
JEM	Justice and Equality Movement
jihad	(Ar.) struggle in the cause of god; holy war
JIU	Joint Integrated Unit
judiyya	(Ar.) customary system of mediation in Darfur based on third-party mediators, known as *ajawid*
kashif	(Ar.) erotic dance performed by women at weddings and private gatherings
Kaytinga	Zaghawa of Fur origin
khalwa	(Ar.) Quranic school
Khatmiyya	(Ar.) principal Sufi sect of northern Sudan
khor	(Ar.) seasonal watercourse
LRA	Lord's Resistance Army
madeih	(Ar.) religious chanting or song that praises the Prophet Muhammad and/or local holy men
mahaliya	(Ar.) locality, an administrative unit
Mahdiyya	(Ar.) period of rule by the Mahdist state, 1885–1898
Majlis	(Ar.) council; legislative assembly
Maliki	(Ar.) one of four schools of Islamic law (others are Hanafi, Shafii and Hanbali)
marissa	a local beer made from various grains but mainly millet
al-mashru' al-hadari	(Ar.) 'civilisational scheme' or 'cultural authenticity scheme', the NIF/NCP project to reorient state and society along Islamist lines
MDTP	Multi-Donor Trust Fund
melik	(Ar.) see *shartay*
merkaz	(Ar.) the centre of a town, also refers to the offices of the district or county government
mujahidin	(Ar.) Muslim undertaking *jihad;* holy warrior

murahalin	(Ar.) cattle guards on Baggara seasonal routes; Baggara tribal militia
mutamad	Commissioner of a locality
Native Administration	System of government through local authorities, established under British administration
nabi	(Ar.) prophet
nazarah	Territorial unit in Native Administration
nazir	(Turk./Ar.) the highest rank in native administration
NCP	National Congress Party
NDA	National Democratic Alliance
NGO	Non-Governmental Organization
NIF	National Islamic Front (became NCP)
Nilotic	Language group including (in southern Sudan) Dinka, Nuer, Luo, Anuak, Pari, Acholi and Shilluk
NPC	National Petroleum Commission
NSCC	New Sudan Council of Churches
Nuba	ethnic and geographical term: peoples of the Nuba Hills of South Kordofan state
Nubia	area of northern Sudan where Nubian languages are spoken; used historically for undefined region south of First Cataract
NUP	Nationalist Unionist Party (now DUP)
OAU	Organization of African Unity (became AU)
OLS	Operation Lifeline Sudan
omda	(Ar.) a local headman, normally of a town, large village or group of villages
ONGC	Oil and Natural Gas Corporation
payam	administrative unit in Southern Sudan, sub-division of county
PCP	Popular Congress Party
PDF	Popular Defence Forces
PDOC	Petrodar Operating Company
Qadiriyya	Sufi order
RCC	Revolutionary Command Council (formed by Nimeiri and the Free Officers after their 1969 coup; and again by the NIF following the 1989 military coup)
SAF	Sudan Armed Forces
Salafiyya	Sunni Islamic movement that takes the pious ancestors, the 'Salaf' of the patristic period of early Islam, as exemplary models
Sammaniyya	Sufi order
SANU	Sudan African National Union (formerly the Sudan African Closed District National Union)
Sayyid	(Ar.) religious title, bespeaking respect

SCP	Sudan Communist Party
sharia	(Ar.) Islamic law, or the sources of Islamic law (literally 'the way', 'the path')
shartay	(Dagu or Kanuri language) hereditary chief responsible for a *dar*
sheikh	(Ar.) local tribal chief or head of a sufi order; can also refer to a religious teacher or other person of social importance
silif	Beja system of customary dispute resolution
SPLM/A	Sudan People's Liberation Movement/Army
SRRA	Sudan Relief and Rehabilitation Association (became SRRC)
SRRC	Sudan Relief and Rehabilitation Commission
Sudd	extensive swamp in southern Sudan formed by the White Nile (from the Arabic *sadd* – a blockage or barrier)
Sufi	Follower of Sufism, Islamic mysticism
Sunni	Branch of Islam that accepts the first four caliphs as the rightful successors to the Muslim prophet Muhammad; followers of this branch
Sunna	the sacred practice of the Muslim prophet Muhammad
tariqa	general term for a Sufi religious order
tembura	spirit cult similar to *zar*
Tijaniyya	Sufi order
TMC	Transitional Military Council (created by senior officers, and led by Siwar al-Dahab, after Nimeiri was overthrown in 1985)
Turkiyya	period of Turco-Egyptian rule in the Sudan, 1821–1885
Umma	(Ar.) political party associated with supporters of the Mahdi family
UNAMID	United Nations–African Union Mission in Darfur
UNESCO	United Nations Education, Scientific and Cultural Organization
UNHCR	Office for the UN High Commissioner for Refugees
UNICEF	United Nations Children's Emergency Fund
UNMIS	United Nations Mission in Sudan
USAID	United States Agency for International Development
Wahhabiyya	See *Salafiyya*
wali	friend of God or Sufi saint; Governor of a state
WCC	World Council of Churches
wilaya	(Ar.) federal state
WNPOC	White Nile Petroleum Operating Company
zar	(Ar.) women's spirit cult in the Nile Valley and elsewhere in north and eastern Africa, also the name given to these spirits
zariba	(Ar.) thorn enclosure to protect livestock; armed camp of slave and ivory traders in the nineteenth century
zikr	See *dhikr*

Map 1.1 Sudan

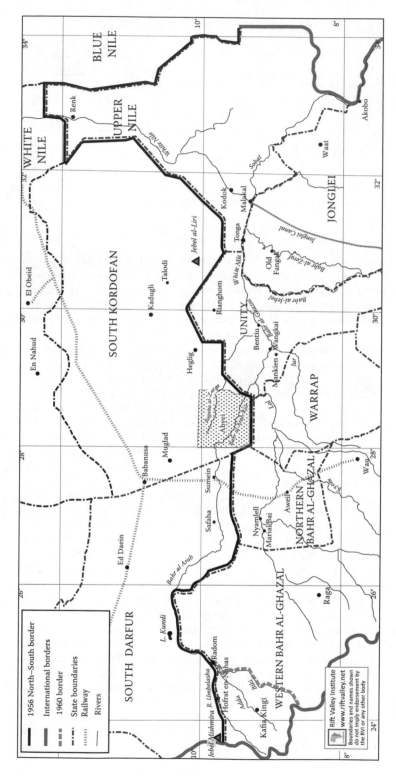

Map 1.2 North-South border area

1

Introduction
Many Sudans

JOHN RYLE
& JUSTIN WILLIS

The future of Sudan, in the second decade of the twenty-first century, is filled with uncertainty. As of 2011 it ceased to be a unified nation state; and the process of territorial separation of north from south could well be accompanied by a renewal of conflict. The Sudan that was created in the nineteenth century through invasion and imperial rule by Egypt and Britain no longer exists. This represents a radical change.

Whatever happens in coming years, however, events will continue to be shaped by the legacy of nineteenth-century state-building, by the conquests that preceded imperial rule and the political projects that followed it in the post-independence era. An understanding of events as they unfold today needs to be informed by a knowledge of what lies behind them: an understanding of the geographical, cultural and historical components of the country that has been created over the past two centuries, and the repeating patterns of state formation and decay which have shaped and been shaped by its political institutions and economic history.

In 2004, in order to focus attention on these issues of politics and development in Sudan, the Rift Valley Institute organized the first Sudan field course. The course has been held each year since, then, usually in Rumbek Senior Secondary School, in Lakes State, in Southern Sudan. It consists of a week of intensive teaching covering all aspects of the country and brings together a teaching staff – mostly professional academics, both Sudanese and non-Sudanese – and a student body composed of diplomats, humanitarian workers, development professionals and graduate students from Sudanese universities. *The Sudan Handbook* reflects the spirit of collective enquiry, diversity of views and sharing of expertise that has characterized the course from its early days.

The Course began at a moment of optimism. By early 2004 it had become clear that, despite many delays, the negotiations in Kenya between the Government of Sudan and the Sudan People's Liberation Movement, first at Machakos and then at Naivasha, would soon lead to a binding peace agreement. The accords which had already been signed offered a commitment from both sides to a comprehensive political transformation, one that would address fundamental issues of inequality, injustice and popular representation. There seemed a real possibility that the conditions of life for millions of people all over Sudan might be dramatically improved.

1

But it was also clear that the conflicts which had ravaged the country for decades could not simply be wished away by signatures on a peace agreement. These conflicts were the product of long-established patterns of authoritarianism on the part of the Sudanese state that would prove hard to break away from. They were themselves generated or exacerbated by earlier projects of national transformation that had been pursued with little or no regard for the interests and opinions of most of those affected by them. There was clearly a danger that an elite peace agreement between the warring parties – the Comprehensive Peace Agreement was finally signed in Naivasha the following year – might have the same outcome.

In 2004 it was already apparent that the oil industry would bring new wealth to Sudan. Oil served both to fuel the war and to create a potential peace dividend, a factor that helped bring the belligerents to the negotiating table. Even before the peace agreement the violent interventions in the oil areas that occurred during the war were coming to an end. But it seemed that the wartime sufferings of the Sudanese might be about to be replaced by new problems of peace.

The years following the CPA were to see sudden unplanned influxes of capital, a huge increase in the presence of both oil workers and aid workers, grand development projects, most of them undertaken in haste, with little local consultation and no sense of historical context. These projects seemed likely, at the local level, to exacerbate existing conflicts or create new ones. What began to manifest itself was the latest variant of what Joseph Conrad referred to as a 'fantastic invasion', the intervention in Africa by outside forces: a new phase of foreign involvement in the national affairs of Sudan under the auspices of an amalgam of commercial interest, humanitarianism, peace-building and counter-terrorism.

The Sudan course was designed to offer, among other things, a critical perspective on such developments, based on an analysis of the role of the state in Sudanese history and the stratagems it had developed over time for extending its power to the peripheries of the country. The course included a consideration of the history of development and the impact of previous international interventions. It drew attention to the risk of repetition of the errors of the past, and the ways in which aid and development could contribute to political disequilibrium.

For a short course this was a tall order. Sudan's borders encompass a huge diversity of territory, peoples and ways of life. It would be implausible to claim that a one-week event could provide a comprehensive understanding of a country or its people. And clearly it did not. What the course provided was as much useful knowledge – and as coherent an analytical approach – as it was possible to fit into six days of intensive, dawn-to-dusk study. The staff of the course has certainly reflected the diversity of the field: Sudanese academics and activists from almost every region of the country have taught on the course in the past seven years, alongside expatriate specialists whose views and fields of expertise are equally various. Although the course is short, it offers something unavailable elsewhere. And the risk of presumption on the part of those who make it their business to study Sudan is clearly eclipsed by the greater risk of ignorance – by the suppression of free speech on the part of governments in Sudan, by the decay of standards in higher education and by institutional amnesia on the part of international agencies and representatives of donor nations. It may be argued, in fact, that those who have had the privilege of living in Sudan as researchers and scholars have an obligation to find ways to impart their knowledge to a new generation that has the chance to influence future events. Such was the thinking of those who devised and taught on the course.

In the years since 2004, the optimism of Naivasha has evaporated. And it has become clear that the concerns which drove the establishment of the Sudan course were all too justified. The Comprehensive Peace Agreement has been undermined; largely owing to the embedded authoritarianism of the Sudanese political elite. The war in Darfur, in western Sudan, has generated a repetition of the horrors of the war in the south. And the resolution of this conflict in the west has become entwined with the north-south peace process. The global response to the decay of political goodwill in the years following the Comprehensive Peace Agreement has been disjointed: there has been widespread condemnation of the actions of the Government of Sudan; at the same time donor countries have significantly increased levels of aid. China and other Asian countries have expanded their capital investment, particularly in the Sudan oil industry, while Egypt and other middle-eastern countries are involved in large-scale hydrological projects on the Nile.

Never has it been clearer that the problems of Sudan stem from the concentration of economic and political power at the centre of the country and from the destructive means that the central state has employed to maintain and extend that power. Yet the diversity of Sudan is its most salient characteristic; and no political dispensation will work that does not recognize this. The Handbook aims, accordingly, to provide a sampling of knowledge about all areas of the territory that has historically constituted Sudan, and the multiple cultural and political realities within it: the peoples who live there, their past and their present, and their relation to successive governments. It offers a critique of the ambitions of the state and of the practice of political power, in the hope that the long story of misgovernment in Sudan may yet be modified.

Mapping Sudan

One way of looking at Sudan's history used on the Sudan Course is as a story of maps: of making maps, arguing over them, and remaking them. Maps of Sudan show not just how the borders of the country have changed over time, but how the very idea of a country with the name Sudan came into being, relatively recently in history. Map-making also offers an extended metaphor for the construction of knowledge, a way of understanding the many layers of information about the country that are offered by different disciplines, and their relation to the lived realities of Sudanese people.

In the early nineteenth century, when Muhammad Ali of Egypt sent his armies south, there was no single name for the lands they were to conquer. For hundreds of years, the belt of Africa south of the Twentieth Parallel North had been known generally as *Bilad al-Sudan*, 'Land of the Blacks', but on the largely empty spaces of the maps which showed the territories south of Egypt there were multiple names – Nubia, Kordofan, Sennar, Darfur. For want of any other general term to describe the realm over which Muhammad Ali and his descendants gradually, and erratically, asserted their control from the 1820s to the 1870s – a realm that included the ancient centres of civilization in the Nile valley, the deserts of the north, the forests of Equatoria and the swamps and savannahs in between, and whose inhabitants included Arabs and non-Arabs, Muslims and non-Muslims, city dwellers and nomads and sedentary farmers – in the absence of a term to signify this vast realm, the word 'Sudan' crept into use, first in Egypt, then in Europe.

In 1880s, when Europeans wrote of the state created by the Mahdi after the collapse of Egyptian rule, they called it 'the Sudan' – though the Mahdi and his followers did not use this term. At the end of the 1890s, with the defeat of the Mahdists and the establishment of Anglo-Egyptian rule, 'the Sudan' became fixed as the title of a political unit, its borders defined partly by the historic claims of Egypt and more immediately by the claims of Britain, Belgium, France and Ethiopia to the land around it. There were still many empty spaces on the maps; but now the word Sudan was written across them.

Whether the Sudan – or simply Sudan, as it is now more usually called – should stay the shape shown on those maps has been the subject of intermittent debate ever since. In the first half of the twentieth-century, the major question was whether Sudan should exist at all as a separate entity, or whether it should rather become a part of a greater Egypt. As this debate faded, rather abruptly after independence in the 1950s, the debate – and violent conflict – came instead to revolve around the shape and political nature of Sudan itself. Should Sudan incorporate all of the territory ruled by the Anglo-Egyptian state, or should this colonial creation dissolve with the departure of the foreign rulers who had brought it? If the state was to maintain the physical shape of the Anglo-Egyptian Sudan, how could it move beyond the stern, centralizing ethos which had maintained imperial rule? For more than fifty years these questions have persisted. The central state has been challenged from the South and the West and the East. And today the Sudan created through those acts of nineteenth-century imperial expansion, having failed to escape its authoritarian heritage, has ceased to exist.

But that will not end the questions over where lines should be drawn on maps, or over what Sudan is, or was, or should be. The legacy of map-making is a complex one. The outline of Sudan on the map was itself not completely fixed by 1900: in the early twentieth century, the 'Lado Enclave' in the south-west, which was briefly a personal domain of King Leopold of Belgium, ruler of the Congo Free State, became part of Sudan; in 1916 the western sultanate of Darfur, which had largely maintained its independence and only briefly been under Egyptian rule, was violently incorporated into 'the Sudan' by the British; in the 1930s, a wedge of land in the north-west was given to the Italian colony of Libya. Even now, in the extreme north-east and south-east, Sudan's borders remain the subject of dispute, with the Halaib Triangle and the Ilemi Triangle, formally claimed by Sudan, effectively controlled, respectively, by Egypt and Kenya.

And within those borders, there have also been multiple disputes. As the spaces on the maps have been filled in – with the lineaments of rivers and hills, internal administrative boundaries, the names of settlements, the territories of particular communities – the accumulation and recording of knowledge has itself functioned as a kind of violent incorporation. Here, as elsewhere, maps have been an essential tool of government: for administration, ordering and control, and in fulfilment of the state's ambitions to change the lives of people through the provision of services.

The Anglo-Egyptian government was quick to create a survey department, which by the 1930s had produced maps for the whole of the Sudan; until relatively recently these maps were still the best available for much of the country. Mapping made administration possible, but the cartographic enterprise is never a simple recording of knowledge. Names – and the spaces they described – were changed and distorted, as strangers (whether Europeans, Egyptians, or people from other parts of the Sudan) struggled with pronunciation and spelling, or with the existence of competing claims to land on the part of different communities on the ground. The act of mapping can be a process of physical dispossession: entire communities may find that maps misplace them, or omit them, and so compromise their established use of land or water. It can also involve social or cultural depletion: the name for the hill where you live may, deliberately or inadvertently, be obliterated by cartographers in favour of the name given to it by your neighbour, an ethnic group that has more educated members and administrative influence and harbours expansionist ideas. Or your community may find itself arbitrarily confined – by the drawing of a line on the map – to an administrative unit with other people whose lives and language are very different.

Today, maps are again at the centre of political debates over Sudan's future. The argument over the boundary line between north and south Sudan has shown both the power and the weakness of cartography. When the Comprehensive Peace Agreement (CPA) stipulated that the Abyei dispute should be settled through a commission which would determine the boundaries of the Ngok chiefdoms that were transferred to Kordofan in 1905, it both acknowledged the potential power of maps and showed a misplaced faith in their straightforwardness. There were no maps which showed those boundaries as they were; and when the chosen Commission tried to create one as the basis for a judgment, it was rejected as inaccurate. The CPA also referred to the provincial boundaries of 1 January 1956 as marking the line between north and south – a line which may become an international border. Choosing a date, and a definition, gave those who drafted the agreement the feeling that they had made an unambiguous decision, sanctioned by the authority of the map. Yet that line is uncertain; both because there were multiple minor changes in administrative boundaries over the years, and because of confusions and errors in the maps of the 1950s, which make exact delineation of the boundary problematic. The precise boundary between north and south will take a long time to agree on. The quarrel over this line and other, pre-existing border disputes between Sudan and Egypt, Kenya and Ethiopia, mean that the very shape of Sudan has become problematic once again.

Local Knowledge, Global Power

The story of the maps of Sudan also illustrates the problem of knowledge itself. It is a reminder that the developing technologies of information gathering – compass and rule, plane table and alidade, aerial survey and satellite image – exist in a relation of tension with local knowledge, with indigenous understandings of rights in land and natural resources, and the meanings given to features of the natural world. Reconciling these two forms of knowledge is a process similar to what cartographers call 'ground-truthing' – the process of walking the land and discussing its features with those who live there. Only such a process can turn latitude and longitude, and contours and boundary lines, into a landscape which is recognizable to those who live in it.

The work of getting to know a place and its inhabitants has too often been neglected by the agents of development, by aid officials and government employees in a hurry to finish a survey, or complete a project. Enduring errors in cartography, on the one hand, and long-term failure of projects, on the other, are the result of such haste. Ground-truthing is time-consuming; and it is not without its own areas of ambiguity. Thus there may be competing truths on the ground: different ways of seeing the landscape; more than one name for the same feature; and more than one claim to a single area of land. Maps that show local understandings of landscape are more complicated than those that simply impose borders and names. And development programmes that engage long term with local institutions are far harder to design and maintain.

Sudan's economic history in the modern era, by contrast, has been characterized by top-down state interventions. These have been ostensibly designed to improve, to make more productive. The extent of governmental ambitions has varied, but the servants of a succession of regimes have all have believed that they possess kinds of knowledge which are superior to local knowledge; it is those kinds of knowledge which have informed their policies and give them the right to instruct, cajole and sometimes coerce, and to reshape the land. The imperial project, and the state-building projects that succeeded it – in Sudan as elsewhere – incorporated mapping as an element in the imposition of order on places and populations under their control. The maps reveal the authoritarian character of the project. The aim is transformation. The assumption, all too often, is the superior knowledge of the government servant or technical consultant.

In the Condominium era the government of the Anglo-Egyptian Sudan produced an *Almanac*: a small reference book for the use of officials. The information in the *Almanac* included weights and measures, ranks and titles, travel times and postage costs; within its pages an official could find instructions for building a platform on which to take the salute from his subject, or details of the penetrating power of a .303 bullet at different ranges. The *Almanac* was a summary guide to the knowledge by which Sudan and its people were ordered and ruled: practical in its relevance to the tasks of administration, and at the same time reassuring to those it was intended for in its evocation of a system of knowledge which reached far beyond Sudan itself. With map in hand and *Almanac* in pocket, the official was a travelling locus of order. Of course, the *Almanac* did not contain all the information that an official might require. Local knowledge was sometimes required to help implement projects of change, whether these involved collecting tax, setting up a market or imposing new laws. The official might well need to know who lived in a place, the name for a river, or the time of year when people planted certain crops. And they took copious notes on such things. But the nature of the project was decided by the superior knowledge brought by the state and its experts, just as the defining elements of the map – the need for borders, unambiguous names, points and lines – were ordained elsewhere.

The *Almanac* carried by officials of the Condominium is no more, but successive generations of officials and experts have continued to apply external sources of systematized knowledge in a not dissimilar way, particularly in the rural areas of Sudan. Experts still come from outside – from Britain or Egypt, as in earlier generations – or from the US, China or India. And, increasingly, they come from within Sudan itself. This does not mean that the projects that Sudanese specialists design are drawn up in any more productive consultation with the communities they affect. The language of such projects is likely to invoke an idea of national development, or a global philanthropic imperative, or the pure spirit of exploitative resource extraction. It may assert the need to earn foreign exchange, or raise revenue from taxes, or ensure food security, or provide health services. What such projects seldom do is stress local knowledge and self-determination. Most development projects in Sudan are still driven by a state which sees its subjects from a distance, from a commanding height: they are large-scale projects driven by the urgent needs of the state for resources and revenues, to be forced through without consultation; dams, oil wells and pipelines plotted onto the spaces on the maps, imposed on the landscape, and then recorded by new maps.

Other projects are devised by international agencies who see their work as a matter of global poverty reduction and their 'clients' as undifferentiated members of a class of needy people. But the poverty they seek to alleviate is largely the result of the policies of the governments under whose auspices they work. Effective intervention in such a paradoxical situation needs to be informed by a careful understanding of local interests and long-term development possibilities. It is only in this nexus between local knowledge and global information that sustainability is possible.

Yet international experts rely heavily on forgetting. Sudan's past is littered with development projects. Some have vanished without trace, others have spawned monstrous offspring, like the mechanized farming schemes in the East and the central belt. These were imagined as the route to food security and prosperity, but have instead generated insecurity and conflict across swathes of land. The history of deleterious development interventions is rarely considered. And few experts are prepared to locate themselves in this history of failure and unintended consequences. For them, Sudan's history is too often told simply as a story of conflicts produced by local rivalries, probably between one ethnic group and another, usually over resources, sometimes over religion, which have raged despite the best efforts of benign interventions to settle them. This history is conceived as a *tabula rasa*.

The old *Almanac* was important to colonial officials, not simply because it gave them useful information; but more fundamentally, because it offered reassurance that they belonged to a system of knowledge which was internally consistent and which transcended the communities which they governed, one that was not constrained by the complicated local histories they found themselves unknowingly intervening in. It was this which gave them confidence and self-belief – in combination with their access to superior technologies of communication and, on occasion, violent coercion. This kind of ideological reinforcement has made generations of experts powerful. The awareness that there are other kinds of knowledge – that there might be more than one kind of chief, that the river has different names, that people's movements across the landscape follow a logic of their own, and that they may owe no loyalty to governments nor any other power – such awareness is liable to complicate both the lives of experts and the rule of autocrats.

Many Sudans

Debate over what shape Sudan should be, and over the relationship between the state and its people have characterized political discussion in Sudan since well before Independence. Such debates are bound up with the telling and retelling of history, as people explain, justify and make claims through reference to the past. In the South, the recent history of the Sudan is represented as a history of lost opportunities, of agreements with the government in Khartoum that have been repeatedly dishonoured. Before that, for many Southerners the story of Sudan is a story of slavery, of the nineteenth century depredations of raiders from the north. But among the people of the riverain north the story is different. Here slaves are invisible; the main story is one of struggle for independence from external powers – external, that is, to the country that was not yet then Sudan. Thus, in Khartoum, primary school children are trained to re-enact the story of Mek Nimr, a traditional leader who, in 1822, killed the tyrannical son of Muhammad Ali of Egypt. These schoolchildren, growing up in a divided country, are rehearsing what is seen in the north – or parts of the north - as the seminal, unifying moment in the history of Sudanese nationalism. Yet Mek Nimr himself lived before there was anywhere called Sudan and had no idea of a Sudan, or of himself as Sudanese. And in southern Sudan, few people have ever heard of him.

A version of Sudanese history which celebrates the idea of a unified state, shaped by the encounter with Egyptian and British colonialism has been inscribed onto the map of Khartoum, where the names of streets are a roll-call of characters from a northern nationalist version of history: Mahdist generals, the sectarian leaders of the early twentieth-century and the young men of the White Flag movement who proclaimed resistance to British rule in the 1920s. But not all the people who live in Sudan share a sense of the significance of these names. In Khartoum, the name of Abu Garga may be synonymous with heroic national struggle against Egypt or Ethiopia; but in the Nuba Mountains it evokes another bleak episode in a history of state violence; in Equatoria it means nothing. For southerners, Zubeir Pasha Street brings to mind not a great national figure, but a slave trader.

The Islamist project of the 1980s was an attempt to impose a new kind of national identity on Sudan, one that saw the country's religious and cultural diversity as something to be overcome in the name of a single unifying belief system. Some Islamist thinkers hailed 1989 as the moment of final liberation from colonial rule, blaming the country's troubles after independence on the corrupting power of a secular western imperialism that sought to continue its control of the country. But for most southerners and many northerners the Islamist vision of the country was anathema, denying the value of their culture and the meaning of their historical experience. The civil war in southern Sudan was aptly called a war of visions.

Sudan, it may be argued, has no single history; it has multiple histories, a clamour of competing versions of what matters about the past. The diversity within Sudan consists not just of the great plenitude of communities, languages, belief systems and ways of life that it contains. It also includes a radical diversity in ideas about what Sudan is that are entertained by members of these communities. Different histories, and different ways of understanding the relation of particular communities to the centres of power and to the governments that have tried to assert control over them – these histories are playing a key role in the current transformation of the Sudanese state.

As Sudan enters a new phase of radical political and administrative restructuring, it becomes more important than ever to understand the variant histories that exist in the minds of Sudanese themselves. There are, it is clear, many Sudans, both real and imaginary – and many more possible Sudans. No account of these myriad visions of the country can be definitive. The Sudan Handbook does not aspire to be a new *Almanac*. It does not offer a systematic account of the country, nor does it provide information in a form meant to be applied to the design of development projects. What it offers, in the spirit of engagement with Sudanese visions of the future, is a critical guide to current knowledge, a collection of essays on key aspects of the country, written from a range of disciplinary points of view. In these essays are a variety of perspectives on the past and present of the lands that lie within the historical boundaries of Sudan - and the peoples that have lived and continue to live there.

2

Land & Water

JUSTIN WILLIS
OMER EGEMI
& PHILIP WINTER

The Anglo-Egyptian Condominium of Sudan was the largest of the political units created by imperialism in Africa. It has grown and shrunk a little over time, gaining Darfur in 1916 and losing a corner to Italian-ruled Libya in 1934, taking its overall size to just below one million square miles (2.4 million square kilometres). But the territory controlled, at least nominally, by the Sudanese state remained – up until 2011 – larger than that ruled by any other African government.

The Condominium was divided for most of its existence into nine provinces. Six of these came to be considered as 'northern', and the other three as 'southern'. These provinces were subdivided in the 1970s, restored briefly as states in a major administrative restructuring in 1991, then divided again in 1994, in a further restructuring which produced 26 states. (One of these, West Kordofan, was subsequently merged into two of the others). Although Sudan has had a state system for two decades, it is not uncommon to hear people using the old system of nine provinces.

The terrain covered by these states and provinces ranges from the Nubian desert in the far north – the easternmost extension of the Sahara, where there is virtually no rainfall – to the swamps and forests a thousand miles (1600 kilometres) southward, where up to 200 centimetres of seasonal rain a year swells rivers, brings floods and feeds a permanent swamp in the central southern plains. In the far north, along the Twenty-second Parallel, Sudan borders Egypt; in the south, around the Fourth Parallel, just north of the equator, it marches with the countries of east and central Africa.

The two regions are linked by the Nile. The White Nile flows from its source in Rwanda and Uganda into the southern part of Sudan, where it is known as Bahr al-Jebel, the River of the Mountain. It flows past Juba, the southern capital, then slows and spreads out in the swamplands of the Sudd (a name derived from the Arabic word for obstacle). As the Bahr al-Jebel flows through the Sudd it is fed by a number of other rivers, the most important being the Bahr al-Ghazal, which is created by the waterways of the Nile-Congo watershed. The White Nile proper begins when the Bahr al-Ghazal meets the Bahr al-Jabal. The Sobat, the last of the southern tributaries, meets the White Nile at Malakal, bringing with it water from Ethiopia. After Malakal the river is uninterrupted until it reaches the Jebel Aulia dam south of Khartoum. Then, in Khartoum, it meets the Blue

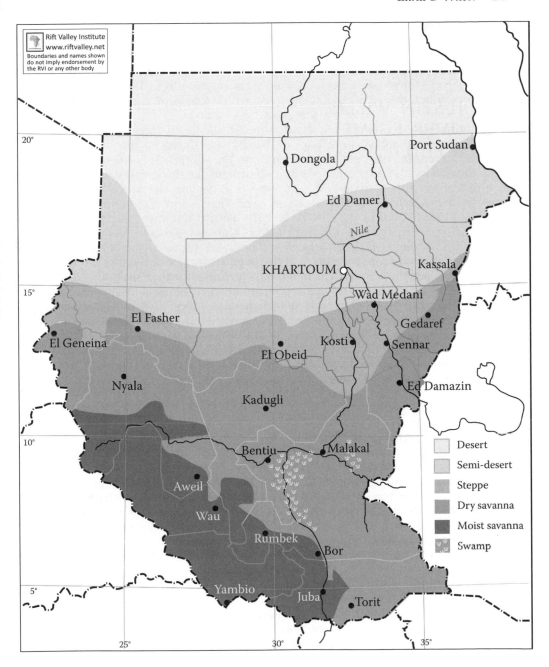

Map 2.1 Terrain

Nile, flowing from Ethiopia, which, over the course of a year, carries more water than the White Nile itself.

From here the river becomes a ribbon of green, with intensive cultivation for a mile or two each side, and the desert beyond. Cultivated areas are punctuated by steep rocky stretches where cultivation is not possible. The Nile has no significant tributaries after the Atbara river, which joins it a few hundred miles north of Khartoum, just before the great bend that takes the Nile on a loop through the Nubian desert. From Atbara through the desert the river flows alone for a thousand miles until it reaches Lake Nasser, and thence to Lower Egypt and the Mediterranean. Between Khartoum and the Egyptian border there are numerous cataracts – rapids and shallows that limit the navigability of the river. Five out of the six cataracts are – or were – in Sudan; the Second Cataract, however, has lain beneath the waters of Lake Nasser since the construction of the Aswan High Dam in the 1960s; and the Fourth Cataract near Meroe has recently been submerged by the construction of the Hamadab or Meroe dam.

Access to water is of vital importance both for the everyday existence of Sudanese farmers and pastoralists and for large-scale state-sponsored economic development. For those dependent on crops or grazing it is matter of survival. At state level, giant hydrological projects such as the Hamadab Dam, and the Roseires Dam on the Blue Nile hold out the promise of hydroelectricity and agricultural development through irrigation projects, but these have often had disruptive effects on local populations. In the sphere of international relations, moreover, hydropolitics has long dominated Sudan's relations with Egypt, since Egypt's population, which at 80 million is more than twice the size of Sudan's, is completely dependent on the flow of the river to bring water and alluvial silt to the agricultural areas of the Nile Delta.

Landscape and History

Sudan's geography, then, like its history, appears to be dominated by the Nile. In northern Sudan, most of the population now live along the river; the major cities, industry, wealth and power are all concentrated there. Greater Khartoum, at the junction of the Blue and White Niles – comprising the three cities of Khartoum, Khartoum North and Omdurman and their surrounding camps and shanty towns – is overwhelmingly the largest urban centre in the country. It would be easy to think that this pattern of development is the unavoidable consequence of a natural landscape; but this is no more inevitable than is the shape of Sudan itself: Sudan's geography is the product of political and historical factors, as well as conditions imposed by nature.

Though large in area, Sudan has never been particularly populous. The population in 1903 was estimated at less than two million – a figure probably pitched deliberately low by British officials anxious to emphasize the loss of life under Mahdist rule. Within a few years the population estimates were being adjusted rapidly upwards, and in 1955-56 the first – and last – plausible census of the whole of Sudan put the population at just over 10 million. 39 per cent of these regarded themselves, according to the census, as members of Arab tribes, and 51 per cent spoke Arabic as their first language. The most recent census, in 2008, recorded a total population of 39 million, but it probably understates the population both of Darfur (recorded as 7.5 million) and of southern Sudan (8.2 million),

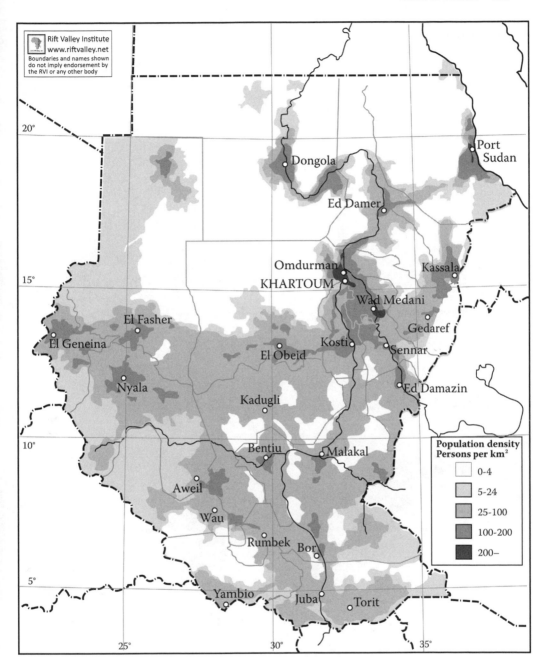

Map 2.2 Population Density

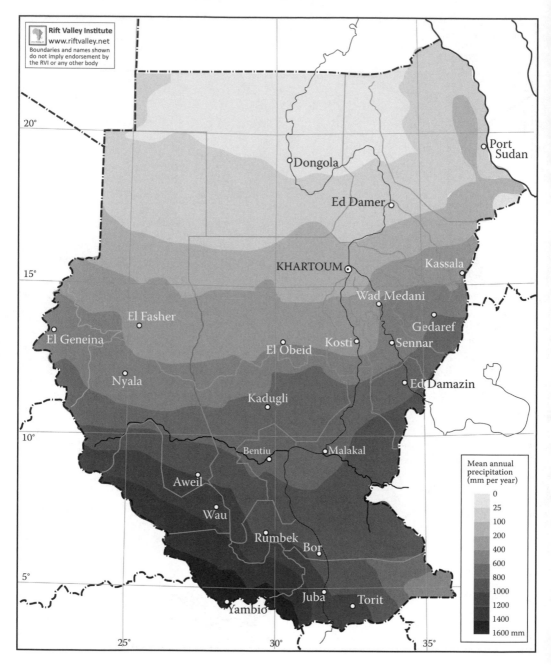

Map 2.3 Rainfall

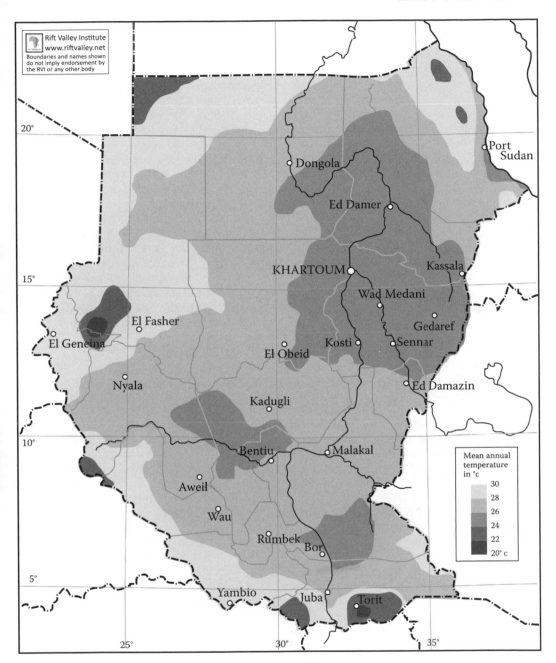

Map 2.4 Temperature

either as a result of flawed data collection or manipulation of the results. The uncertainty over how many people actually live in Sudan is the most striking example of a recurrent problem: in Sudan, statistics are generally unreliable, or contested, or both.

However many people there are in Sudan today, one thing is clear: they rely heavily on an economy which is overwhelmingly agricultural and pastoral. This assertion may seem surprising, given the apparent economic importance of the oil industry; but few Sudanese live from the profits of oil. They live from the crops they grow (mainly sorghum – *dura* in Arabic – and millet) and the herds they tend (camels, cattle, sheep and goats). Farming and stock-raising are important activities all over Sudan. Even the extreme north-west, towards the Libyan border, an arid and effectively desert land, plays a part in livelihood strategies: camel keepers who spend much of the year in Kordofan will drive their herds to these remote lands to catch the *gizzu*, the brief grazing offered by the tiny amount of rain which falls there, which feeds the camels in the breeding season. In Kordofan itself, and in Darfur, even in areas where the annual rainfall seems small, there is cultivation; people farm seasonally along the edge of water courses; they plant to take advantage of rain when it falls. And they move their livestock where the grazing is: seasonally, following established patterns, but also opportunistically. Thus, even in areas where the annual rainfall seems pitifully low, people can live from the land and from their herds. To do so successfully over a long period requires a degree of flexibility; being able to move the herds, or plant where the rain is falling.

The ability to move and to make use of different types of land has also been important for those who live on and around mountains. For the people who live in the Nuba hills of South Kordofan – not a single group, linguistically or culturally, but rather many different, small groups – the most successful livelihood strategies have involved a combination of farming garden plots around their homes on the hills, and planting grain seasonally on larger fields down in the plains. For pastoralists, here and elsewhere, who need to move their herds seasonally for them to survive, this transhumant grazing strategy has encouraged collective, kin-based notions of land tenure which emphasize the rights of occasional use rather than outright ownership of land by individuals. A consistent theme of the modern history of Sudan has been the tension between these flexible strategies of land use and the new demands of administrative boundaries, individual ownership and entrepreneurial investment.

Roughly speaking, in Sudan, the further south, the more rain there is. This rule is not invariable. Where there is high ground there is more rain, around Jebel Marra in Darfur or in the Nuba hills, for example; and the extreme south-eastern corner of Sudan is relatively arid. But in general, the overall amount of rainfall and the extent to which it is spread through the year both increase towards the south. The area of the three old southern provinces – Upper Nile, Bahr al-Ghazal and Equatoria – is generally much greener than the north. The wettest part of Sudan lies on its borders with the Democratic Republic of Congo and the Central African Republic. Everywhere, the rain is seasonal, and there are some months which are likely to see more rain than others – even in the south-west, where it may rain in any month, there is a pronounced seasonality to the rain. This is the product of the inter-tropical convergence zone, the shifting meeting place of high-altitude air streams.

There are also significant differences of soil type, which combine with the pattern of rainfall to produce varying kinds of vegetation. From north to south, roughly speaking, the soil changes from sandy to clayish to the hard red, lateritic soils known as ironstone. In the south, the distinction between the ironstone plateau of the south-west and the flood-prone, clayish black cotton soils which lie east and north of them is striking, affecting vegetation and the possibilities of movement. The black cotton swells and grows sticky in the rain; it shrinks and cracks as it dries. The clay plains at the heart of the south are largely grassland. Here travel is very difficult when the rains are heavy. The ironstone plateau is more wooded and movement is easier.

Landscape and Technology

Over the last hundred years in most parts of Sudan, human intervention has reshaped the landscape and the possibilities of movement and communication. Railways and telegraph lines were the first innovations; under Turco-Egyptian rule in the nineteenth century, a telegraph line reached Khartoum from Cairo. Railway construction from Egypt south into Sudan made little headway under Turco-Egyptian rule; but the Anglo-Egyptian invasion, the 'reconquest' of 1896-98, rolled forward on the iron rails which carried the steam train. Within a few years of the establishment of the Condominium a programme of railway building connected Khartoum with Egypt, with the new Red Sea harbour at Port Sudan, and with Kordofan's provincial capital at El-Obeid. In the 1950s and early 1960s, a further programme of investment took the railway to Nyala in 1959 and, three years later, to Wau, in the south. (Today, there are plans, not yet realized, to link the south to east Africa by rail.)

Like the political dispensation, the railways placed riverain northern Sudan at the centre; all traffic had to pass through Khartoum, and the links to the outside world also lay through the three cities. Steamer services were established from Khartoum up the river to Juba, but the road network of Anglo-Egyptian Sudan was limited. When, after 1956, a succession of independent governments began to develop this road network, it too focused on the riverain north: that was where the roads led, and where the roads were best.

In the 1970s, the railway network was deliberately run down: perhaps because it was inefficient, perhaps because Nimeiri's government resented the political power of the railway workers union. As a consequence, Sudan's railways were barely functioning by the late 1990s (though there was a small amount of new construction to service the oil industry), but a new programme of road building re-emphasized the dominance of the northern riverain centre – a programme which has accelerated since around 2002, creating tarmac roads from Khartoum north to Wadi Halfa, and improving and developing the roads from Khartoum to the east and to the Gezira, as well as resurfacing the main roads in Greater Khartoum. The failure to complete an asphalted road westwards, that would link Darfur to the rest of the country, regarded by many Darfurians as a deliberate act of neglect, has been a contributory cause of civil conflict in the region.

While scant and unreliable rainfall have made flexibility and mobility important attributes across much of northern Sudan; the Nile has always offered an incentive for a different livelihood strategy, one which focuses on investment and the development of claims on land along the line of the river itself. The annual flooding of some sections of the river creates a very local landscape of fertile, moist alluvial soil, which shifts a little each year as the river makes little changes in course. This seasonal floodland has for millennia been an outstand-ing resource for cultivators. In more recent times, the steady elaboration of pumping technology – from scoops, to water wheels, to petrol-driven pumps, to schemes for dams and networks of irrigation canals – has created new oppor-tunities for the growing of crops. The effective use of land across much of Sudan has relied on flexibility and mobility, but the developing technologies of riverain agriculture have placed a premium on fixed investment and the control of defined areas.

Controlling the Nile

These possibilities for development are the product of the particular nature of the Nile river – or rather, rivers – as well as the increasing application of capital and technology to control them. The furthest source of the Nile is in Rwanda: from there, water flows into Lake Victoria, through Uganda and Lake Albert (or Rutanzige, as it is also called). This is the water that becomes the White Nile – which, having rushed down the slope from Uganda towards Juba, then meanders its way slowly through the southern part of Sudan, taking its colour and its name from suspended particles of pale clay. The gradient north of Juba is very slight indeed, and the river moves uncertainly, its pace further slowed by the Sudd, great masses of floating vegetation that turn the river into a lengthy stretch of swamp that grows in the wet season and shrinks in the dry, with meandering channels that can make navigation difficult. The Sudd is hard to navigate by boat, and its seasonal expansion across the clayish soils is a menace to land travel, but it is a redoubt for wildlife, creating a remarkable resource for its inhabitants – in the dry season there is a bonanza of fish and opportunities to plant in the moist and fertile soil as the water recedes. For people who live by combining cattle-herding, fishing and seasonal agriculture, as many do in southern Sudan, the particular flow of the White Nile shapes their livelihoods.

The Sudd soaks up seasonal changes and the White Nile emerges from it, south of Malakal, as a relatively predictable river, with a fairly constant flow of water through the year. At Khartoum, it joins with another, very different Nile. The Blue Nile has a shorter journey than the White; it rushes down to Khartoum from the highlands of Ethiopia, crossing mostly hard ground, with no meander-ing along the way. It is a very changeable river. When there is no rain in the Ethiopian highlands, there is little water in the Blue Nile; when the rains fall, the river swells rapidly and dramatically. Between May and August, its volume rises by around 1,000 per cent; by February, it is back to its lowest point. Because of this rapid flow, it does not create a vast wetland like the Sudd; there are some local, minor changes in its course, but the fertile alluvial soils which it deposits – the *jerif* – lie closely along the course of the river itself.

It is the waters of the Blue Nile – and those of its smaller sibling, the Atbara – which make the Nile north of Khartoum swell and recede with the seasons each year. North of Khartoum, the river goes down a series of steps in the landscape, which produce the cataracts, long an obstruction to river traffic. Along this stretch of river, as along the Blue Nile, the seasonal generosity of the river was closely bound to its banks, and settlement and farming have always clung closely to the edge of the water. In Egypt, the seasonality of the Nile was the basis of the annual inundation from which Egypt's agriculture was developed.

It was Egypt's reliance on the waters of the Nile which helped to create Sudan; in the late nineteenth century, Egypt's British masters could not countenance the thought that any other European power might control the flood which made Egypt's fields fruitful, and so they insisted on the need for a campaign to defeat the Mahdist state. It was also Egypt's reliance on the Nile which was to set in train the succession of grand hydraulic schemes, planned under the condominium, some of which are finally being built today. Shortly after the defeat of the Mahdists, the Aswan Low Dam was completed on Egypt's southern border with Sudan; its aim was to control the seasonality of the Nile, ensuring a reliable supply of water for Egyptian agriculture. The Sennar Dam, which was completed in 1925, was intended to create new opportunities for irrigation along the line of the Nile in Sudan itself, with the growing of cotton for export being the key aim. The dam at Jebel Aulia, on the White Nile (1937), was mainly intended to further regulate the water flow to Egypt, though it also provided some water for local irrigation; the Khashm el Girba dam on the Atbara (1964) was built primarily to ensure a water supply for the population that was displaced when the Aswan Dam was raised.

Over time, however, hydro-electric power has come to be the principal rationale for dam-building, with irrigation becoming something of a by-product: the Roseires Dam (1966) on the Blue Nile, currently being raised to create a larger irrigated area, was originally built to generate power, and the recently completed Merowe dam, which has obliterated the fourth cataract, is primarily a hydro-electric project. Dams have exerted a remarkable fascination over a succession of Sudanese regimes, encouraging the focusing of investment and schemes for development along the line of the Nile, particularly in northern Sudan where the river is more tractable; symptomatically, the Government of Southern Sudan is considering its own grand dam scheme, between Nimule and Juba, to generate electricity.

There has been one other scheme of intervention on the Nile; intended not to dam up the river but to make it flow. This was the Jonglei scheme, the plan for an immense canal which would bypass the Sudd and carry the waters of the Nile straight to Malakal and then beyond. Initially conceived as part of a water-management plan, one that had Egyptian interests at its core, the scheme was revived in the 1970s under the guise of development, presented as a plan to make the Sudd productive and create irrigation prospects in the Southern Region. The project was viewed with suspicion by many southerners, and there were significant uncertainties over its possible effect on the environment; there were public protests in southern towns; and the digging of the canal was abandoned in 1984 after the SPLA attacked the construction camp.

While hydraulic projects have been at the centre of state ideas of development in Sudan, there has been an alternative model of agricultural development, which took the focus away from the Nile. After some experiments in the 1940s, the government decided in the 1950s to systematically promote mechanized rainland farming in the belt of land that forms what has been called the transitional zone, between the Tenth Parallel north and the fourteenth. In the 1970s, the radical government of Jaafar Nimeiri threw new energy into this, and considerable areas of land in what were then Blue Nile and southern Kordofan provinces were assigned to mechanized farming schemes, in the hope that they would produce grain which could be exported to Saudi Arabia and the gulf countries in exchange for hard currency. While some of the investors who put money into these farms evidently prospered, mechanized farming has been seen as problematic by development specialists. By taking up land which, from the state's point of view, no one 'owned' but which was used on an occasional basis by small-scale cultivators, or as seasonal grazing resources, or migration routes, these giant farms compromised the livelihoods of people who relied on flexibility; and the land itself was in some cases quickly exhausted.

In the last few decades, as a result of state intervention, civil war, famine, and, in some areas of the north, increasingly unreliable rainfall – and the consequent disruption of traditional systems of food production – Sudan has seen dramatically accelerated population displacement. Millions of people have been forced to move. Rural-urban migration has resulted in dramatic changes in the population landscape, notably the mushrooming growth of cities in central Sudan, especially the capital region of Khartoum. Sudan's porous international borders with Chad, Eritrea and Ethiopia mean that it has also played host to many hundreds of thousands of refugees from wars in these countries. These shifts in population have far-reaching implications for the natural environment, producing deforestation around urban centres and necessitating food aid where self-sufficiency has been lost.

Natural Resources

Away from the river and the grand projects, Sudan has other kinds of natural wealth. One of the least visible, but most consistently important, is gum arabic, which is an important source of income for the inhabitants of a wide belt across the savannah zone between the Tenth Parallel and the Fourteenth Parallel. An edible glue which exudes from the bark of an acacia tree, *Acacia senegalensis* or *Acacia Seyal*, gum arabic is used in producing pharmaceuticals, cosmetics, paints and foodstuffs, including most soft drinks. Sudan presently produces around 25,000 tonnes a year, or half of the world's annual production; most of it coming from Kordofan, where gum gardens do well in dry and sandy conditions. There is little cultivation involved; gum arabic collection is generally a seasonal occupation of poor farmers. At present, a government monopoly over the export trade limits the returns to these farmers, and provides significant revenue to the state. The shea or lulu tree (*Butyrospermum parkii*), source of the shea butter used in cosmetics, occurs in a swathe across Sudan, south of the gum arabic belt. Lulu is a cash crop whose potential has yet to be fully exploited. Elsewhere in Sudan, timber is a potential export commodity. In the south, in particular, there are significant resources of hardwood, growing on the ironstone; during the war, much was felled by army officers in the government garrison at Wau and exported by train and aircraft to the north.

Wildlife remains a threatened and undermanaged resource in Sudan. The Sudd, in particular, is one of Africa's great conservation challenges. The fish and game of the Sudd and other areas of the south helped sustain its inhabitants through two civil wars, but conservation organizations are only now beginning to do surveys to determine what is left of the once-plentiful wildlife. Southern Sudan is home to two of Africa's three main mammal migrations, that of the white-eared kob (*Kobus kobus leucotis*) and that of the tiang (*Damaliscus korrigum lunatus*). These seasonal movements rival the migration of the wildebeest of the Serengeti in scale and extent. Kob and tiang migrate north and south on the plains east of the Nile, the kob from the Guom Swamps past the Boma plateau and back, the tiang from the Duk Ridge to and from the floodplains of the Kidepo river. The meeting of these two species with the reedbuck (*Redunca redunca*) and Mongalla gazelle (*Eudorcas albonotata*), at the turning point of their respective seasonal movements, is a spectacular event. There are indications, though, that the paths of the migrations are changing in response to human activity. Southern Sudan is home to many rare species, such as the giant eland (*Taurotragus derbianus)* and the shoe-bill stork (*Balaeniceps rex*), the provincial symbol of greater Bahr al-Ghazal and now the symbol of Lakes state. Other charismatic vertebrates have suffered considerably. The elephant population, more than 150,000 in 1976, is a fraction of that today. The northern white rhino is probably extinct in Sudan. Ivory, one of the country's principal exports in the nineteenth century, is now subject to international prohibitions – but can still be found on sale in the *suqs* of Omdurman.

Minerals

With the exception of oil, Sudan's mineral resources seem mostly to be spread around its borders. In the past, copper was mined in the far west of Sudan, at the site known as Hofrat en Nahas; deposits remain, but there has been no commercial working of these in recent times, and an exploratory programme by a major international mining company was abandoned in 1999, as it seemed that the reserves were not commercially viable. In the Ingessana hills, in the east, there are deposits of chrome ore. In the 1970s, chromium was produced locally, but today there is only export of the ore itself; in 2006, Sudan produced 20,000 tonnes of ore. The hills of eastern Sudan have a long tradition of gold working which stretches back to antiquity. Commercial exploitation of this was intermittent in the nineteenth and twentieth centuries, but since 1991 there has been consistent production by a company majority-owned by the Sudanese government. Production of gold may be falling; very different figures are given by different sources: a recent government claim that Sudan produces 20,000 kg of gold a year, much of it from artisanal panning of alluvial gold, is well above other estimates, which put the figure at 4-5,000 kg. Eastern Sudan also has large deposits of gypsum, and in 2006 14,000 tonnes a year were being mined.

Oil

Sudan's oil is mostly quite far from the northern riverain area. One of the striking aspects of the exploitation of this resource has been the efficiency with which the revenue from it has – despite the distance involved – been largely channelled to Greater Khartoum (though the revenues are now shared with the Government of Southern Sudan). The oil concessions run across Sudan, mostly sloping down from west to east, from southern Darfur to eastern Equatoria; there are concession blocks around Khartoum and in the east, but it is not clear what reserves these northern fields may actually hold. Most of the known oil reserves are in the south. The pipelines run north to Khartoum state, where one refinery is located, and then on to Port Sudan, where there is another refinery, and from where the oil is shipped, most going to the China and Japan.

Not all of Sudan's oil is the same. That from the border area whether greater Bahr al-Ghazal meets Kordofan, which was the first area to be commercially exploited, is called Nile blend; it is of a higher quality than the Dar blend which comes from Upper Nile. Fula blend, from the Kordofan-Darfur borderland, is used for domestic consumption.

Since commercial production began, in 1999, oil has transformed the economy of the central state – though not of Sudan as a whole. In 2008, oil accounted for 95 per cent of Sudan's exports, by value, and for 60 per cent of overall government revenue; during the CPA period, the Government of Southern Sudan has developed as an institution which is completely dependent on oil, which provides 98 per cent of its revenue. This governmental dependence is the corollary of a very high level of state involvement in the oil industry. While the precise terms vary in different concession blocks, the basic model has been for joint ventures between government corporations and foreign investors. These allow close government control; they have also allowed the elaboration of a corporate system in northern Sudan, in which there is a very close relationship between government and private sector. The oil industry appears to represent the most extreme manifestation of Sudan's distinctive political geography, in which the northern riverain area dominates, and derives wealth from, the rest of the country.

When the oil runs out in Sudan, sometime in the next few decades, water is likely to reassert itself as the country's key economic resource. The construction of dams on the Nile, the generation of electricity as an alternative power source, and the establishment of associated agricultural schemes are the main components of Khartoum's development strategy in the north. In the south, the Jonglei Canal, abandoned in 1983 at the start of the north-south civil war, may be revived. But the effect of a new Jonglei Canal project on dry season grazing and on the wildlife resources of Sudan – and on public opinion – is hard to predict. It is also possible that the waters of the Nile may become a source of international conflict. Sudan is one of nine countries involved in the Nile Basin initiative (an independent south Sudan would make this ten), which has attempted to renegotiate the international agreements that regulate the use of water by riparian states. The agreements give Egypt and Sudan the right to the lion's share in the use of the Nile waters. According to the Nile Waters Agreement of 1929 (and its 1959 amendment), Sudan's share is 18.5 billion cubic metres. Together with Egypt's 55.5 billion cubic metres, the claims of the two northernmost riverain countries account for almost 90 per cent of the annual flow of the Nile. Conflict over this resource has long been a source of friction with the other Nile Basin countries; many years of negotiation have failed to resolve their differences.

Recommended Reading

Tothill, J.D. (ed.). *Agriculture in the Sudan*. London: Oxford University Press, 1948.

Barbour, K.M. *The Republic of the Sudan: a Regional Geography*. London: University of London, 1961.

Howell, Paul, Lock, Michael and Cobb, Stephen (eds). *The Jonglei Canal: Impact and Opportunity*. Cambridge: Cambridge University Press, 1988.

Collins, Robert O. *The Waters of the Nile: Hydropolitics and the Jonglei Canal, 1900–88*. Oxford: Clarendon Press, 1990 and Princeton: Markus Weiner, 1996.

3

Early States on the Nile

ABDELRAHMAN ALI MOHAMMED
& DEREK WELSBY

Sudan, Nubia and Egypt

Discussions of Sudan's history before the late nineteenth century are complicated by differences between present-day political and cultural boundaries and those of earlier periods. The first cataract of the Nile near present-day Aswan is a key reference point. From the emergence of the Pharaonic state around 3000 BCE onwards, the southern border of Egypt lay hereabouts. Egypt often controlled territory further south, but to the Egyptians the land beyond the cataract remained an alien realm. In later periods, although the location of the frontier fluctuated , a major cultural boundary remained. Following the Mahdist revolt in the 1880s and the expulsion of Egypt from Sudan, Egyptian control was maintained as far south as Wadi Halfa, and in January 1899 the official frontier between the two countries was fixed along the Twenty-second Parallel, which lies just north of the Second Cataract. In any treatment of the history of Sudan prior to this time, the part of Egypt that lies south of the First Cataract must be included.

Not only boundaries, but geographical and cultural terminology change over time. Thus the term Nubia may be used historically to describe an extensive cultural zone, reaching as far north as the First Cataract, but in the present day it has a more restricted definition, signifying those reaches of the river north of the Nile bend where speakers of Nubian languages reside.

The Rediscovery of Sudan's Ancient Past

For those to the north of Sudan, interest in the lands that lie southwards extends back over five millennia. Egyptians came to Sudan as traders, prospectors and conquerors. The fifth century Greek historian Herodotus recorded tales of the lands to the south of Egypt. The Romans invaded the region and sent a fact-finding mission which may have reached as far south as the Sudd. Byzantine missionaries proselytized upstream of the Nile confluence as far as Soba East, the capital of the medieval kingdom of Alwa; Muslim travellers traversed the northern part of the country; and a Catalan speaker, perhaps a pilgrim, visited the southern Dongola Reach in the thirteenth century. These visitors were followed by the prolific Ottoman writer Evliya Çelebi in the seventeeth century. The history of the region may seem to be characterized by the expansion of northern powers southwards. At certain times, though, the powers that arose south of the First Cataract, that is to say in what is now northern Sudan, were able to push back and conquer the lands to the north.

The first significant contribution to uncovering Sudan's past came when the Scottish traveller James Bruce passed through a field of ruins near the village of Begrawiya in 1772 and correctly identified it as the site of Meroe, the Kushite capital in the first Millennium BCE and early centuries CE. From the early nineteenth century, Sudan drew the interest of a new kind of European scholar – many of them from a background in Egyptological or Middle Eastern studies. Almost all their activities were focused on the northern Nile Valley. The excavations organized and financed by Henry Wellcome, the pharmaceutical entrepreneur, at Jebel Moya in the Gezira, between the Blue Nile and White Nile, were a rare exception to the rule.

These researchers sought out the major monumental sites that could be associated with Egypt and the Classical World. In central Sudan and southern Sudan such remains did not exist and those areas were almost totally neglected, as were the desert regions to the east and west of the Nile. Southern Sudan became the preserve of the anthropologist and ethnographer, and this imbalance in the available data persists to this day, partly as the result of the long periods of insecurity in the south. Darfur, like the south, has also been little explored by archaeologists to date.

The Sudan Antiquities Service

The Sudan Antiquities Service was established in 1903, but for many years it was run on a part-time basis. The first Commissioner was not appointed until 1939, and the Service was not systematically organized until the 1950s. Throughout the 1960s and 1970s the Service concentrated its efforts on the UNESCO Campaign to Save the Monuments of Nubia that accompanied the construction of the Aswan High Dam in Egypt. Today Sudan is seeing a rapid increase in human settlement, particularly around the main urban centres. Archaeological remains are increasingly threatened by this periurban expansion, and by dam construction schemes – as with earlier major development projects such as the construction of dams at Sennar and Jebel Aulia in the 1920s and 1930s and Roseires in the 1960s, and the development of the Gezira cotton scheme. Until recently such schemes were undertaken without any archaeological rescue operations with consequent loss of valuable information on important sites. Awareness of the importance of the archaeological heritage is now reflected in government programmes which aim to protect the country's cultural heritage. The Antiquities Ordinance of 1999 includes a provision that development projects may be initiated only after the completion of archaeological studies.

Hunters, Gatherers, Early Farmers

Traces of some of the earliest inhabitants of Sudan have been reported in the Dongola Reach at the site of Kaddanarti, just to the north of Kerma. Recent excavations at the island of Sai resulted in the discovery of a well-preserved settlement spanning the period between 300,000 to 200,000 years BCE, and provided new information about the early human occupation of this region of the Nile Valley. Red and yellow iron oxide was collected here, apparently for use as pigments, and this has been claimed as evidence of early artistic activity. The climate at that time was relatively humid but became arid soon after.

The earliest and most representative Palaeolithic site in central Sudan is Khor Abu Anga in Omdurman, discovered in 1949. The site is associated with the long period of human history in which our ancestors used simple stone tools and lived by hunting and gathering. Other sites from this era have been recorded in Wadi Halfa and Argin, while later Lower and Middle Palaeolithic sites were also found in the Dongola Reach. A cemetery at Jebel Sahaba dated towards the end of the Palaeolithic period has been called the earliest war cemetery in the world. Here lie the remains of up to 53 men, women and children, most of them slain by stone-tipped arrows.

Mesolithic populations were hunter-gatherers who developed sedentary societies with a food-collecting economy. In Sudan, they lived along the Nile and its tributaries, exploiting riverine resources, producing pottery and utilizing tools of stone and bone. The Mesolithic period (8500-5500 BCE) in the Nile Valley was first noted as a result of excavation at Khartoum hospital by A.J Arkell, a British colonial administrator and archaeologist. Arkell's excavations in 1949 at esh-Shaheinab provided the first evidence of the Early Neolithic period (4900-3800 BCE) in central Sudan. This period is characterized by a more systematic food producing economy, with the harvesting of wild grains of barley and sorghum and herding of cattle and goats. During this period the climate in the Sahara was warm and humid.

The First Urban Civilization and Relations with Egypt

Towards the end of the Neolithic, extensive urban settlement began in the Northern Dongola Reach; evidence for this has been located beneath one of the cemeteries at Kerma. Until recently considered to be a small rural settlement, it is clear that in the third millennium BCE there was a large urban complex here surrounded by massive and complex defences. Within the timber and earthwork ramparts are many circular timber huts, rectilinear structures and storage pits. The town predates the development of urbanism elsewhere in sub-Saharan Africa by several millennia. Presumably built on the banks of a channel of the Nile, the town may have been abandoned as the river channel shifted further to the west.

Around 2500 BCE another urban centre developed four kilometres to the west. This town became the metropolis of what was known to the Egyptians as the Kingdom of Kush. Like its predecessor it had elaborate defences, an important religious quarter at its heart and innumerable domestic buildings, administrative and industrial complexes. The rulers of Kush rapidly assumed control of the Nile Valley from the upstream end of the Fourth Cataract at Mograt Island to the island of Sai. The material culture of this kingdom, known by the name of its type site, Kerma, is distinctive. It is typified by extremely fine handmade pottery, amongst the best ever made in the Nile Valley, black-topped red ware with a metallic sheen on the black interior and, in case of Kerma Ancien pottery, finely decorated below the rim.

The kingdom of Kush was a major trading partner of ancient Egypt, situated athwart the land route that linked Egypt and the Mediterranean world with central Africa. Its trading networks were extensive and may have included areas far to the south east near Kassala on what is now the Eritrean border, perhaps one of the regions known to the Egyptians as Punt. The trade items passing through Kerma – ivory, animal skins, hard woods, gold and slaves among them – brought great wealth to the town and this is displayed in the royal tombs. The main cemetery, on the site of the pre-Kerma settlement, covers an area of nearly 90 hectares. It is estimated to contain between 30,000 to 40,000 burials. One, perhaps of a king of the middle period of the Kerma kingdom is a grave 11.7 metres in diameter and 2 metres deep, covered by a mound 25 metres across; on the south side there is a crescent of over 4000 cattle skulls. The tombs of the later Kerma kings were even more impressive. Buried under mounds up to 90 metres in diameter they were accompanied to their deaths by as many as 400 sacrificed humans, amongst whom may have been members of the king's family, retainers and prisoners of war.

The respect shown for the military prowess of the Kushites by the Egyptians is demonstrated on the one hand by the units of archers drawn from this region in the Egyptian army and, on the other, by the massive fortifications the Egyptians built during the Twelfth Dynasty to protect their southern border. These forts have names such as 'Warding off the bows'. During the period 1750-1650 BCE, Egyptian power was on the wane. In the north, the Hyksos, an Asiatic people, occupied the Delta. During this period the kingdom of Kush occupied all the territory up to the First Cataract and raided with impunity deep into Egypt.

A recently studied inscription from el-Kab 125 kilometres north of the First Cataract begins thus: 'Listen you, who are alive upon earth ... Kush came ... aroused along his length, he having stirred up the tribes of Wawat ... the land of Punt and the Medjaw...' The Egyptian pharaoh Kamose bemoaned the fact that 'when a chieftain is in Avaris and another in Kush and I sit in league with an Asiatic and a Nubian, every man [is] holding his slice of Egypt.'

With the resurgence of Egyptian power, particularly under Ahmose (c.1550-1525 BCE) the Egyptians went on the offensive. After ousting the Hyksos from the Delta, Ahmose turned his attentions south. By 1500 BCE Thutmose I had vanquished the Kushite king in a major battle at the Third Cataract and set up his boundary stela, a carved stone marker, far upstream at Kurgus.

Egyptian control lasted until the early eleventh century BCE, evidenced by a string of major fortified towns extending as far as Jebel Barkal, a site the Egyptians believed to be the southern ancestral home of their state god Amun. Although the Egyptian domination is evident in the urban centres, its impact on the bulk of the population within its territory may have been much less significant. It appears that when Egypt abandoned its conquests south of the First Cataract, indigenous culture once again came to the fore. This is indicated in funerary customs, ceramic production and architecture.

The Rise and Fall of Kush

The situation in Nubia in the few centuries after the Egyptian withdrawal is unclear. We have hints of an important power base at Qasr Ibrim where there was an impressive fortified stronghold, but it was at el-Kurru, twelve kilometres

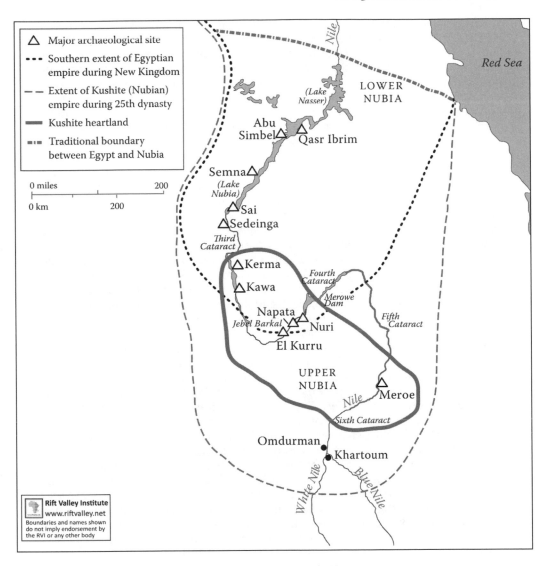

Map 3.1 Ancient Nubia

downstream from the rock massif of Jebel Barkal, that a new state arose which was destined to dominate the Nile Valley from the confluence of the two Niles as far as the Mediterranean. Here there was a clear development of graves, tomb superstructures and funerary customs from indigenous pit graves to extended mummified burials in elaborately decorated rock-cut tombs crowned by dressed-stone pyramids. This sequence, documenting the adoption of many aspects of Egyptian religion and funerary culture appears to have been very rapid, spanning a period of only 200 years. This was presumably mirrored by an equally rapid expansion of the state, its leaders rising from local chieftains to become kings of a vast empire.

Unfortunately we know virtually nothing of how this transformation was achieved. What does seem clear is that the early Kushite rulers embraced the Egyptian mythology relating to Jebel Barkal, acquiring the knowledge to allow them to understand the many Egyptian inscriptions and reliefs decorating the temples at the mountain's foot. This material made it clear that Egypt had claimed its legitimacy to rule Kush by its control of the southern home of Amun in the *jebel* itself. It was, therefore, as champions of the Egyptian state god Amun – by then also a Kushite god – that the Kushite king Kashta in the mid eighth century BCE took over control of southern Egypt. His successor Piankhi (Piye) went on to conquer the whole of Egypt and to rule, briefly, the largest empire ever seen on the Nile, only surpassed by that of Mohammed Ali in the 1820s, over 2500 years later.

Kushite control of Egypt was brief. Faced with an aggressive Assyria (against whom Kush fought first in the Levant) Kushite rule in Egypt was finally broken with the sacking of Thebes by the Assyrians in 663 BCE. Although forced to retire to the south, the Kushites maintained control over a vast tract of the Nile Valley well upstream of modern-day Khartoum. How far their writ extended to the east and west of the Nile is unclear, but Kushite sites are known deep in the Bayuda, over a hundred kilometres up the Wadi Howar in the Libyan Desert and in the Butana. In the first few centuries of its existence a religious centre developed at Napata, the name given to the region around Jebel Barkal, but a major urban centre was already in existence at Meroe far to the south. The importance of Meroe was further enhanced when the royal burial ground was relocated there in the early third century BCE. For visitors today, the pyramid fields of Meroe are one of Sudan's most spectacular archeological sites.

Kushite culture is an interesting amalgam of influences from Egypt merged with local sub-Saharan African traditions. Over its 1200-year history this culture developed dramatically, partly as a result of cultural and political changes in its original source of inspiration, Egypt. In the early period Kush assimilated Pharaonic Egyptian culture and adopted Egyptian as its written language for monumental inscriptions. However, as Egypt itself came under the control of a succession of foreign rulers – Persians, Macedonians and Romans – so the influences on Kush changed. Although the Kushites had presumably always had their own language it was only around the third century BCE that a writing system was developed. Thereafter monumental inscriptions and graffiti alike were largely written in this language, now known as Meroitic, which is still very little understood.

Whereas Egypt, a province of the Roman Empire, embraced Christianity during the third and fourth centuries CE, the Kushites remained true to ancestral gods, both local and of Egyptian origin. But the Kushite state collapsed in the fourth century CE. The state, being a generally very thin strip of territory extending over more than 2000 kilometres along the Nile, was inherently unstable. The wealth and power of the kings based at Meroe will have been what held it together; most of this was derived from the control of trade from central Africa. In the third century CE, however, the volume of this trade was reduced by the impoverishment of the Roman Empire and the rise of another trade route through Axum on the Ethiopian plateau. Although Kushite culture survived to an extent, the territorial integrity of the state was lost.

The Christian Kingdoms of Nubia

Historical sources record that by the mid sixth century CE there were three successor states, Nobadia in the north with its capital at Faras, Makuria in the centre with its capital at Old Dongola, and Alwa (Alodia) in the south with its capital at Soba East. It was these three states which were converted to Christianity by missionaries sent from Byzantine Egypt and Constantinople. This marked a pivotal moment in the cultural history of the Middle Nile Valley; the arrival and possibly rapid adoption of the new religion wiped away millennia of Egyptian and indigenous religious traditions, signalling, notably, the end of the 5000-year old practice of human sacrifice.

The adoption of Christianity doubtless brought important political benefits, allying the Nubian states with Byzantium, the regional superpower. However, the balance of power in the region was shattered in the early seventh century by the Persian conquest of Egypt. Although the Byzantines re-established their control, the armies of Islam dealt a crushing blow both to Byzantium and the Sassanian Empire in the 630s; and the Arab invasion of Egypt in 639 produced a permanent change in the politics of the region. The highly aggressive new masters of Egypt immediately advanced into Nubia under Abdullahi bin el-Sarh. Here, though, they met both a hostile landscape and a bellicose enemy whose prowess with the bow made a deep impression on the would-be conquerors. One Arab source reports 'the Muslims had never suffered a loss like the one they had in Nubia.' Returning a decade later and laying siege to Old Dongola, hostilities were brought to a close with the signing of a peace accord, the *Baqt*, which guaranteed the territorial integrity of Nubia. Over the following centuries the Nubian kingdoms Makuria, Alwa and Nobadia developed a vibrant culture.

The Coming of Islam

Although Christianity remained the dominant religion on the Middle Nile until the thirteenth century, Arab settlers began to arrive much earlier, first along the Red Sea coast by way of Egypt and then westwards to the Nile and beyond. Contact between Arabia and Sudan had existed long before Islam. There were two main routes: the first ran across the Sinai Desert through Egypt and into the Sudan; the second was across the Bab el-Mandab into Abyssinia and then northward, or directly across the Red Sea. Ninth-century Islamic tombstones from Khor Nubt in the Eastern Desert provide early evidence for this Arab penetration. Later migrations of Arab groups from the Arabian Peninsula to Sudan contributed a great deal to its Islamic culture, and led to the building of ports and towns at Badi, Aidhab and Suakin and, in the post-medieval period, at Sennar and El-Fasher.

There is clear evidence for the presence of Muslims within the Christian communities of Nubia. A large Muslim community, for example, presumably traders, is recorded on the banks of the Blue Nile within the Alwan capital in the tenth century. It was at the time of the Crusades that attitudes to Christian Nubia in the Muslim world seem to have changed. The first major breach of the peaceful coexistence of Muslims and Christians on the Nile took place under Salah ed-Din, by then the ruler of Egypt, who sent his brother Shams ed-Dawla to attack Nubia in 1173. The next two centuries saw a round of invasions, many reaching the Makurian capital. These were often precipitated by rival pretenders to the Makurian throne soliciting assistance from the Arabs to the north. In 1317, what may have been the audience hall of the Makurian kings at Old Dongola, was converted into a mosque; soon afterwards the ruler of the Christian kingdom is recorded as being a Muslim.

The decline of Alwa, the Christian kingdom to the south, is largely undocumented. The great red-brick churches excavated in the capital seem to have been occupied by squatters as early as the thirteenth century. A very late source, the Funj Chronicle, reports that Soba was overthrown in 1504 by a coalition of Arabs and the Funj of Sennar, under their leaders Abdallah Gamaa and Omarah Dongus. The Funj state occupied the Gezira between the Blue and the White Niles and the upper reaches of the Blue Nile and extended its control into Kordofan and to the Red Sea in the region of Suakin. The emergence of this state facilitated the emergence of Islamic kingdoms in other parts of the Sudan, such as the Fur and el-Masabaat kingdom in western Sudan, the Sheikhdom of el-Abdallab, with its capital firstly in Gerri and later at Halfaya near Khartoum, and the Sheikhdom of the Red Sea and Fazogli.

Egypt was under Ottoman control from the early sixteenth century, and there was an Ottoman presence on Sudan's Red Sea coast, at Suakin, from 1524. In the Nile Valley the Ottoman frontier was pushed south from Aswan to the First Cataract, then on to the Third Cataract. Advancing north down the Nile, the expanding Funj came face to face with the Ottomans pushing in the opposite direction. After a battle at Hannek near the Third Cataract in 1584, the protagonists left a wide loosely controlled region between the Ottoman outpost on Sai Island and the area of direct Funj control, corresponding to the ancient boundary between Nobatia and Makuria. This frontier marked the southern limit of the Ottoman Empire's North African territory. By the early nineteenth century, however, Ottoman control over the north had lapsed and the Funj state was in terminal decline.

Recommended Reading

Adams, William Y. *Nubia: Corridor to Africa.* London: Princeton, 1997.
Edwards, David N. *The Nubian Past: an Archaeology of the Sudan.* London: Routledge, 2004.
Hassan, Yusuf F. (ed.) *Sudan in Africa.* Khartoum: University of Khartoum Press, 1971.
Török, Laszlo. *The Kingdom of Kush. Handbook of the Napatan-Meroitic Civilization.* Leiden: Brill, 1997.
Welsby, Derek A. *The Kingdom of Kush, the Napatan and Meroitic Empires.* London: The British Museum Press, 1996.
Welsby, Derek A. *The Medieval Kingdoms of Nubia: Pagans, Christians and Muslims on the Middle Nile.* London: The British Museum Press, 2002.

4

Peoples & Cultures
of Two Sudans

JOHN RYLE

Whether Sudan is considered as a single country or two, cultural diversity and ethnic complexity are among its most immediately striking features. Between them, north and South Sudan are host to two world religions, myriad local belief systems and hundreds of indigenous languages (rivalling Africa's most polyglot nations, Nigeria, Cameroon and the Democratic Republic of Congo). The modes of livelihood of contemporary Sudanese range from the daily commute of the urban middle-class in the expanding suburbs of Khartoum to the long-range migrations of camel pastoralists in the arid lands of eastern Sudan. And from the deal-making of merchants and itinerant street-traders and the field labour of tenant-farmers in the Gezira to the domestic cultivations of Equatorian forest-dwellers and the seasonal movement of cattle keepers in the swamps and savannahs of Bahr al-Ghazal.

Ethnic groups in Sudan are numerous; and individual and group identities have multiple aspects. Sudanese people differentiate themselves – or have been differentiated by others – using a range of overlapping criteria: lines of descent, common language, place of origin, mode of livelihood, physical characteristics, and political or religious affiliation. The resulting categories may appear to perpetuate difference, but they also enable its opposite: the ordering of relations of exchange and cooperation between communities. Ethnic and other categories change and crosscut one another, reflecting shared histories.

Sudan's inhabitants have been progressively linked together over centuries by patterns of trade and migration, and by an emerging political economy that has changed their relations to state power and to each other. Their labour – and their ancestors' labour – has been exploited, often by force, and their livelihoods modified or transformed. They have been both victims and instruments of political turbulence and military devastation. Such disruptive episodes, particularly in recent times, have forced many, particularly those living outside the northern heartland in the Nile valley, to move in order to survive, engendering further economic and cultural transformations.

Understanding these Sudanese communities and the relations between them requires an approach that combines geographical, historical and anthropological forms of knowledge. For this purpose, Sudan may be divided into seven regions: the northern heartland that lies along the Nile between Dongola and Khartoum and between the Blue and White Niles; Nubia in the far north towards Egypt; the

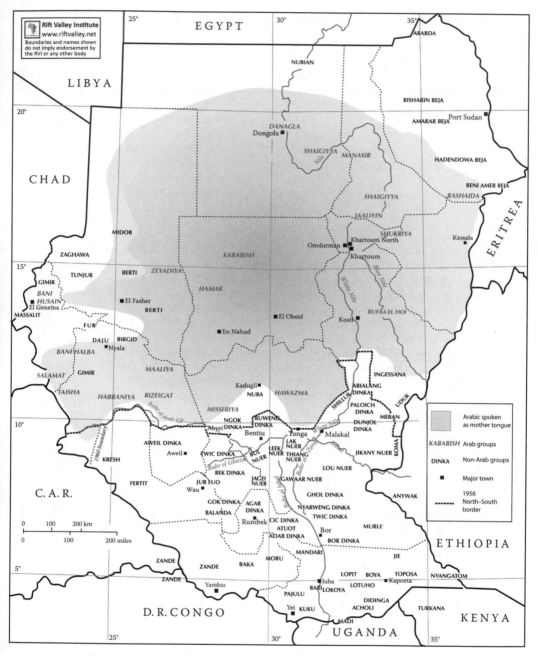

Map 4.1 *Principal ethnic and ethnolinguistic groups in Sudan and approximate home territories*

desert region in the east stretching to the Red Sea hills and the coast; Darfur and Kordofan in the west; the north-south borderlands along the Tenth Parallel; the floodplain of the White Nile forming the southern heartland; and, finally, beyond it, the wooded ironstone plateau of Equatoria.

People from all these regions of Sudan have long been resident in major towns all across the country (and in neighbouring African countries, and – more recently – in the cities of Europe, North America and Australia). Yet local origin and a sense of belonging based on kinship or common language remain the primary components of identity for most Sudanese, even for those born and raised far from their places of familial or ancestral origin, as many are. Kinship is the fundamental language of social association; and the greater the distance from the centres of power and the reach of central government the greater the importance likely to be accorded to it, and the less compunction in invoking it.

Some aspects of the cultural diversity of the north and south Sudan may be understood as the product of long-term movements of people into or across geographical zones, and corresponding changes in their modes of production, a process that starts with the first expansion of early humans into north-eastern Africa. This diversity is also the product of much more recent events, and processes of interaction and redefinition that are still in progress. As the Anglo-Sudanese novelist Jamal Mahjoub has written, Sudan has a multi-layered history, one that has 'crystallized from the crucible of possibility'.

Migration, Settlement and State Formation

In prehistoric Eastern Africa, the unchronicled migrations of hunters and gatherers were followed, first, by the introduction of domesticated animals from Asia, notably the long-horned, auroch-like cattle whose descendants are still the source of livelihood for stock-keepers in south Sudan and the north-south borderlands, then – around the fifth millennium BCE – by the introduction of agriculture. The states that arose in the Nile Valley thereafter owed their wealth and power to the ability to produce food surpluses from the labour of slaves, usually raided from populations further south (raids that were themselves carried out by slave armies) and to the extraction of natural resources such as gold, ivory, skins and timber. This pattern of accumulation endured through the rise and fall of the Nubian kingdoms of the pre-Christian era, through the Christian kingdoms of the middle ages, into the Muslim polities of the sixteenth century, and beyond. Its legacy in interethnic relations can still be seen in Sudan today.

In the current era, the most significant event in Sudan's demographic and social history has been the process of Arabization and Islamization, an epochal change that transformed indigenous societies across the African continent. After the advent of Islam in the seventh century, a pre-existing pattern of small-scale population exchange between Arabia and Africa was succeeded by a long-term process which combined the physical migration of people from the Arabian peninsula with extensive assimilation between these migrants and indigenous African populations, and the establishment of trade networks that linked Egypt and the Middle East to West Africa. In time, this was to bring a new religion, a new language and a new source of social organization to a region stretching from Senegal to the Red Sea, the region known to the Arabs as Bilad al-Sudan, 'the land of black people'.

Following the first Islamic conquests of North Africa, small numbers of armed traders followed the Nile Valley southward to Nubia: a seventh-century agreement records the establishment of relations between the new Muslim rulers of Egypt and the indigenous Nubian kings, marked by an annual tribute of slaves. Later, in the fourteenth century, conflict in Egypt encouraged Arab migration southwards to Nubia, and, from the sixteenth century onwards, the Arabization of the central area of Sudan gathered pace.

This cultural penetration has been characterized by historians as a predominantly non-violent process, involving the progressive assimilation of indigenous populations by marriage and proselytization. By this account the paradigmatic bearers of Islam were itinerant holy men and teachers (who were sometimes also traders). With them came the slow spread of literacy and a new grammar of kinship, one that gave recently Islamicized communities the opportunity to create lines of patrilineal descent linking them to the family of the Prophet Mohamed or his followers, thus merging diverse local cultures into an Arab ethnic identity. The legend of the wise stranger, a founding ancestor of Arab origin who is given the daughter of a local ruler in marriage and becomes ruler in his turn, is widespread among communities in the north and west of Sudan.

From the sixteenth century onwards new centres of power emerged in the region that was to become Sudan: the Funj kingdom in the Nile Valley around Sennar – an area that is still a key part of the heartland of the modern northern Sudanese state – and, in the west, the Fur sultanate and the Masalit sultanate, both of which endured into the twentieth century. The rulers and the subjects of the Fur and Masalit sultanates were Muslims, but most of them did not embrace an Arab identity in the way that some of the Funj peoples and others closer to the Nile came to do. Nor did they abandon their native languages. Today, considerable sections of the population of northern Sudan – in Darfur and elsewhere, while practising Islam and speaking one of the Sudanese dialects of Arabic as a lingua franca, retain their own languages. They remain culturally distinct from Arab communities living alongside or among them. These differences may be underlined locally, in rural areas, by differences in modes of livelihood – most Arab groups in Darfur, for example, are primarily nomadic pastoralists; while many of the non-Arab groups are sedentary farmers. But ethnicity and livelihood do not map onto each other with any consistency: non-Arabs can be pastoralists; groups and individuals of Arab origin may settle and become farmers.

Arab Identities in Northern Sudan

The historical limits of Arabization can be seen in the overall distribution of languages and cultures in contemporary Sudan. In the central areas of northern Sudan in the Nile Valley, the great majority of the inhabitants identify as belonging to one or another of a dozen or more Arab tribal groups: they practise Islam, claim Arab descent and speak only Arabic. These children of the river, *awlad al-bahr*, have dominated the post-Independence state. In the far north and in the east of the country, however, as in Darfur, non-Arabic languages are still spoken and non-Arab identities maintained.

In the east, the Beja, an indigenous people over a million strong, who occupy most of Red Sea State (and whose presence there is recorded from antiquity), preserve, for the most part, clear cultural differences from neighbouring Arab communities, whether they continue the traditional Beja life as rural camel-breeders, or live in towns such as Port Sudan, where many have been compelled to migrate by drought. Here, Arabic may be the language of religion, of government and commerce, but Bedawi, the Beja language, forms the fabric of everyday domestic life. In Nubia, between Wadi Halfa, on the border with Egypt, and Dongola to the south, several indigenous languages are still spoken, at least by those of an older generation. And traces of pre-Islamic Nubian culture can be discerned upstream from Dongola, among the more Arabized peoples towards the centre of the country. South of Khartoum, beyond Kosti, the limit of Arab-Islamic cultural influence coincides, more or less, with the border between north and south Sudan (though a form of Arabic is the lingua franca of the south).

Today something over half of the inhabitants of northern Sudan – between fifteen and twenty million people – would define themselves as belonging to one or another group of Arab, or Afro-Arab, descent. Most of these descent groups fall, in theory, under one of two higher-order groups, Jaali and Juhayna. The logic of patrilineality is liable to break down on examination, however; there is often a lack of fit between particular Arab tribal identities and these overarching categories. The sedentary peoples of the central Nile valley mostly define themselves as Jaali (to be distinguished from the Jaaliyin, a Jaali subgroup), and many claim lineages which link them to a common ancestor, Ibrahim Jaal, and through him to al-Abbas, uncle of the Prophet Mohamed. The other overarching Arab group, the Juhayna, includes most present-day nomadic groups, and a number that were historically nomadic but have long been settled.

The educated elites of three groups in the central Nile valley, groups that came to prominence in the Turco-Egyptian and Condominium periods, have, to a significant extent, monopolized state power in the post-independence era. The Jaaliyin, a Jaali subgroup with an historic centre in Shendi, are the first of these. Jaaliyin have also, historically, dominated trade and business in the towns and cities of the north and, until the second civil war, in the south. The second of the key groups in northern politics is drawn from the Shaigiya, a tribal confederacy known historically for initial resistance to the Turco-Egyptian invasion of Sudan and subsequent cooperation with the invaders, and later for their domination of Sudan's armed forces. The third of the triumvirate of riverain groups from which the political elites have been drawn is the Danagla, the people of Dongola in southern Nubia. Danagla are found in every town and city of the north (as are Shagiya and Jaaliyin), while the original Dongolawi communities maintain a traditional rural life as date-farmers, cultivating the strip of fertile land along the banks of the river downstream of the great Nile bend, where a Nubian language continues to be spoken, adding a significant undertone to an otherwise Arab-inflected cultural identity.

Beyond the northern Sudanese heartland, away from the two Niles, in Kordofan and parts of Darfur, is the territory of nomadic Arab camel and cattle pastoralists. Many Arabs in Kordofan and Darfur trace their ancestry, nominally at least, to a second wave of migration sometime after the seventeenth century, which entered Sudan from the east. Their traditions and ways of life – and their historical origins – are distinct from those of the farming people living along the river and the latter's urbanized relatives in the cities of the heartland. This difference is reflected in a paradoxical use of the term 'Arab' in riverain communities: it may be used as a self-description, or in a pejorative sense to refer to these desert-dwelling nomads.

The Kababish, an historically recent confederation of camel keepers who live in the arid lands of northern Kordofan, have been seen as typifying the way of life of the desert-dwelling Arab peoples – though since the 1980s many of them have lived in poverty on the fringes of Omdurman, having lost their livestock to droughts and misgovernment. In northern Kordofan and in northern Darfur there are numerous other such groups of Abbala – camel-keeping tribes – wresting a living from the harsh environment, as herders and harvesters of gum Arabic. Further south, in southern Darfur and southern Kordofan – in the northern part of the north-south borderlands – where greater rainfall expands the possibilities of livestock husbandry, is a broad belt of cattle-keeping Arab peoples, known collectively as Baggara (their name derived from the Arabic term for cow). Baggara groups include the Hawazma, Misseriya, Rizeigat, Taisha and Habbaniya. To a still greater extent than other Arab incomers, these cattle nomads of the west have politically and economically assimilated indigenous populations, while themselves being physically assimilated, an ancestry visible in skin tones that are darker than those of most other Arab Sudanese, as dark as many southerners.

Skin-colour, it may be noted, though it is not a matter of indifference to Sudanese, does not map onto ethnic divisions, here or elsewhere. Thus the Juhayna group also includes the Shukriya in the Butana region and the mainly pastoralist Rufaa al-Hoi and Kenana on the Blue Nile. The latter two groups tend to be paler-skinned than other Sudanese, with more recent narratives of arrival from the Arabian peninsula. (The most recent of all Arab migrants to Sudan are the Rashaida, who settled in the eastern borderlands in the 1860s.)

From the 1920s onwards Sudanese nationalists, mainly from riverain groups, worked to develop a self-consciously Sudanese Arabic cultural identity. After independence, accordingly, a policy of arabization, *tariib*, was adopted by successive governments in Khartoum and propagated in every region of the country. But government policies of Arabization and Islamization, which involved, among other measures, the expulsion of western missionaries from the south and the replacement of English with Arabic as the language of instruction in southern schools, served to sharpen differences rather than elide them. The near-monopoly of political power on the part of elites from the central riverain region encouraged the growth of an idea of Arab racial supremacy. Southerners, in particular, were often targets of ethnic prejudice that invoked an earlier history of enslavement of people from the south. This contributed, in time, to insurgencies in the peripheries, first in the south and then in the west. In the civil wars that followed successive governments in Khartoum resorted to an ethnically based counter-insurgency policy that involved the use of tribal militias recruited from Arab groups to attack non-Arab communities in areas of rebel support, a strategy that has provoked polarization of these communities.

The Limits of Arab Influence

In the heart of Darfur, the forebears of the non-Arab Fur established the Darfur sultanate on the fertile slopes of the Jebel Marra massif, and ruled there, from the seventeenth to the twentieth century (with an interruption during the Mahdiyya), over an ethnically heterogenous population that included both nomadic Arab groups and non-Arab farming communities. Today, though, Fur territory and other parts of the Darfur region are in increasingly disputed political space. Due to a significant extent to the government's use of militias drawn from Arab nomadic groups and the ethnic divide-and-rule strategy of which this is a part, tribal identities in Darfur have become militarized; and rights to land brutally contested.

Another non-Arab group involved in the Darfur conflict is the Zaghawa, whose territory extends across the border into Chad. Traditionally camel pastoralists, over the last two generations many Zaghawa have metamorphosed into transnational traders. Their truck convoys span the Sahara – from the oases of the Sahara to Suq Libya on the outskirts of Omdurman. But Zaghawa communities, too, have participated in and suffered from the effects of civil war. In recent years large numbers of Darfuris – including Zaghawa, Fur, Masalit and other ethnic groups – have been driven from their villages and forced into displaced camps on the outskirts of towns, contributing to a wider drift towards urbanization.

In scattered communities in western Sudan and, to a greater extent, in the central Nile Valley – particularly in the Gezira – descendants of migrants from West Africa have a significant presence. Before the advent of air travel, Muslims from West Africa travelled through Sudan on the overland pilgrimage route to Mecca; some remained, encouraged by the opportunities offered by colonial development schemes, and settled as wage labourers, principally in the Gezira, on the vast irrigated cotton-growing project between the Blue and White Nile southeast of Khartoum. The majority of these settlers were Hausa from northern Nigeria; the rest were drawn from other West African ethnic groups, some of them speaking Hausa as a lingua franca. In Sudan the settlers became known as Fellata (originally a term for the Fulani, one of the non-Hausa groups). The term was applied by other Sudanese to all descendants of West Africans and acquired a pejorative connotation. Today the term 'Hausa' is often used to refer to all Sudanese of West African descent, but communities of Fulani-speakers, mainly seasonal cattle nomads, maintain distinct cultural features. In recent years Sudanese Hausa have begun to assert an Arab identity, illustrating the flexibility in ethnic affiliation that is a persistent theme in Sudanese history.

Among the indigenous non-Arab peoples of northern Sudan, the hill-dwelling Nuba of southern Kordofan are the most culturally and linguistically diverse. Dozens of language groups are represented in a few thousand square kilometres of the Nuba mountains. Some originate from as far north as Nubia, but Nuba communities have their historical origins in many different areas of the country, diverse populations having been displaced over long periods of time and found refuge in these mountain redoubts. Today, some Nuba are Muslims; some Christians; some are neither; most groups are patrilineal, reckoning descent through a line of male ancestors as Arab, or Arabized, peoples do, but some are matrilineal, a form of social organization with a pre-Islamic origin. They share their territory, often acrimoniously, both with transhumant Baggara pastoralists and with the large-scale agricultural schemes established in recent decades by incomers in the valleys between the hills.

The Nuba (known outside Sudan for their traditions of wrestling and body decoration), are connected to northern Sudanese central riverain culture and economy through labour migration. For several generations there has been large-scale recruitment of Nuba into the ranks of the Sudanese Armed Forces. Yet during the second civil war in the south, resistance to acculturation and to the economic domination of the centre drove many, under the leadership of Yousif Kuwa, a Miri Nuba, to join the SPLA. (Raised as a Muslim, Yousif Kuwa described his political awakening in cultural terms, explaining that he had grown up believing he was an Arab, until he heard the Arab headmaster of his school say: 'What is the use of teaching these Nuba, who are only going to work as servants in houses?') Despite the lack of a common language – apart from Arabic – and their existence as distinct communities living in different hill areas, an emerging political consciousness gave some Nuba a sense of common destiny.

There are also similar, smaller, hilly redoubts on the Ethiopian border, home to groups such as the Ingessana (Gamk in their own language), and the Uduk ('Kwanim Pa in their own language). These too are, increasingly, affected by the expansion of the state and its attempts to control the periphery, and the conflicts this has brought in its wake.

Chiefs and Tribes

In the twentieth century, under British rule in Sudan, tribal identities such as these, in rural areas of the north and the south, were institutionalized in a system of indirect rule that was adapted from colonial administration in British West Africa. In Sudan the British administrators aimed to restore the authority of certain of the ruling families and structures of authority that had been destroyed during the preceding era of the Mahdiyya. Where these did not exist they were created. Local leaders and men of influence in rural areas were recognized as *omdas*, sultans or chiefs, in a system known as *idarra ahliya*, native administration,

Native administration served to increase the power of local elites, and perpetuate and sometimes deepen ethnic distinctions. Some groups were amalgamated with one another by edict; others were effectively created as an indirect result of the colonial dispensation. British rule thus simultaneously exploited the mutability of ethnicity and exalted the frequently mythical notion of common descent on which many ethnic identities were based. Native administration in northern Sudan also involved the recognition of collective rights to tribal lands or *dur* (plural of *dar*, homeland or territory), which further entrenched the authority of leading families of those groups recognized by the government, and left, in some cases, a problematic legacy of land tenure. Although the system of native administration was formally abolished by the regime of Jaafar Nimeiri in 1971, elements of the system of rule through chiefs and *omdas* have endured, and some have been restored in recent years, both by the government in the north and by the government in the south.

Tribal identity may be reinforced in other ways. Some Sudanese carry outward signs revealing ethnicity. Despite official disapprobation, traditions of facial scarring, *shulukh*, continue in rural areas of both north and south. Ritualized surgery of this kind may be for beautification or for therapeutic purposes; or it may provide an indication of the community into which a person has been born. The once-commonplace T or H shaped facial scars of Jaali men and women and the three horizontal lines of the Shaigiya are seen less frequently today, but the candelabra forehead marks on Dinka men from Bor, or the horizontal lines of the Nuer are a relatively frequent sight. (Scarification is a coming-of-age ritual among the Nuer and the Dinka, a procedure that, for boys, follows earlier removal of the lower front teeth.)

A contentious type of body modification that is widely practised in various forms in northern Sudan is female circumcision, or genital cutting. Anthropological accounts of the lives of women in communities in the north stress local understandings of this practice as part of a symbolic affirmation of female fertility, ritually separate from the world of men. Female circumcision is the subject of a continuing campaign in Sudan for its abolition or modification. Male circumcision is ubiquitous among Muslims in Sudan, and is also practised by some non-Muslim groups in the south.

In the south, although the respective roles of men and women are closely defined by cultural practice, there is generally less physical segregation in social relations. Despite extensive mixing between Sudanese from north and south over centuries, formal unions between people from the northern riverain areas and those from the south are not frequent. The absence of female circumcision in southern communities is not the only obstacle, nor even the main one. Many communities in the north, for instance, favour marriage between certain categories of cousin; and other biases may come into play. Within the north, unions between people from riverain communities and those from the west, or other peripheral regions, may not be regarded with favour by the families involved.

Peoples and Cultures of the South

South of the Tenth Parallel, Arab and Islamic influence diminishes markedly. But the peoples of the south are as varied in their ways of life and the moral worlds they inhabit as those of the north. Until the mid-nineteenth century much of what is now southern Sudan was sequestered from the north by impassable swamplands, but under Turco-Egyptian administration in the nineteenth century, Upper Nile and Bahr al-Ghazal and areas to the south were opened as a hunting ground for slaves, a time that is not forgotten in collective memory. In the twentieth century the British colonial administration discouraged Arab and Islamic influence in most of the region, and attempted, usually successfully, to establish rule through chiefs, a system similar to the native administration in the north, while missionary activity and Christian influence grew. Today, many in the south are adherents of indigenous religions; others have been Christians for generations; a few are Muslims; some span more than one world of belief.

Southerners live variously as sedentary farmers and as agro-pastoralists. In many parts of the south there is a general aspiration to ownership of cattle. Cattle give status; and are an important element in patterns of exchange and cooperation, particularly in marriage negotiations, often across apparent boundaries of ethnicity. But almost all of those commonly referred to as cattle pastoralists also grow crops, and most practise seasonal fishing: the choice of livelihood strategy is driven by geographical circumstance as much as ethnic identity. In terms of indigenous political organization of the peoples of the south there is also wide variation: some southerners live in communities under the authority of a hereditary monarch; others are reluctant to acknowledge any political authority at all, internal or external.

The pattern of life of southern societies, as with those in the north, is framed by the environment they inhabit. The basin of the White Nile, the pastoral domain of southern Sudan, is a vast, grass-covered clay plain, parched in the dry season and swampy in the rains. The population of the floodplain and surrounding areas have adapted to these extremes of climate by seasonal movement towards and away from the Nile or its many tributaries, moving annually between wet-season villages, where they cultivate a range of crops including *dura* (sorghum) and maize, and dry-season cattle camps, close to rivers, where their herds can find grazing until the rains come again.

Chief among these communities are the Dinka (Jaang or Monyjaang in Dinka) and Nuer (Naath in Nuer), peoples with closely-related languages and similar ways of life. Other communities pursuing a primarily pastoral existence include the Murle of Jonglei, the Mandari of Central Equatoria and the Toposa and Nyangatom in Eastern Equatoria. Though they generally practise mixed agriculture, gaining a living from seasonal crops and fishing, as well as from livestock husbandry, cattle are prominent in the culture of these groups: exchanged in marriage, seized in raids, imitated in dances and celebrated in song. Conflicts over livestock and access to water and grazing are commonplace. Recurrent feuding between tribes or tribal sections is also widespread. The resultant cycle of revenge killings has traditionally been resolved by the payment of cattle as blood price. In recent times, however, settlement mechanisms have been strained by the spread of firearms and the exacerbation of feuds by wider political and military conflicts.

Until the time of the Condominium, communities in the south lived largely beyond the influence of any state, recognizing only diffuse and localized forms of authority. In the nineteenth century the size and range of Nuer communities expanded at the expense of the Dinka in the east; Dinka communities in turn expanded further south and west. Intermarriage between them continues to be routine. Among the Nuer and the Dinka, religious leaders, known in academic literature as prophets, have had a significant influence. Prophets had a role in resistance to British colonialism; and their teachings, particularly those of the Nuer prophet Ngungdeng Bong, are still invoked to explain current political events. In the recent civil war, Dinka and Nuer took a leading role in southern resistance to rule from Khartoum. Ambivalence towards central authority remains widespread among members of these communities, despite the fact that they are well represented in the government of South Sudan.

Related to the Dinka and Nuer linguistically and through shared mythology are the Shilluk, or Collo. The Shilluk live north of the Nuer, mainly on the west bank of the White Nile, between Malakal and Renk. They are part of the archipelago of Luo-speaking communities that extends south to the Great Lakes region of Central Africa and is distributed widely across southern Sudan, where it includes – besides the Shilluk – the Anuak of Jonglei, the Jur-Luo of Bahr al-Ghazal and the Acholi and Pari of Lafon in Eastern Equatoria. Unlike the Dinka and Nuer, Shilluk political organization was historically centralized under a monarchy with divine authority established near the town of Fashoda. Interaction between the Shilluk kingdom and the polities to the north has been continuous since the time of the mediaeval Funj sultanate; yet there is strikingly little Islamic influence among the Shilluk. (This is in contrast to the Dinka groups across the Nile on the east bank, the Abialang and Dungjol Dinka, who are now mostly Muslim). The Shilluk king, the Reth, still exerts a powerful influence on the affairs of the Shilluk people.

The south-western area of Sudan, the fertile wooded country on the ironstone plateau between the floodplain and the Nile-Congo divide and towards the border with Uganda, is the home of a number of communities who live largely by agriculture. The Bari-speaking peoples of Central Equatoria, living on each side of the White Nile, include the Kuku of Kajo-Keji, the Madi, the Pajulu and – around Juba – the Bari themselves. In Western Equatoria, the Zande occupy an extensive area from Maridi, through Yambio to Tambura. The last two towns are named after Zande kings, scions of a conquering aristocracy, the Avongura, who created the Zande empire in the eighteenth century – incorporating indigenous peoples – in the area where Sudan, the Central African Republic and the Democratic Republic of Congo now meet. The military-political organization of the Zande was dismantled by European colonial powers, but it has left an enduring cultural and ethnolinguistic legacy.

Between the Zande and the Dinka to the north, and extending west to Wau and Raga, live a range of much smaller groups, historically subject to absorption by their larger neighbours, from the Jur-Bel and Jur-Modo and Bongo in Lakes and Warrap to the Fertit peoples in Western Bahr al-Ghazal, who extend to the border with Darfur. Finally, east of Juba, in the mountainous areas of Eastern Equatoria, are a number of sizeable groups, notably the Lotuko, the Acholi and the Didinga, who practise mixed economies of agriculture and livestock raising.

Migration and Nation

A survey of the peoples of Sudan, and glimpses of the histories that have shaped the social categories through which they exist, can provide only a bare indication of the lived experience of language and culture. The story of Sudanese people – as of people in most times and places – is one of movement: of expansion, contraction, displacement, migration, and sometimes decimation. At the individual and group level Sudanese still survive by moving: seasonally for grazing, for work, or for education, unseasonally to escape war and famine. Increasingly also, they are likely to migrate permanently from rural to urban areas. The towns and cities of Sudan have grown rapidly: first, Greater Khartoum and, more recently, former provincial centres such as Nyala and Juba, the latter now the burgeoning capital of South Sudan. Villages become suburbs or slums; villagers become townsfolk.

The displaced and migrant populations of Sudan are sustained, as they have always been, by kin-based affinities. But kinship takes its place in an expanding set of social bonds, of personal loyalties and patron-client relationships. Individual Sudanese, like others, negotiate overlapping identities in the realms of ethnicity, language, religion and professional roles, adapting to circumstances, invoking collective histories and acquiring new social repertoires as required for survival. Indigenous languages are likely to be a casualty of the large-scale movement of people and accompanying social changes. In the era of two Sudans, the challenge remains: to widen the moral community to include all citizens and all dimensions of the cultures they inhabit. This is a vision of nationhood that has yet to find consistent political expression, either in the north or in the south.

Recommended Reading

Asad, Talal. *The Kababish Arabs: Power, Authority and Consent in a Nomadic Tribe.* London: Hurst, 1970.

Cunnison, Ian. *The Baggara Arabs.* Oxford: Oxford University Press, 1966.

de Waal, Alex. 'Who are the Darfurians?', *African Affairs* 104, 415 (2005): 181-205.

James, Wendy. *War and Survival in Sudan's Frontierlands: Voices from the Blue Nile.* Oxford, Oxford University Press, 2nd edition, 2009.

Hutchinson, Sharon. *Nuer Dilemmas: Coping with Money, War and the State.* Berkeley, University of California Press, 1996.

Sharkey, Heather. 'Arab identity and ideology in Sudan'. *African Affairs* 107, 426 (2008): 21-43.

Hassan, Yusuf Fadl. *The Arabs and the Sudan: From the Seventh to the Early Sixteenth Century.* Edinburgh: Edinburgh University Press, 1967.

Francis Deng. *War of Visions: Conflict of Identities in the Sudan.* Washington DC: Brookings Institution, 1995.

5
Religious Practice & Belief
WENDY JAMES

Conventional writing on religion in the Sudan, by historians or theologians, tends to take as quite distinct topics the spread of Islam on the one hand and of Christianity on the other; or else it focuses on other belief systems – on contemporary 'tribal' religions – as though they existed in isolation. However, modern anthropological or sociological studies of actual Sudanese communities show how difficult it is to disentangle the story of the world religions from each other, or from their respective involvement with the legacies of pre-existing beliefs or the vibrancy of current locally-rooted ceremonial practices. The latter category we can take to include many domestic rituals connected with the cycle of life, maturation, healing, and death. These rituals are found across the country alongside the major public affirmations and rites that we rightly dignify as African traditional religion.

Beneath the initial appearance of a community as 'Muslim', 'Christian', or 'traditional African' lie many layers of complicated memory and accommodation to other traditions. The dominant patterns of inequality which are so well established in many Sudanese communities, including gender relations, patronage and clientage, differences between locals and incomers, and the legacy of historical relations between slaves and their owners, find surprisingly robust expression in religious activity. Tensions may surface more explicitly in the symbolic discourse of religious practice than is usually possible in the everyday language of life as led in the towns and villages, or for that matter, in the language of national political life.

Historical Background: Islam, the Dialectics of Authority vs Charisma

As the Turco-Egyptian rule in the Sudan was beginning to crumble in the early 1880s, and the Mahdist movement was gaining supporters, the Dutch traveller J.M. Schuver was on his way through the country, aiming to explore unknown routes up the Blue Nile and into Abyssinia. He was following an inland track towards Sennar, away from the main route by the river itself. Noticing groups of white-draped youths and children shuffling around bright evening fires, reciting as they went, he recognized these as Quranic schools, each under the eye of a pious cleric. He gives us a very sympathetic portrait of these often itinerant holy men (*feki* in colloquial Arabic, *fugara* in the plural form) who typically had a simple way of life dedicated to spiritual pursuits, providing the necessary Muslim blessings at family rituals, and medicines or protective amulets for dealing with illness and misfortunes. At one place Schuver came upon what he termed a 'real rural seminary' hidden in the woodland, away from the eyes of passing caravans and bands of soldiers. Here was a gathering of *fugara* and numerous groups of youths under instruction. Schuver considered he had visited one of those centres of 'Sudanese patriotism fused with religious enthusiasm'. These, he thought, would 'join hatred against the unbelievers to resentment against the Turkish tyranny' and play a part in the insurrection already threatening.

This scene resonates for us today, especially since the resurgence of militant Islamist politics a century after Schuver's travels. We may ask, to what extent have there been earlier periods when 'patriotism' has been 'fused with religious enthusiasm'? How far has governmental authority in the past been associated with one or other dominant form of religious orthodoxy? And how far has there always been a tendency in Sudan towards charismatic sources of resistance to such authority?

Scholars concur in suggesting that Sunni Islam was first introduced into the middle Nile valley during the medieval period, when the former Christian-run kingdoms of Nubia were weakening politically. By the early sixteenth century, political rule had been established over large parts of the region under a new dynasty, known as the Funj, based at Sennar on the Blue Nile. The Funj kingdom inherited not only political, but ritual and ceremonial practices which had much in common with those of the older Nubian kingdoms and also of the Nilotic Sudan, as we know from modern studies of the Shilluk kingdom, a polity that emerged later further up the Nile.

The new rulers at Sennar were soon to adopt Muslim ways, though in Jay Spaulding's phrase, Islam remained an 'exotic royal cult' for some time. By the seventeenth century, there was an increase in the number of Muslim missionaries visiting Sennar, including men of Sudanese origin (initially trained abroad), who helped win acceptance for the Maliki school of Islamic law; and the first mosque in the Funj kingdom was built, providing orthodox education and literacy in Arabic. The Sufi school of Islam, which sought mystical union with the higher powers through asceticism and spiritual exercises, also became established. Sufism brought to the Sudan the *tariqa* or religious brotherhood, a new form of social organization – still important today – in which authority was vested in a leader recognized as having special spiritual power or *baraka*. This was passed on from a teacher or spiritual master to his followers, often to his own son. The Sufi communities, mainly locally-based, though affiliated to the Qadiriya order, flourished both in urban areas and in rural areas where syncretism with pre-Islamic beliefs was relatively unproblematic.

The characteristic Sufi mode of worship has long been the *dhikr* or *zikr,* in which the names of God are chanted, often in conjunction with music, songs and circular dancing, occasionally producing trance. As trade and towns developed through the eighteenth century, these communities were often granted land and a tax-free status. Sufi centres proved an attraction for many of the poorer urban migrants, including debtors and asylum seekers in search of a new life; the leaders of these communities thus became spokesmen for the masses, some remembered as folk-heroes, their *baraka* transmitted onward and their tombs revered as shrines.

Meanwhile, the new bourgeoisie in the towns of the Sudanese heartland began to proclaim themselves Arabs, constructing putative family links back to well-known names from the early days of Islam. The success of the new Arabized merchant families rested on the possession of slaves, who laboured in the home and in the fields. This served to entrench social distinctions in a world which extended legal and social protection to Muslims but not to non-believers from outside its bounds. Similar processes and responses to the arrival of Islam in the Funj kingdom were evident in the sultanate of Darfur, though in this case of a robust indigenous polity with its own very distinctive political culture, on a less massive scale, and at a later date.

The Ottoman conquest of the old Funj kingdom in 1821, and the succeeding period of 'Turco-Egyptian' rule which lasted until its overthrow by the Mahdists in 1885, saw an intensification of exploitative trade into new peripheries of the south and west, including slaving and forced military recruitment. This period saw the further spread and consolidation of the Sufi orders. In the west, the growth of the Tijaniyya tariqa was linked with increased immigration of West Africans. In the Nile valley the Khatmiyya Order drew in members from many different backgrounds, paving the way for the quasi-national movement of the Mahdiyya. Muhammad Ahmad, the Mahdi, was himself originally a Sheikh of the Sammaniyya Order, but Mahdism aspired to transcend these orders; it was a campaign for the purification of Islam along reformist lines, aiming to return to the basic principles of early Islam, to the Quran and the *sunna*. Having found support through the existing various Sufi *tariqas* of popular Islam across the country, Muhammad Ahmad then sought to suppress them in the name of the national movement – and to foster, in Schuver's words as quoted above, a fusion of Sudanese patriotism with religious enthusiasm.

Following the Mahdiyya, and for the greater part of the twentieth century up to and beyond independence in 1956, mainstream political developments in the northern Sudan took their shape from the sectarian rivalries that had already been established. In particular, the followers of the Mahdist movement them-selves were reconstituted as a quasi-religious brotherhood, the Ansar, which underpinned the rise of the modern political party of the Umma. It drew its main strength from the west of the country. The rival Khatmiyya movement found modern political identity as the Democratic Unionist Party, its regional strong-holds being rather in the central Nile Valley and eastern and south-eastern adjacent areas. Despite major political shifts at the centre of government, there is still broad support in northern Sudanese society for the old sectarian movements.

Academic study of Islam in modern Sudan has typically emphasized its local historical memory and manifestations, and often its accommodation with pre-Islamic or alternative indigenous forms. A study of the Berti of Darfur – an entirely Muslim, Arabic-speaking community – has shown how, although their vernacular language had disappeared by the 1990s, a variety of local rituals endured. These were particularly important in women's lives, as part of an integrated system of 'practical religion'. Berti did not see any contradiction between Islamic observances (mainly the concern of men) and the various rites which constituted *al-ada*, or 'custom', an Arabic term adopted widely across the Sudan. The implication is that that these were considered 'harmless customs' rather than a threat to the purity of faith.

At Jebel Miri, in the Nuba area of South Kordofan, at least until the 1970s, people still spoke their own language and practised local music, dances and ritual when at home. However, they were comfortable speaking Arabic, using Arabic names and following Islamic practices and manners when they switched from the village to outside agricultural employment or city life – as many young men did, on a seasonal basis. Interestingly, young women at home were permitted to sing in Arabic and play the popular *daluka* music they had heard in local market towns or on the national radio; but as soon as they married and set up house in Miri, they had to limit themselves to the local rituals, grindstone songs and others drawn from the repertoire of the vernacular tradition.

Studies of modern Muslim communities in the central heartland of the Nile valley have examined the complexity of people's lives in relation to the spiritual sphere. By focusing, in many cases, on the lives of women and their struggle to cope with personal events and the ups and downs of family fortunes, these studies reveal a layering of religious belief and practice that owes more to the continual recreation of vernacular ideas than to the formalities of the mosque, or the profession of faith, prayer, fasting, alms-giving and pilgrimage that constitute the five pillars of the Islam. They reflect also the tensions inherent in concepts of gender in the cultures of central Sudan, and the ambivalent stance of the Islamic authorities in relation to those spiritual cults, which are largely controlled by women.

In the village of Hofriyat, downstream from Khartoum, in the 1980s, as described by Janice Boddy, women lived largely in an everyday world of their own; their lives were contained within the village, within the walls of their compounds. Their attitudes, and their persons, were carefully groomed for reproduction within the extended family. This was achieved in part through the operation of pharaonic circumcision, the most radical form of genital cutting, an operation that secured for them, and for their future husbands, a state of being understood both as moral cleanliness and as bodily integrity.

The women of Hofriyat were well aware, nevertheless, of a wider horizon: the world of men's activities, of history, of foreign ways, a world in counterpoint to their own. They were conscious of the danger of looming spirits from that outside world, spirits that could descend upon them and interfere with their fertility and the health of their children. Within formal Islam (and indeed Orthodox Christianity) there is a limited acknowledgment of such undefined spiritual presences, but in the Nile Valley (as also in Christian Ethiopia) these spirits are recognized more explicitly in a women's spirit cult called *zar*. *Zar* (plural *zayran*) is the name of these characterful, often dangerous beings. Women are particularly vulnerable to possession by them. Once affected, they cannot get rid of the attentions of the *zar*; they must become accommodated to it as a part of their lives. The spirits are typically figures from Sudanese history; they have names, costumes, and habits – and demand offerings. When possessed, a woman may act out the part – now a part of herself – of an Ethiopian princess, an Arabian sheikh; even a British district officer, complete with sun-helmet, whisky and cigarettes. The women in charge of the *zar* cult hold elaborate ceremonies in which the various *zayran* are called down, through the music and song they specially respond to, and possess the women involved.

Sennar is a bustling town with a mixed population and its religious life (today including four churches) reflects this scene. In Sennar, some women are practitioners of *zar*; some are involved in the parallel cult of *tembura* (which emerged historically from ex-slave and displaced military communities). There is also a holy woman of the family of the Khalifa Abdallahi, the successor to the Mahdi, who acts as a consultant to patients in the manner of the ubiquitous *feki* or holy man of the Islamic tradition. Within the 'Three Towns' (Khartoum, Khartoum North and Omdurman) the *tembura* cult is also active among former military families (many of slave descent) in Omdurman. The spirit world is acted out there in the hierarchies of Sudanese military history, with all its accompaniment of bugles, uniforms, and marching.

Christianity, Ancient and Modern: Anglo-Egyptian Policies and their Aftermath

Christianity is the other key world religion of the modern Sudan. Its history goes back further than Islam. But apart from archaeological remains, there are few signs left in the modern Sudan of the string of Christian kingdoms which extended along the Nile valley in medieval times, and were linked with Ethiopia. In the early medieval period, as far as we know, Christian teaching and practice was largely confined to a monastic elite, but its impression on ordinary Nubian communities is suggested by the persistence of the cross in some aspects of popular culture. The small number of Coptic Christians in Sudan today are more recent arrivals from Egypt, who came, along with Greek and other trading and professional families, in the wake of the Ottoman conquest in the nineteenth century. It was in the middle of that century too that Christian missionaries from the West, specifically Catholic priests of the order of the Verona Fathers, under the inspiring leadership of Daniel Comboni, began to establish outposts in the southern regions of the Sudan.

From its inception, the Anglo-Egyptian Condominium government was, understandably, very sensitive to religious questions. It gave what support it could to the more orthodox and conservative forms of Islam wherever these were already established in the country. Any signs of continuing Mahdism or other Muslim 'fanaticism' were thoroughly investigated, and various charismatic figures, such as claimants to the title of *nabi* Isa – part of a millennial expectation of the coming 'prophet Jesus', which was a problem for the British in the western Sudan especially after the conquest of Darfur – were kept under control. The old Sufi *tariqas* did re-emerge, while the Mahdi's own followers in the Ansar became something like a Sufi order themselves, but rarely caused concern to the government.

In the south, however, the influential religious leaders of the Nilotic peoples, especially those whom later scholarship described as 'prophets', were the object of extreme suspicion and regarded as rebels, or potential rebels, against government rule. The Nuer prophet Guek, for example, son of the prophet Ngundeng, was killed by British-led forces in a punitive campaign which was the direct outcome of this suspicion in 1929, and his body hung on a tree as a warning to others. Everywhere the government sought those they deemed legitimate tribal chiefs, as distinct from charismatic ritual figures, as the true leaders of the people.

Under British administration Christian missionary organizations were welcomed, though under considerable restrictions. They were allocated spheres of influence where it was assumed they would not be a provocation to Muslim feelings: across the south, below the Twelfth Parallel, and later in parts of the

Nuba Hills. Very broadly, the Roman Catholic sphere occupied the country west of a line drawn from Tembura to Meshra-al-Rek and then from there along the west bank of the Nile to just north of Kodok (Fashoda). The American Mission (Presbyterian) was assigned the east bank of the Nile from Kodok to west of Tonga, together with the hinterland north and south of the Sobat River all the way to the frontier with Abyssinia. The Anglican CMS had all the intermediate country south toward the frontier, except for the east bank of the Nile south of the Fifth Parallel which had been a part of Uganda. The latter area was a free zone between spheres of influence, but had been extensively exploited by the Verona Fathers.

In all cases, missions were expected not only to preach on religious matters but to teach practical skills which would contribute to the development of the country. Missions which openly preferred to concentrate on evangelism as such, like the SIM (the Sudan Interior Mission, later Serving in Mission), were discouraged. Latecomers to the system, they were allowed to work only in remote areas where it was supposed they could not do much damage – such as the north-eastern corner of Upper Nile near the Ethiopian border. In this case, two districts where the SIM had already established itself were transferred to Blue Nile province in 1953, shortly before Sudanese independence. This meant that these Christian congregations found themselves in a province of northern Sudan, creating a fraught situation within a very few years, after the outbreak of the first civil war.

Perhaps the main reason for the broad coherence of the Christian tradition as it exists today in the southern Sudan lies in the shared experience of marginality which so many southerners have experienced in the modern nation. During the Condominium period, what became known as the 'Southern policy' attempted to rein in the influence of Islam and the Arabic language in the south, while granting responsibilities for education as well as religious prosletyizing entirely to the mission organizations in their respective areas. With the beginnings of insurgency in the south starting in 1955, the newly independent government of Sudan of 1956 began to blame the missions for creating unrest. Within a few years, their permissions and visas had been curtailed, and all foreign personnel in the field had been expelled – among the last to go were from the Blue Nile in 1964. Local churches were thus rapidly 'Sudanized' – initially a simple handover – and in the conditions of war displacement, partial recovery during the 1970s, and the return of war from 1983, the role of the Christian faith understandably expanded.

Despite the sectarian rivalries that might once have been expected, the various Christian churches based in the south, with their central institutions largely in Khartoum, have worked together effectively. The Sudan Council of Churches, founded in 1965 (shortly after the expulsion of foreign missionaries) and paralleled by the New Sudan Council of Churches during the war years from 1989-2005, has played a significant part in national affairs. There have been only a few signs of the splits and unorthodox innovations found in many other regions of African Christianity. On the whole, in the Christian regions of the Sudan, the aspirational and emotional appeal of religious activity has remained under the authority of established church organizations – though these of course now extend into rural areas, in a way that the medieval monasteries established in the first phase of Christianization of the country could never have done. Moreover, of course, the modern mission enterprise as a whole has aspired to bring the message of the gospels to the people in their own languages – a sharp contrast with the prime value placed upon the classical Arabic of the Quran in the teachings and propagation of Islam. Further, we could note that although early Christian instruction, and Bible translation especially on the Protestant side, tended to relegate much local belief and practice to the realm of Satan, there has been an increasing willingness, in both Catholic and Protestant mission endeavours, to respect existing cultural practices. The leadership of virtually all churches in the Sudan is now in Sudanese hands. Although Christianity has been the dominant public form of religious affiliation across the south from before the 1950s, as well as in parts of the neighbouring regions of southern Kordofan and Blue Nile, there are very few detailed accounts of mission- or church-based communities and the way they, like their compatriots in the Islamic regions, have had to come to terms with older beliefs and practices in the intimacy of the domestic sphere.

Christian teaching in practice has often been conveyed in a *lingua franca*. In Sudan, colloquial Arabic has played a role which should not be underestimated. Portions of the Bible were translated into colloquial Sudanese Arabic in the years from 1927 to1964, and a complete New Testament appeared in 1978. Work is ongoing at present on a version in Juba Arabic. Moreover, services and sermons across the country are often translated into colloquial Arabic side-by-side with a local language, as congregations are now very often mixed.

Indigenous Roots: 'Traditional African Religion'

What was there before the world religions established themselves in Sudan? We can visit the extraordinary physical legacies of the ancient past: Meroe, for instance, the pyramid field north of Khartoum, or Jebel Barkal, with their royal temples, carvings of gods, and engraved texts (not yet fully deciphered). In other regions that have remained beyond the reach of the world religions until very recently, we have ample evidence of highly developed cosmological, moral and spiritual systems which had, and to a good extent still have, a degree of autonomy. Their continuing influence depends upon their connection with regional centres of charismatic leadership and in some cases institutional political authority. Though without written scriptures, systems of ritual and belief such as those of the Shilluk, Dinka, or the Nuer, kindred peoples of southern Sudan, rest on a history of the material construction of sacred sites and associated social connectivity and discipleship. When we note the existence in old Meroe of what archaeologists term 'pyramids' built from the fourth century BC to the third century CE, we may also recall the prophet Ngundeng's Mound, in what is now Jonglei state, built in the late nineteenth century; or reading about the court system and royal rituals of the Funj kingdom and its dynastic connections with the outlying provinces of Sennar articulated through kinship networks defined by women, we can recognize parallels with the ceremonial and social structure of the modern Shilluk or Anuak kingdoms. It is not too fanciful to suggest that these features of social life reflect pre-modern institutions that once formed part of shared cultural traditions in the Nile Valley.

Beyond the most public and formal expressions of indigenous religious systems, it is important to recognize that the elaborate life-rituals of many groups across the Sudan are still central to their everyday beliefs. Initiation to male or female adulthood, perhaps to formal age-sets, as well as domestic rituals of birth, marriage and death are still key to personal life and belief among a large number of communities, whether nominally Muslim or Christian. Such practices may be oriented to notions of morality, spirituality and of the afterworld which have little to do with the world religions. This is especially true with respect to the understanding and treatment of episodes of illness and other misfortune. However, the tendency in much ethnographic literature to dignify every minor belief as a part of local religion is not always helpful. In my own accounts of the Uduk people of Southern Blue Nile I have generally avoided the term, preferring to reserve it for contexts in which a centralized conception of divinity, as distinct from humanity, is associated with social authority. In those cases where we can indeed convincingly speak of traditional African religion, the formal manifestations of cosmology and public ritual rest within a rich seedbed of practices concerning human life and death at the domestic or private level.

The old term 'animism' has recently gained currency in the language both of missionaries and of journalists writing about the southern Sudan, as though this somehow dignified pre-Islamic and pre-Christian beliefs by putting them on the same plane. There are problems with the term 'animism', however, and I have preferred to write of 'traditional African religions'. In the first place, animism belongs to a former era of anthropological debate about 'primitive religion' and has not escaped its association with the ascription of limited intellectual and moral capacity to believers. Second, the notion of animism focuses on 'beliefs' almost in a vacuum, without recognizing the forms of religious authority which go with political leadership, or the historical continuity of those forms as reflected in the material record of sacred sites. In its blandness it fails to capture the strength, and indeed inherent claims to validity, and translatability, of the ideas it describes – that is, in effect, the universal quality of their spiritual apprehension. It thus underestimates the emotional complexity of people's lives outside the church and schoolroom context, and overestimates the singularity and specificity of conversion. Third, in journalese, 'animists' is used selectively. It appears only in relation to the southern Sudan, not other places such as Ethiopia, or East and West Africa, or Britain, or America, or Japan.

The great indigenous traditions of the upper Nile, mainly those of the large-scale, predominantly pastoral, transhumant Nilotic-speaking peoples, were the focus of an early generation of anthropological research in Sudan. Interpretive accounts of their beliefs and practices, strikingly resonant with those of the peoples of the ancient Middle East as represented in the Old Testament, are among those now regarded as classics in the anthropology of religion. The writings of E. E. Evans-Pritchard led the way, following up his early work on the logical character of Azande thought with his study of what he boldly called 'Nuer Religion'. Of course, the Nuer being a largely preliterate society, indigenous Nuer 'theology' and 'belief' had to be approached through the translation of language in use, and the observation of rituals, rather than sacred texts. Evans-Pritchard showed how the ways in which Nuer referred to various manifestations of *kuoth* or 'Spirit', how they offered prayers and sacrifices and discussed relations between the human and the spiritual revealed a whole cosmology, which at its apex justified the translation 'God'. Myths and songs, historical memories of great prophetic leaders, and rituals conducted at the sacred sites associated with them – in particular the remains of Ngundeng's Mound, the shrine built by the prophet Ngundeng and partially destroyed by the British – continue to reconstitute the tangible world of 'Nuer religion'. The classic work on Dinka society, Godfrey Lienhardt's *Divinity and Experience*, focuses on the translatability of personal experience and specifically upon the forms that a human apprehension of the divine may take. It emphasizes the existential reality of *nhialic* as an ultimate divine presence in relation to the history of human beings, along with various lesser 'divinities' associated with the emergence of particular clans. In Dinka cosmology there are also relatively autonomous 'free' divinities and 'Powers' (*jok*) of the kind that can cause harm to human life, but can also be occasionally placated or exorcized. Among the Dinka, maintenance of peaceful and proper relations between human beings themselves, and between them and Divinity, is the responsibility of local ritual specialists known as Masters of the Fishing Spear. These are born to priestly lineages, as distinct from the more common warrior lineages, and inherit physically from their fathers a special capacity for spiritual insight. In the Dinka lands of the mid-twentieth century, there was thus still a geographical and social integrity to the typical home community, comfortable with its local hierarchy of social and religious authority. The spiritual powers associated with a person's home can catch up with them after they have left: a diagnosis of possession by 'free' divinities or dangerous Powers is very likely to be made if a person falls ill when they are geographically displaced and probably detached from kin.

Today, of course, no part of the country can be properly isolated for study from constant patterns of human movement, resulting in the cross-fertilization of ideas and practices, the transportation of religious authority from one place to another, and uncertainties over what had once been eternal truths. But there is no doubt about the resilience and power of indigenous religious forms in the upper Nile, nor about their appeal to scholars prepared to accept them on their own terms. They have inspired many smaller-scale studies of vernacular religious belief and practice in the south as well as in other marginal areas of the country, where a presumption of the strength and autonomy of 'traditional' forms is not always as justified.

The power of older religious experience and convictions deeply held from childhood can even outlast conversion. In a well-documented case, the son of a Dinka Master of the Fishing Spear was captured by slavers in the late nineteenth century, and eventually rescued by a missionary who brought him to Britain. Sensing his proper vocation, he became a Methodist lay preacher, living in Wakefield, Barnsley and finally Scunthorpe, becoming famous as 'the Black Evangelist of the North'. In his autobiography, Salim Wilson (alias Hatashil Masha Kathish) ascribed his religious inspiration to memories of his father, the special qualities of his lineage, and his Dinka heritage.

Contemporary Civil War, Displacements, and Religious Ferment

The disturbances and displacements suffered by people during the recent decades of civil war have fuelled new religious aspirations and commitments across the south and adjoining areas. They have created new patterns of religious ferment across the country, provoking not only newly strident declarations of faith but also an apparent resurgence of 'old' beliefs and of indigenous elements within the framework of the mainstream world religions. In the south and the north-south border areas, rural families literally having to flee for their lives are known to have held impromptu prayer meetings under trees as they camped along the way, and have attributed their survival to their faith in the God of the Bible. In the refugee camps of neighbouring countries, where different groups of Sudanese from the south, the Nuba Hills or the Blue Nile met with each other and found support among locals of the host countries, a sense of belonging to a wider world through one's church membership was important. Much international aid also came via Christian organizations or secular Western organizations perceived as Christian, who were often able to provide moral support as well as material. Within the south, even during the war, commitment to the Christian faith deepened and there was a spread of daughter churches into rural areas where they had not existed before. Even domestic dwellings in some areas began to display simple wooden crosses on the roof. With the ongoing return of the displaced to their former homes, the re-establishment of churches in both the physical and moral sense is proving a key element in post-war recovery.

What has been the role of religion in Sudan's civil wars? It is not helpful to reduce the 1963-72 and 1983-2005 civil wars to a struggle between Islam and Christianity as such. But the element of religious rhetoric, there from the start, did intensify, especially with the appearance of the National Islamic Front which took power in the coup of 1989 (later being transformed into the National Congress Party). The NIF represented a further fusion of patriotism with religious enthusiasm, in this case stemming from the growth of the modern Muslim Brotherhood, from its roots in the older Wahhabiyya or Salafiyya movement of Saudi Arabia. Military strategy increasingly justified campaigns against un-believers as *jihad*, holy war. These campaigns extended, paradoxically, into some areas, such as parts of the Nuba Hills, where the people were actually Muslims. Similar strategies of counter-insurgency, with accompanying religious rhetoric, spread to Darfur from 2003 onwards. This was a region where Christian mission-aries had never been allowed to operate and virtually all the population were at least nominally Muslim. The language of religion thereafter seemed to morph into racial terminology. Although splits occurred within the NIF, and the coalition of interests at the centre of the state has adopted a muted rhetoric, the extremist voices of the new political Islam, for example in attempting to control women's dress in the capital city, are still heard across the world.

Meanwhile, in the camps of refugees and displaced people that have burgeoned in Sudan and across its borders, and in and around military garrisons, there is evidence of new forms of mixing and matching of religious ideas and obser-vances. Among the Blue Nile refugees who spent a generation in camps in Ethiopia, there have been strange visions of angels, monsters, and of Jesus calling people home. At other times, the local diviners have started to make diagnoses of possession by *tembura* spirits – the same as those invoked in Omdurman and Sennar – a pan-Sudanese phenomenon which they had not been acquainted with before.

Something of the fervent mix of hope, suffering and excitement that marks the current religious scene in the Sudan is well illustrated by the remarkable attention paid to a Catholic saint, St Josephine Bakhita, in several parts of the country. Born in Darfur in the mid-nineteenth century, she was snatched by slave-traders, bought eventually by an Italian diplomat, and ended her days in Rome, as a nun, in 1947. She was canonized in 2000, the first native Sudanese saint. With the outbreak of major conflict in Darfur, her fame spread through the whole of the substantial Catholic community in Sudan and among non-Christian Darfuri Sudanese refugees in Cairo. A Reuters report of 5 September 2008 described a packed service in St. Bakhita parish church, situated in Jabarona, an IDP camp outside Khartoum, punctuated with songs honouring the saint. Most of the church members, the report explained, were southerners who had originally fled north during the civil war, but after the fighting escalated in Darfur they turned to the saint for solace. A displaced person from the Nuba Hills said: 'We all pray through her intercession to God to give us the grace to find forgiveness for Darfur and for all the conflicts in Sudan.' Outside, children were playing soccer under a huge mural of the saint's face. Though Josephine is scarcely remembered in Darfur itself, her face now appears on hats, key rings, badges and women's brightly printed clothes in Juba. In 2006 Bakhita Radio 91 FM, run by the Catholic Archdiocese of Juba, went on air, broadcasting a range of programmes relating to social affairs and community development in English, Arabic, Bari, Madi, Acholi, and Dinka.

Since the time of J. M. Schuver, many others from outside the Sudan who have come to know the country, whether from travel or reading, have been struck by the extent to which Sudanese life is steeped in religion. This impression corresponds, to a marked extent, to the feelings and memories and commitments of Sudanese themselves. Religious feeling and observance in Sudan is not necessarily a matter of formal adherence to the mainstream faiths; it may occur outside the rituals of the mosque or the church. Today, there are new complications in the field of religion. Competing political visions draw both on religious rhetoric, and on the national and international resources offered by organizations supported by the world religions. But the religious landscape of the Sudan is many-layered; not all of it is visible or predictable. I have indicated some of the interactions in real communities between various levels of practice and belief. Among these are many which have spread to become more widely recognizable. The ceaseless movement of people in Sudan in the present day – the growth of trade networks and labour migration, the intermixing of status and gender roles, the long history of war and displacement – these factors create the occasion for the development of new pan-Sudanese religious phenomena, constructed from a dialogue between new global religious trends and the country's own very rich heritage of belief and practice.

Recommended Reading

Karrar, Ali Salih. *The Sufi Brotherhoods in the Sudan.* London: C. Hurst and Co, 1992.

Boddy, Janice. *Wombs and Alien Spirits: Women, Men and the Zar Cult in Northern Sudan.* Madison, WI: Wisconsin University Press, 1989.

Evans-Pritchard, E. E. *Nuer Religion.* Oxford: Clarendon Press, 1956.

Holy, Ladislav. *Religion and Custom in a Muslim Society: The Berti of Sudan.* Cambridge: Cambridge University Press, 1991.

James, Wendy. *The Listening Ebony: Moral Knowledge, Religion, and Power among the Uduk of Sudan.* Oxford: Clarendon Press, 1988.

Johnson, Douglas H. *Nuer Prophets: A History of Prophecy from the Upper Nile in the Nineteenth and Twentieth Centuries.* Oxford: Clarendon Press, 1994.

Lienhardt, Godfrey. *Divinity and Experience: The Religion of the Dinka.* Oxford: Clarendon Press, 1961.

Trimingham, J. Spencer. *Islam in the Sudan.* London: Oxford University Press, 1949.

6

The Ambitions of the State

JUSTIN WILLIS

Since the early nineteenth century, central states in the Sudan have had two consistent characteristics. They have been authoritarian, perceiving themselves as representing a political culture superior to and distinct from that of the majority of the people whom they rule. And they have been weak. Not weak in an absolute sense, since they have often been able to deploy considerable force against their own people; but weak in that they have lacked the resources to pursue their ambitions effectively. This weakness, combined with distrust of their own subjects, has helped create a further consistent characteristic of successive regimes in Sudan: they have tried to coopt forms of local or 'traditional' authority which they believe they need, but which they see as inferior and distinct. Where these states have differed has been in the extent of their ambition and particularly, how far they seek to change, rather than simply dominate and exploit, the people whom they rule.

Central states in Sudan have also tended to be extractive, supporting themselves by taxing or directly engaging in the export of raw materials – slaves, ivory, cotton, grain or petroleum. As is the case across much of Africa, that extractive role has emphasized their position as gatekeeper states, whose existence is predicated on their ability to mediate between powerful external forces and subject peoples. The rulers of the Sudan have often looked beyond Sudan itself for their cultural and political models and their economic and military support.

There were states in the Sudan long before the early nineteenth century. But they have left little mark on Sudan's modern political culture. Although the material remains of these earlier states are well represented in the National Museum in Khartoum (the incidental by-product of the construction of the Aswan High Dam in the 1960s which submerged many of the ancient monuments of Nubia), official culture in Sudan today makes little of them: there are no roads named for them, nor public celebration of the long history of state formation in the Nile Valley that they represent. Even the Muslim states that succeeded them, Darfur and Sennar, are scantily acknowledged. There is still less acknowledgement of the small states on the fringes of present-day Sudan, such as the Zande chiefdoms or states of Western Equatoria, or of the long history of stateless societies in Bahr al-Ghazal and Upper Nile.

The invisibility of this political heritage at the centre of political power is significant. The history of the modern state began in the northern Sudan in

54

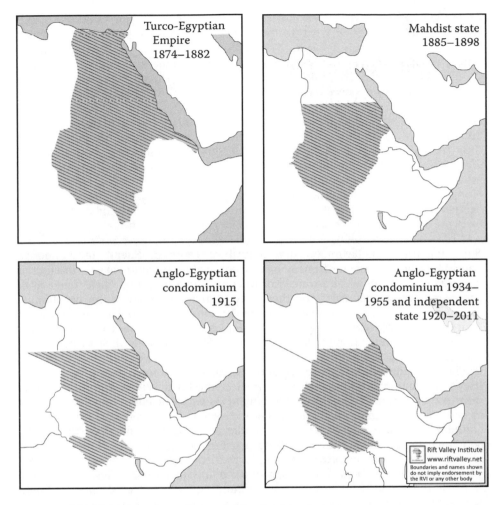

Map 6.1 State formation and changing boundaries

1821, with the invasion by the Turco-Egyptian forces of Muhammad Ali, the Albanian soldier who clawed his way to power in Egypt in the confused aftermath of Napoleon's invasion. Nominally the servant of the Ottoman Sultan, Muhammad Ali constantly sought to develop his independence by acquiring wealth and resources of his own. He extended his authority southwards up the Nile in the quest for slaves to man his army and gold to fill his treasury.

In both of these aims he was disappointed; slaves were obtained, but the creation of a slave army for Egypt was not a success, and the gold deposits in the Sudan proved to be less rich than Muhammad Ali had hoped. But Sudan was thus created as a colony of Egypt. It was far enough from Cairo – and different enough from Egypt – to require a distinct and distinctive administration, based in the newly-created town of Khartoum. In the new administration military men played a major role as local governors and inspectors. Little supervision was exercised over these local officials: they were expected to defray the costs of their own presence, and of the soldiers who supported them, from locally-raised tax; and contribute revenue back to Egypt. Thus was created what Sudanese call the Turkiyya; the Turco-Egyptian state. Service in the Sudan was not viewed as desirable: officials were far from home and never had enough soldiers to enforce their orders, nor enough money to pay their soldiers. They could be brutal, possessing a considerable advantage over the populace in terms of military technology, but because they were so few they relied on cooperation with local figures of authority. They sought out individuals through whom they could work, and the abuses suffered by the populace were the work of these local agents, as well as of the 'Turks'.

The combined effect of these impositions was enough to encourage a substantial migration away from the riverain areas of the north, where communications were most developed, and administration at its most effective – and taxes were at their highest. Some of these migrants pressed south, beyond the uncertain boundary of Turco-Egyptian authority, along the line of the river into areas populated by people who were neither Muslim nor Arab. Here these migrants sought to recoup their fortunes through trade in ivory and slaves – the international demand for which increased substantially up to the 1870s.

From the early 1860s, the central state – hitherto restricted to the largely Muslim and Arab communities of Kordofan and Sennar – began to play an ineffectual game of catch-up with these traders. There were two motives. One was the desire to tax this developing trade more effectively to remedy the chronic financial deficit of the state. The other, ironically, was the pursuit of imperial respectability, coupled with a new ambition: Egypt, still ruled by the descendants of Muhammad Ali, was attempting to create an African empire, but it was doing so under the eyes of a Europe which was committed to abolishing the slave trade. So from the end of the 1860s the agents of the state, pressing further south along the river towards Uganda, and south-west into what was becoming known as Bahr al-Ghazal, relying on their superior firepower as they did so, were ostensibly suppressing the slave trade. A motley assemblage of European adventurers joined the Circassian administrative elite as officers in the Turco-Egyptian army. But suppression of the slave trade was beyond their capacity: it was too important a source of income for the administration; and many of their own foot soldiers were themselves slaves.

The Turco-Egyptian state was a clear example of an authoritarian polity whose internal weakness prevented it from realizing its ambitions. Its expansion was interrupted in the 1880s by a complex movement that has come to be called Mahdism. At the centre of this movement was Muhammad Ahmad ibn Abdallah, from the Dongola area of the Nile, a minor Sufi leader who in 1881 declared himself to be the Mahdi: the Expected One, whose appearance on earth presages the second coming of the messiah, *Nabi Isa*, (the prophet Jesus). Inspired by this idea the followers of Muhammad Ahmad defeated the forces of the Turco-Egyptian state in a series of battles which culminated in the capture of Khartoum and the killing of Charles George Gordon, the British officer who had been sent to organize an Egyptian withdrawal, but who unwisely stayed on to try and defeat the Mahdi. It is worth noting that the Mahdi's messianic declaration did not have an instantaneous effect. The movement took some years to establish itself and its appeal did not extend much beyond central and western Sudan. The Mahdi's final capture of Khartoum in January 1885, after a long-drawn out siege, struck a powerful symbolic blow against the Turco-Egyptian adminis-tration, but as a military feat it was unremarkable: the town was poorly fortified and ill defended.

The reasons for the Mahdi's ultimate success have been much debated. It has usually been argued that it was the weakness and brutality of the state which encouraged popular revolt against it; some have suggested that the attempts to abolish the slave trade and the institution of slavery further irritated influential traders and property owners. There are other arguments concerned with the internal dynamics of Islam. The Mahdi's movement fits into a wider pattern of nineteenth-century Islamic radicalism – not the reformist movements of the Middle East, but movements of renewal, which looked to restore a pristine Islamic purity to states which had become compromised. Such movements swept much of West Africa from the late eighteenth century onwards. Built on the dissatis-factions of those on the margin of the Islamic world, they appealed to those who had most reason to fear enslavement. Adherence to Islam offered a less arbitrary political system, one which took account of religion and not skin colour. The latter aspect may be significant in the case of Sudan: the Mahdi's forces were swelled – perhaps decisively so – by recruits from the south of the country, often of slave origin, who had been forced into military service under Turco-Egyptian rule. Many of these southerners, whose homelands lay outside the Islamized areas of the north, fought for the Mahdists, as they had fought for the Turco-Egyptians, because they were forced to do so; but a significant number may have seen support for the Mahdi as a way of improving their status.

Whatever his aspirations and those of his followers, the Mahdi did not succeed in establishing a more just and equitable state. He died shortly after Khartoum was captured; in his place, one of his deputies, Abdallahi al-Taisha, from one of the Arab cattle pastoralist groups of southern Darfur, became Khalifa ('successor'). The Khalifa ruled from Omdurman, across the river from Khartoum. Omdurman thus acquired the role it has continued to occupy as the centre of northern Sudan's political culture, consciously indigenous in style, in contrast to the straight streets of Khartoum, the capital that was built by the Turks. The Khalifa's relations with the riverain population of the north were tense and his hold over the north of Sudan uncertain. In the parts of the south which the Turco-Egyptian state had claimed, he had almost no power. Tales of widespread starvation, brutality and the death of more than half the population under the Khalifa's rule were spread by the British to build support for their schemes of revenge against the killers of Gordon. These stories were undoubtedly exaggerated, but the Khalifa's state was not strong, and in the last few years of the nineteenth century it was destroyed by an advancing army of Egyptian and British troops.

Egypt itself had come under British occupation in 1882. (Egyptian political and financial instability were seen as a threat to imperial interests.) In 1896, with the Egyptian government and army under close British control, the 'reconquest' of the Sudan, as it was called in an attempt to emphasize the legitimacy of Egypt's claim, was launched. 'Sudanese' battalions played a central part. These were units of the Egyptian army, officered largely by the British and made up of men from the south of Sudan, often of slave origin. Omdurman was captured in 1898; the Khalifa was killed eleven months later at Um Diwaykrat, in South Kordofan.

The use of Egyptian soldiers and money in the campaign made the overthrow of the Khalifa much easier but it left an uncertain political situation which was not so much resolved as enshrined in the arrangement known as the Condominium. Under the Condominium both Britain and Egypt had sovereignty over the Sudan. This consisted of the territory which had been ruled by Egypt, with its southern boundary more or less defined by the northern boundary of Britain's East African territories. In practice, the British dominated the administration; but the tension over precisely whose colony Sudan was lasted until the end of the Condominium. Rivalry between Britain and Egypt had a significant influence on the independence movement, and during Condominium rule Sudan's ambiguous legal status acted in important ways to constrain and weaken the state.

The 'Reconquest' had complex motivations. Revenge for Gordon – a popular cause with the British public – was one. But the British interest in Egypt was a more important factor. Egypt was far more important to the empire than Sudan could ever be. British investment in Egypt, and the stability of the Egyptian economy, was dependent on the Nile; the Nile flowed through Sudan; so no other European power could be allowed to control the Sudan. It was this simple logic which drove the 'Reconquest' and the continued British presence. Britain was in the Sudan to stop anyone else from being there, and control of the state was primarily for this end.

Despite all the rhetoric and romance that has grown up around the British presence, and the undoubtedly sincere attachment of many British officials to the Sudan, these simple desiderata must not be forgotten. As a result British officials found themselves pursuing sometimes contradictory aims – protecting the way of life and culture of their Sudanese subjects, and also improving and changing their material conditions. Behind these contradictions there remained the simple imperative: the state existed in order to control territory. It was this the relative modesty of this of ambition which helped the Condominium achieve a degree of stability, although it was a stability behind which lay always the threat of force.

The British who dominated the administration of the Anglo-Egyptian prided themselves on the order and regularity of their rule; and through most of the 58 years of the Condominium they assumed that the corollary of such order was an authoritarian central structure. The Governor-general ruled from the palace in Khartoum; beneath him the men of the Sudan Political Service ruled as Governors and Inspectors (later District Commissioners). They were remarkably few in number: a total of three hundred and fifteen men joined the SPS between 1899 and 1939. Each bore responsibility for a vast area of the country; they wielded more or less unlimited authority. Only in the last few years of the

Condominium was there a rush of experimentation with electoral forms of representation – initially at a local level, and then nationally.

The simplicity of administrative structures was dictated to a significant extent by financial exigency. The Condominium began with an enormous budget deficit. This was partly plugged by a subvention from Egypt. This was used in maintaining the military forces of the Condominium, giving it a coercive capacity that was unusually large for a colonial state in Africa. The Condominium made good use of this, emphasising military displays and ceremonies, and in its first decades relying heavily on the use of force to establish its authority, particularly in the south.

But the Egyptian subvention was a threat to British domination of the Condominium, especially after 1922, when Egypt became formally independent of Britain (though remaining, resentfully, under British occupation). A local source of revenue had to be found. The answer was a single economic development strategy: a vast cotton-growing scheme in the Gezira, which started producing significant amounts of cotton in the late 1920s. This did, ultimately, yield considerable taxable revenue – in years when the world market was good – first for the government, which owned a large share of it, and for the companies who invested in it, but also for the Sudanese who held tenancies. It also, of course, promoted the dependence of the emerging economy of Sudan on a single crop, which was largely exported as raw material.

The wealth created by cotton-growing had other effects. The proportion of the profits which flowed to the Sudanese was unevenly distributed; it went to certain individuals and families, often those who already enjoyed some connection with the state, and who were part of the developing social and political culture of the riverain northern heartland. One of those who played this game with some success was the son of the Mahdi. Despite the suspicion and hostility of some officials, Sayyid Abd al-Rahman al-Mahdi (known to officialdom as SAR) obtained a degree of assistance from the British, establishing himself as a wealthy and powerful man. In return he became a reliable supporter of the Condominium government. This was invaluable to the British in times of crisis, such as the two World Wars and the Egyptian revolution of 1919-22. As head of the Ansar sect established by his father, Sayyid Abd al-Rahman was in perpetual rivalry with the head of the Khatmiyya tariqa, Sayyid Ali al-Mirghani (known as SAM). Both combined political and religious leadership with the role of entrepreneur, as their successors do today.

Riverain northern Sudan also provided the bulk of another increasingly wealthy and important group in Sudanese society – those whom the British called the *effendiya* Arabic-speaking Muslims with some formal western education who occupied clerical posts in the lower ranks of the government. British attitudes to this group were decidedly complex; they viewed them as a political danger, they disliked their presumption and their adoption of patterns of dress from outside the Sudan; they identified them – probably accurately – as the most important group in the anti-British and pro-Egyptian agitation of the early 1920s, which culminated in 1924 in the unrest known as the White Flag revolt. After the suppression of the White Flag Movement, the British expelled most Egyptian officials from the Sudan. But the British relied on the *effendiya* – all of them men – to keep the bureaucracy working. They were much cheaper than British employees, and they shared at least some aspects of political culture with them. They were, after all, more often than not the products of Gordon College, or 'Eton on the Nile', created to train a small body of Sudanese in the tasks of the modern state.

By the end of the 1920s, some members of this group were beginning to invest the word 'Sudanese' with a new meaning. Up to this point 'Sudanese' was not a term that most inhabitants of the country would have used to describe themselves. Peoples in the heartland referred to themselves as Arabs. 'Sudanese' (its root form meaning 'black') was a term reserved for people from the south. But in the 1930s educated members of the northern riverain Arab elite began to apply it to themselves as a statement of an aspiring national identity. They also called themselves 'graduates', in self-conscious affirmation of their identity as secondary school graduates.

Suspicion of these educated men as a subversive group was one of the factors that led the British to develop a different system of administration for outlying parts of the country, for the more remote parts of the north and the whole of the south. This sought to engage with local ideas of authority to create an articulation between the centralized state and what were labelled 'traditional' local authorities. 'Native administration', as the British called this approach, had the advantage of keeping the cost of administration low. With its precursors in the Turco-Egyptian administration and successors in several post-independence governments, it can be seen as the longest lasting of all administrative systems in modern Sudanese history.

But British policy towards the south was complex and contradictory. On the one hand the south was made subject to and part of the centralized state run from Khartoum, a state to which southerners had no access and in which the importance of Arabic and Islam was unquestioned; on the other hand, British officials sought – not always consistently – to keep the south distinct and separate, and to exclude from most of its extent not only northern officials but any Muslim or Arab influence. For a time from the end of the 1920s this approach was formalized as 'Southern Policy'. The contradiction encouraged neglect: government-provided education, most British officials thought, was liable to be bad for southerners, bringing them under the influence of the northern 'graduates', so education in the south was for many years left to under-resourced Christian missions. The rush to reverse these policies in the last years of the Condominium, from around 1947, was as belated and ineffectual as the attempt to create a new, more inclusive political culture of representation in the same years.

The ineffectiveness of these measures was partly due to the rapid end of the Condominium. This came much more swiftly than had been anticipated. Celebrated by some as a courageous victory for Sudanese nationalism, the end of the Condominium was more the result of Anglo-Egyptian rivalries and politicking. While Egypt was wriggling free from British control after 1945, Britain and Egypt had each courted and encouraged the small group of graduates who perceived themselves as Sudanese nationalists, seeking to enlist their support one against the other. The result was that at independence, the Sudanese state was more or less handed over on a plate – to the *effendiya* and their allies among the established sectarian groups, Abd al-Rahman al-Mahdi's Ansar, and Ali al-Mirghani's Khatmiyya. The Khatmiyya group nominally favoured union with Egypt; while the graduates associated with Abd al-Rahman al-Mahdi called for an independent Sudan. But as the end of the Condominium drew rapidly closer, these contending parties reached agreement on an independence which gave them control of the central state that the graduates had served as functionaries. This was to the exclusion of the majority of Sudanese.

They took control at a time of rapid state expansion. The expansion was fuelled by good years of cotton prices and by the reformist ambitions of a late colonial regime briefly devoted to projects of social welfare: to the expansion of education, the creation of new development schemes and improvements in wages and conditions for workers. But as the boom years ended shortly after independence these expansionist ambitions proved unsustainable. In politics, the economic downturn was compounded by the assumption of the riverain elite that the pursuit of modern nationhood required that other Sudanese – in the west, in the east, and in the south – accept their culture and their view of the future. The consequences of this narrow vision were already apparent before the end of the Condominium, in the bloody events which followed the Torit mutiny of August 1955, when southern Sudanese, suspicious of the imposition of northern officials in the run-up to independence, turned violently against vulnerable individual northerners in the south.

This contradiction between a northern elite with a restrictive view of nationhood, and a wider population excluded from full participation in the political process, has fuelled half a century of centre-periphery conflicts in post-colonial Sudan. But the problems of governance have not been restricted to war at the margins. After independence, regimes in Khartoum became locked into a cycle of instability. Brief periods of parliamentary rule have been succeeded by lengthy periods of effective dictatorship, in turn ended by popular unrest. Some observers have attributed this destructive cycle to the influence of sectarian politics in the north. They argue that the prolonged rivalry between Ansar and Khatmiyya – between the Mahdi family and the Mirghani family – have had the effect of sabotaging democracy, making it impossible for what were formerly called the 'modern forces', the technocrats, trade unions, teachers, to lead Sudan in the path of development. This is a misleading simplification. Sectarian rivalry, in part a legacy of colonial policies that favoured the two leading families , has certainly been a problem, but the ambitions of the modern forces themselves – shaped by a sense of the superiority of the ideals and culture of the riverain centre they hailed from – exacerbated the crisis of the state, straining its resources to breaking point. Post-independence governments have been authoritarian for the most part. They have had aspirations to transform the country, but lacked the power to realize their goals. Grand ambitions have propelled instability. These included the campaign by General Abboud, who seized power in 1958 and tried to Islamize the south, and President Nimeiri's visions of a country where prosperity would be created by mechanized farming. Resistance to these visions was met with a response that was both authoritarian and weak – Abboud's war in the south, Numeiri's alliance with radical Islam and, in the 1980s, Sadiq al-Mahdi's use of *murahalin* (mounted raiders drawn from Arab pastoralist groups) as military auxiliaries. The reflex authoritarianism of a state convinced of its rightness has also affected politicians and administrators who are not riverain northerners as the southern leader Abel Alier inadvertently revealed when he said of those who resisted the Jonglei Canal Project, that he would 'drive them to paradise with a stick'.

In recent years this particular cycle of instability at the centre seems to have been interrupted. The current regime in Khartoum has held power since 1989, longer than any other since independence. This is partly the result of a new source of economic strength; for the first time since the cotton boom of the early 1950s, a Sudanese government has buoyant revenues – from oil. Much of this money has been spent on maintaining and expanding the apparatus of state violence. But the longevity of the National Congress Party and the Ingaz government may also result from a restriction of ambitions. Since the split in the Party and the expulsion of Hassan al-Turabi and his supporters, the government has retreated from its earlier project of cultural transformation; its concerns are no longer with Islamization, but rather with the extraction of oil wealth, and the spending of this wealth, either abroad or in the central riverain area. All other parts of the Sudan – west, east and south – are significant only as potential sources of oil, or as potential bases for rivals. Khartoum's concern is limited to controlling political challenges and ensuring the speedy extraction of oil. This pragmatic approach places less strain on the regime's resources, but it has fostered a policy of destabilization and disruption of the margins of the state, designed to preempt any challenge to oil extraction or the control of the state.

Paradoxically, it has been the National Congress Party, the longest-lasting of all post-independence regimes, that presided over the break-up of the modern Sudanese state. The pragmatic strategy of the NCP, a strategy of minimal aspiration, is one that served earlier states well. The Fur and Funj states of four hundred years ago had little interest in transforming the political culture or worldview of their subjects; in each, a ruling group survived and maintained itself in power principally by extracting resources – mainly slaves – from peripheral areas, areas they deliberately kept in a state of instability. A similar governing strategy has kept the present government in power. But the periphery has fought back more fiercely than before. It has reclaimed both land and power from the centre. The future may see a return to an earlier political era in another sense, a return to a situation where multiple centres of power vie with each other within the borders of the former Sudanese state.

Recommended Reading

Collins, Robert O. *A History of Modern Sudan*. Cambridge: Cambridge University Press, 2008.

Holt, Peter M. and Daly, Martin W. *A History of the Sudan*. Harlow: Longman, 2000.

Johnson, Douglas. *The Root Causes of Sudan's Civil Wars*. Oxford: James Currey, 2003 & revised edition 2011.

Warburg, Gabriel. *Islam, Sectarianism and Politics in Sudan since the Mahdiyya*. London: C. Hurst and Co, 2003.

Woodward, Peter. *Sudan 1898-1989: The Unstable State*. Boulder: Lynne Riener, 1990 and London: Lester Crook Academic Publishing, 1990.

7

From the Country to the Town

MUNZOUL A. M. ASSAL

Sudan's population has historically been highly mobile, and there are long-established patterns of periodic migration from rural to urban areas. Until the late 1970s this movement from the country to towns was generally temporary, but since the 1980s it has increasingly taken on the character of permanent settlement. During this period, despite decades of war, Sudan's population has been growing at nearly three per cent per annum. This growth has been fastest in a few urban centres, with Khartoum having the greatest share.

Estimates for rates of migration and urbanization vary. By one estimate, in 2005, one in three of Sudan's population was living in towns, half of them in Greater Khartoum (i.e. the 'Three Towns' of Khartoum, Omdurman and Khartoum North, and their satellite settlements). Khartoum has become a megalopolis, one of Eastern Africa's biggest cities. The capital's population grew from 250,000 on the eve of independence in 1956 to nearly three million in 1993. (By then a quarter of all Sudanese were recorded as living in towns or cities.) Fifteen years later, in the census of 2008, though figures have not been officially released, Khartoum's total population is indicated at over five million.

Travelling in Sudan today, in the rural areas and the sprawling informal settlements round the capital and other cities of the northern heartland, it is easy to see the unprecedented extent to which people have been moving from villages into urban centres. The increase is linked to another significant trend. By 2005 one in six people in Sudan were classified as internally displaced. Involuntary displacement has become a key factor in Sudan's rapid urbanization. It has been driven by insecurity, by ecological degradation and by government policies which have concentrated services in few urban centres (notably Khartoum) and undermined traditional rural production.

The Sudanese state has consistently favoured mechanized and irrigated farming over traditional agriculture. This has benefited those who are rich and well-connected, and can provide capital. The growth of mechanized farming schemes since the early 1970s has denied pastoralists access to seasonal grazing and to the migration routes on which they depend; it has driven small-scale farmers off the rainlands they once cultivated. In this way, state policies have directly increased the rates of rural inmigration. Almost all parts of the country are affected in one way or another by this. Though southerners and westerners may have suffered

63

most, movement from the country to the town is not unique to any particular ethnic group or region.

Rural-urban migration is a back-and-forth, bit-by-bit process. Over time, the idea of going home fades away. There are counter-migrations, but the number of these is small; movement between country and town is, overwhelmingly, a one-way process. In burgeoning urban centres, new migrants place a burden on urban infrastructure and public services. And members of migrant households, a majority of which are headed by women, must find a way to eke out a living – as petty traders or labourers or domestic servants – in the already-saturated informal economies of the urban periphery. Still, these urban migrants may be in a better position in terms of opportunities and earning than those they leave behind. The rate of economic growth in Sudan between 2003 and 2008 was well above seven per cent, but urban-rural, regional, and north-south disparities all worsened.

Histories of Migration

There is an established history of movement from western Sudan to the eastern and central parts of the country. Seasonal or short-term migration has long been a livelihood strategy for these communities, and migrants have generally returned to their areas of origin. But a succession of dry years from 1978 to 1987 resulted in the movement of several million people from the west to the cities and agricultural areas of the Nile valley. Those who might once have been short-term migrants became permanently displaced.

This is a trend that has continued. A combination of natural disasters, war and inequalities in resource distribution has led to a point where today, almost half the Sudanese population is estimated to be on the move every year. In southern Sudan the long civil war destabilized a large zone of the country and pushed millions northward, more than two million to Greater Khartoum alone. There have also been major population shifts within other regions. According to the 2008 census – though its results have been disputed –more than half of the population of Darfur now lives in South Darfur State, indicating a radical shift of population away from North and West Darfur.

According to the 1993 population census, a third of all migrants fell within the rural-urban category, while another third moved from one city to another and a quarter from one rural area to another. Only one tenth moved back from the city to the country. This pattern can be explained by the fact that internal migration in Sudan is undertaken as a series of steps. First, migrants may move from the countryside to a town within the same state or region, and then from there to another town in a different region or state. Migration to Greater Khartoum is the final step. According to the 1993 census, half of the migrants in Khartoum came from other towns; not directly from the countryside.

In the 1980s and 1990s the civil war in the south created a generalized state of insecurity in some areas and led to the partial abandonment of traditional production systems. Development projects ceased. The war produced massive population movements. In the south, where most towns were garrisons during the civil war, the pattern was complex. Towns such as Juba, Malakal, Torit and Rumbek became army bases for the Sudan Armed Forces (SAF) or for the Sudan People's Liberation Army (SPLA). Some southerners sought refuge – and access to relief supplies – in towns, others found safety in rural areas. But those who fled from the south to the north all moved to towns, and most moved to Khartoum. The Nuba Mountains, southern Blue Nile and Abyei area were also affected by fighting. People moved as IDPs from these areas to the central parts of Sudan.

Southern Sudan is a partial exception to the rule of no return that applies to most migrants. Since the end of the war in the south there has been a significant returnee population there. The overwhelming majority of southerners in the north during the civil war and beyond moved to major towns and cities. Khartoum, Shendi, Karima, Port Sudan, El-Fasher and El-Obeid are all towns where communities of southerners developed over three decades. While first generation migrants or IDPs were farmers, pastoralists or fishermen, their children grew up in an urban environment and hence acquired skills that cannot be used for farming or other traditional livelihoods strategies. For this reason, instead of returning to rural areas in southern Sudan, returnees prefer to relocate to towns like Juba, Wau or Malakal.

More recently, the war in Darfur has produced large-scale movement from rural areas to displaced camps within the three Darfur states. The towns of Nyala and El-Fasher are growing fast. In 2008, the population of El-Fasher was over half a million, boosted by the presence of three major IDP camps: Abushouk, Zamzam and Al-Salam.

While Greater Khartoum is undoubtedly the first city of the Sudan, Eastern Sudan is – surprisingly – probably the most urbanized part of the country. The urban population in Red Sea State doubled in ten years between 1993 and 2003. Sixty per cent of its population are now recorded as living in towns, mostly Port Sudan, but also Sinkat and Tokar. The increase in the urban population of Red Sea State is, again, the result of rural-urban migration caused by the deterioration of living conditions in the countryside. And the same demographic and economic structures have affected the region as other drought-stricken areas.

Pros and Cons of Migration

There is a positive side to migration. It may offer better work and educational opportunities, moving labour resources to areas where they are most needed. Rural-urban migration is a dynamic process, and it can involve social commitment to both the origin and destination. In western Sudan, it is generally known that families with migrant members are better off than ones without. In this sense, rural-urban migration, or migration generally, can foster integration and entrench people's connections across space. Through migration, different people come together and get exposed to each other's ways of living and thinking. Migration provides possibilities for greater tolerance in multiethnic and multicultural societies.

Yet, there are far-reaching negative consequences also. First, the rural areas lose vital productive resources, especially as the majority of migrants are of working age. This results in the deterioration of productivity of agricultural and pastoral sectors, hence the decline of the contribution of these sectors to the gross national product. Second, the rapid growth of urban population puts pressure on the services and urban infrastructure. Third, inequalities in the town reveal poverty and lack of integration of migrants into the urban system. Khartoum, for example, is currently witnessing a remarkable real-estate development including residential complexes, infrastructure and foreign investment projects. Parts of the city are coming to resemble Dubai or Abu Dhabi, in the Arabian Gulf. Yet, these developments do not benefit the half of Khartoum's population that lives in the vast periphery of the city. The city provides few services to this group. And long-term residents of Khartoum fear that the growth of the city will reinforce ethnic and class polarization. Successive governments have feared what they see as the destructive potential of new-comers and have adopted a security approach to migrants and IDPs, pushing them to the outer edges of the city.

How Migrants Live

How do migrants earn a living? Over the years, they have adopted many strategies. IDPs initially depended on relief food provided by NGOs. Relief food was distributed from 1984 onwards as a result of famine in eastern and western Sudan. But relief distribution was greatly reduced in 1998 and IDPs in Khartoum have been left largely on their own since 2002 when the crisis in Darfur began, and most if not all NGOs directed their attention to the crisis there, or to rehabilitation in the south.

The most challenging issue for migrants is housing. The settlements of the urban poor can be categorized into four kinds: low-density neighbourhoods in remote locations; urban villages; official IDP camps; and informal squatter settle-ments or pockets of habitation. The increase in the urban population has led to land speculation, which means that poor migrants are squeezed out of the market for accommodation. The extent to which they are disenfranchised is evident from the fact that some who have lived in Khartoum for decades are yet to obtain their own residential plots.

Two settlements on the Omdurman side of the Nile – Al-Salam and Al-Fatih – provide clues as to how migrants survive in the city. The naming of Al-Salam camp is itself revealing. While officially called Al-Salam ('peace'), the camp is generally known as Jabarona, meaning 'we were forced'. The name suggests how the relocated groups that were moved there felt about their new location.

Jabarona is on the western periphery of Omdurman, around 15 kilometres from the great market at Suq Libya. It is one of four official IDP camps in Khartoum, established in February 1992 to host IDPs expelled from different parts of Khartoum after their squatter settlements were destroyed by the city authorities. It is ethnically highly diverse: Fur, Dinka, Nuba, Nuer, Shilluk, Azande and members of ethnic groups from Darfur and Kordofan live there. In 2005 the population stood at over 100,000. Some male inhabitants of Jabarona work on building and construction sites in Khartoum; women sell tea, or work in the homes of affluent persons, or brew local beer, *marissa*. Since 1998, with the near cessation of relief supplies, the population of the camp has had to rely increasingly on income from wage labour and the informal economy. Young men and women go for work in areas at a great distance from their homes, where they may stay for the week, returning at weekends. Women commute daily between Jabarona, Suq Libya and other locations where they can find work or set up tea stalls. A few of the educated IDPs work at schools in the camp itself, even though the salaries are far from enough for their family needs. There is considerable dependence on women. Some families subsist on only one meal a day, cooked and served by women in the evening after they are done with work. New arrivals use kinship networks as entry points to the town. They live with relatives or kin groups, who may also help them find work. This leads to ethnic concentration, as migrants of the same ethnic group cluster together.

Networks of kinship are the main source of employment and social protection. Migrants from Darfur, for example, are engaged in menial activities like selling water, vegetables and fruit. Some young migrants join the army and police although there are no reliable statistics on this. Studies show that women selling food and tea are able to make more money than men, although they risk harassment from male customers, particularly as most do not have the necessary licenses from health and tax authorities. In recent years refugees from Ethiopia and Eritrea have competed with Sudanese women in income-earning activities such as tea and food selling and domestic work as house maids or nannies.

In 2003 Jabarona was among the first camps to be redesignated by the city authorities as a regular neighbourhood. The idea was to bring services and provide plots for residents on a legal basis. IDPs who were living in Jabarona at the start of reorganization were given tags to ascertain their eligibility for residential plots. The process of reorganizing involved large-scale demolition. It started in November 2003; the former camp was divided into twelve blocks, each containing about two thousand plots. By the end of 2005, nine blocks had been surveyed and organized. The process of reorganizing Jabarona involved bulldozing thousands of mud-brick houses. Some 25,000 families applied for the new government-allocated plots. Those who were residents in the camp before 1997 were given priority over later arrivals. Of these families 11,000 could afford to pay plot fees and had the necessary documents – birth certificates, a medical assessment of age, or ID cards. But thousands of families who could not provide such documentation were excluded.

Poor migrants and IDPs living in settlements outside the official camps are not part of the programme of legalization of places like Jabarona. During 2009, a series of massive demolitions and relocations took place in a range of squatter settlements in Greater Khartoum. Inhabitants of Soba Al-Aradi, Salama and Mayo, south of the city, were relocated further south in Jebel Awlia, in so-called peace villages, and in Al-Fatih. Al-Fatih is forty kilometres north of Omdurman. The population there has now grown to over 300,000.

Popular committees run the show in Al-Fatih. Their key responsibility is to issue official papers for inhabitants of the resettlement site, a service that must be paid for. Such documents (especially residence certificates) are necessary to access services and get paper work done within the bureaucracy. But most people have no idea how these committees are selected and do not deem them representative. Building plots are available, but few can afford them. Of those who can, many leave, while continuing to rent out the houses they build. Perched on the very edge of the city, they have lost their access to the job market, and to their social networks. Many must return to their former homes to gain a livelihood. And some end up squatting again, in new social housing on the land they previously inhabited but were forced to leave. Although they remain exposed to the risk of further evictions, they see it as a better option than remaining in the sites to which they were relocated.

Conclusion

Over the past two decades there has been a change in the attitude of IDPs and other migrants in urban centres in Sudan. In the 1990s most were trying to secure the basic needs of food and shelter. Since 2003 they have been increasingly claiming social and political rights. While this is a significant shift, it does not mean that their basic needs are now secure. Most of the new urban migrants in Sudan are barely integrated into the social and political system of the cities where they have settled. For social survival they depend on networks of kinship inherited from their communities of origin, For economic survival, they engage in unskilled work with long hours, often far from their homes and involving long periods of travel. They rely, often, on the labour of children: nearly half of the children in migrant settlements do not complete primary education.

The violent events that followed the sudden death of John Garang in August 2005, when youths rampaged in Khartoum and dozens of peoples were killed, revealed the fragile nature of the social fabric. Local media commentators linked the rampage to angry southerners from migrant communities, but it soon became clear that, though ethnic difference was an element, those who engaged in burning, killing and looting included marginalized people from all over the country. The events in Khartoum were shocking to some in the north, long insulated from the violence endemic in other parts of the country; and separatist voices became louder in the aftermath. Ominously, the riots also revealed the existence of armed militias in the city. Should north and south Sudan separate, and should there be conflict between the two new states, there is likely to be further intercommunal strife in the urban periphery of Khartoum, where so many southerners live.

Rural-urban migration and urbanization can lead to the integration of different ethnic groups. But Sudan's protracted instability and conflict has defeated the melting-pot powers of urban centres, and what we see instead is a reconstitution of ethnic identities. This process is reinforced by the failure of the state to ensure that the basic needs of the poor are met. State policies of revitalizing tribal and ethnic identities also contribute. Policies such as 'return to the roots', which have tried to establish forms of tribal administration among urban migrants, have led to people affirming their tribal or ethnic identities in search of security. New forms of native administration have emerged: sultans are appointed with jurisdiction over communities of southern IDPs in Khartoum and the local courts they organize are recognized by the authorities.

There is little evidence that migration to Khartoum and other major cities will be halted or even reduced in the near future. While authorities are busy managing urban social and spatial problems, largely unsuccessfully, they ignore the structural causes of the massive population movements in the country. Internal migration in Sudan is a response to civil crisis and the collapse of livelihoods in rural areas. But the authorities are unable to manage the migration; and Khartoum society is unable to assimilate the migrants. One outcome of this will likely be the creation of the same patterns of marginalization, frustration and militarization that have been manifest in the geographical peripheries of Sudan over the past decades.

Recommended Reading

Abusharaf, Rogaia. *Transforming Displaced Women in Sudan: Politics and the Body in a Squatter Settlement.* Chicago: The University of Chicago Press, 2009.

Ahmed, Abdel Ghaffar Mohamed. 'Rural production systems in Sudan: a general perspective', in *Beyond Conflict in the Horn of Africa: Prospects for Peace Recovery and Development in Ethiopia, Eritrea, Somalia and Sudan*, edited by Doornbos, Martin, Cliffe, L., Ahmed, A.G.M. London: James Currey, 1992: 133-42.

Assal, Munzoul. 'Rights and decisions to return: internally displaced persons in post-war Sudan', in *Forced Displacements: Whose Needs are Right?*, edited by Grabska, Katarzyna and Mehta, Lyla. London: Palgrave McMillan, 2008: 239-58.

De Geoffroy, Agnès. 'From internal to international displacement in Sudan.' Paper prepared for the migration and refugee movements in the Middle East and North Africa. American University in Cairo, 2007.

Pantuliano, Sara, et al. *The Long Road Home: Opportunities and Obstacles to the Reintegration of IDPs and Refugees Returning to Southern Sudan and the Three Areas.* London: Overseas Development Institute, 2007.

Young, Helen, et al. *Darfur – Livelihoods under Siege.* Feinstein International Famine Centre, Tufts University, 2005.

8

From Slaves to Oil
LAURA JAMES

Introduction

Sudan's economy has been based, since early times, on natural resource extraction for the benefit of the state. This has involved the exploitation, first, of gold, then ivory and slaves, and, more recently, water – the latter especially in irrigated agricultural projects. Finally, in recent years, oil has become the most significant export. The history of resource extraction has built up a concentration of wealth and power in the northern Nile states. And the production of oil since the late 1990s, while it has transformed the economy, has reinforced existing patterns of wealth distribution. Although agriculture is still the single most important sector in the Sudanese economy, providing jobs for about two-thirds of the working population, oil has now become the main driver of the economy, sharply pushing up GDP growth since the opening of the first export pipeline in 1999. This has had a knock-on effect on other sectors, including manufacturing, construction and services.

This chapter outlines the history of resource extraction, culminating in the development of the Sudanese oil industry over the past decade. It surveys the main oil producing fields, the varied quality of the crude oil produced, and the limitations of the country's export and refinery infrastructure. It explores how these affect political relations between north and south, covering issues of corruption, transparency, conflict, sanctions, new exploration and future prospects. It considers the relation of the new oil economy to the old economy of agricultural production and its implications for government spending in north and south Sudan.

Oil has dramatically boosted government revenue in north and south, but has also created new demands for spending and decentralization. As a result, fiscal discipline has slipped in recent years, with both the national and the southern governments struggling to balance their budgets. This has had a negative impact on the banking sector and put pressure on the exchange rate. It has also further boosted the large public debt, most of which is in arrears.

The growth of the petroleum sector has had even more dramatic consequences for patterns of trade and investment in Sudan, with oil now accounting for around 95 per cent of export revenue, and import spending rising to fund oil-related expansion and infrastructure. China has emerged as the country's principal trade partner. Flows of money out of the country have increased, owing in part to repatriation of profits by foreign firms, resulting in a widening of the current-account deficit – financed largely by Asian investment in the oil sector. Sudan's post-oil economy is therefore increasingly dependent on international partners – and vulnerable to a new set of domestic and international risks.

The Pre-oil Era

Like most African countries, Sudan depends on the exploitation of natural resources for its economic growth, and the distribution of the benefits from the extraction of those resources has been a key factor determining the country's social and political structure. Over many centuries before the European colonial era, a pattern was established whereby the resources found to the south – gold and ivory and people – were traded down the River Nile to the north. Slaves, generically known as 'Nubians', were raided from outlying regions and traded to Egypt by the kingdoms established along the central Nile. In 1820, when the Egyptian ruler Muhammad Ali invaded Sudan, exploitation of these resources was one of his major aims. The slave trade peaked in the 1870s. Under the Mahdiyya, civil disorder in northern Sudan led to a decline in the trade. Under the Anglo-Egyptian Condominium it was banned, but the early years of the Condominium saw a similar pattern of other resources being traded from south to north. At the same time there was a move to exploit a wider range of natural resources in the north, through the establishment of commercial agricultural projects, notably the irrigated cotton-growing scheme in the Gezira.

This scheme, which was intended to be the foundation of Sudan's new economy, came to demonstrate the dangers of national dependence on a single commodity. When it was formulated in the 1920s, with the intention of sourcing raw cotton to feed the textile industry in Lancashire, in the United Kingdom, international prices were high. They collapsed in the Great Depression. And the effect of the Gezira scheme was to further distort the country's economic structure. An awareness of its huge importance for the national economy meant that available resources came to be even more closely concentrated in northern areas. Moreover, servicing the massive debt owed by Sudan to British bond-holders financing the scheme put a huge burden on government finances which was particularly acute whenever cotton prices (and therefore government revenues from the scheme) fell; service payments accounted for as much as one third of government revenue in the 1930s.

Beyond cotton, Sudan under the Condominium also saw the development of a number of other cash crops, including gum arabic, sesame, groundnuts and sugar. Attempts to systematize the trade in livestock and livestock products ran up against infrastructural constraints, such as inadequate veterinary services. However, agricultural diversification was hindered not only by the fact that the international prices of most commodities fluctuated wildly during the interwar period, but also by British colonial policy. In order to protect government revenue from taxes on imports of products such as coffee and tobacco, there was an explicit drive to discourage the development of processing industries or even the planting of a greater range of cash crops, especially in the south of the country. As a result, Sudan's dependence on cotton increased, with the Gezira project joined by a similar irrigated scheme at Tokar and the development of rain-fed cotton-growing in Nuba and Equatoria.

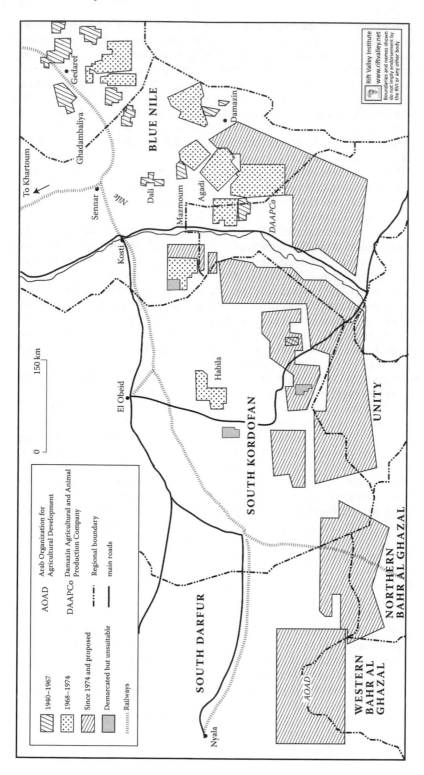

Map 8.1 Agricultural schemes

As the international cotton market boomed after the Second World War, Sudan saw an acceleration of economic growth and developed even more cotton projects, such as the Zande scheme in the south. Many of these were poorly planned, with little account taken of access to roads and markets. Increased dependence on cotton led to massive fluctuations in government revenue in line with international prices. This unpredictability limited the authorities' scope to make the most of the good years. There was an intermittent risk of rising inflation. The uneven distribution of agricultural projects across the country exacerbated existing inequalities, as investment remained heavily focused in urban riverain areas in the north of Sudan, while most of the South, and Darfur and much of the East were relatively neglected. The few agricultural schemes started in the south did not thrive. Investment faltered in the wake of Sudanese independence in 1956 as insecurity increased in the run-up to the long north–south civil war.

Throughout most of the twentieth century, Sudan's economy remained largely agricultural, with growth rates rising and falling depending on harvests. The 1970s saw a plethora of irrigated and rain-fed mechanized farming schemes, funded in part by Arab countries, in an attempt to make the most of Sudan's climatic conditions in order to turn it into the oft-proclaimed 'breadbasket' of Africa and the Middle East. The controversial Jonglei Canal project in southern Sudan, which was intended to increase the availability of water for agricultural projects in northern Sudan and Egypt, was also revived. As food prices fell, however, most of these plans failed, leaving Sudan with the legacy of a greatly increased public debt.

The government suffered a major debt crisis in 1977–78, and although it was tided over by US financial assistance, the 1980s saw a fiscal squeeze, with the privatization of nationalized corporations and significantly fewer development projects. Instead, the north–south civil war saw a revival of the old trade in people in the new guise of labour migration. Large-scale displacement of southerners provided a pool of cheap, indentured labour for the north's expanding irrigated and rain-fed mechanized projects. By that time, however, a new economic model was on the horizon. International companies exploring for oil in the south began to discover several likely prospects, raising the likelihood that Sudan would soon have a much more valuable natural resource to exploit.

The Advent of Oil

The commercial exploitation of Sudan's oil resources since the 1990s has effected a transformation of the economy. At the same time it has reinforced, rather than undermined, existing geographic patterns of wealth distribution. Oil has become the country's dominant export commodity, and international interest in the sector has led to a sharp rise in foreign investment flows, with some spillover into the non-hydrocarbons economy, including some infrastructural development. Government revenue has surged, allowing a strong rise in public spending.

The general outline of these changes is clear, but the detail of the numbers is liable to be disputed. Reliable information on the Sudanese economy is difficult to obtain. Although both the central Bank and the IMF provide figures, they are sometimes of questionable quality. The international data relies on information collected on behalf of the state; this may be influenced by political considerations, or simply be unreliable. Economic activity in much of the south of the country, and in northern regions that are difficult to access, such as Darfur, is largely excluded.

Despite this proviso, the available information gives a broad idea of the country's current economic structure. Sudan's gross domestic product (GDP) at current prices appears to be fairly evenly divided between agriculture, services and industry. In real terms, oil still accounted for only around 17 per cent of the real economy in 2009, with even official data suggesting that services and agriculture, at around 35 per cent each, remained much more important. Meanwhile, industrial activity beyond the oil sector was still relatively minor, at just over 10 per cent of the total.

In employment terms, agriculture is still by far the single most important sector, providing work for at least two-thirds of the working population. In addition, it remains the foundation of the rural economy across vast expanses of the country, rendering a large number of people vulnerable to risks of disruption from climate and conflict. But agricultural products are no longer the most important source of export earnings, with their contribution dropping from 100 per cent to around six per cent in the 15 years to 2009. Even before that, cotton, traditionally the bedrock of the export trade, had declined in importance, displaced by livestock and sesame. Other significant commercial exports are gum arabic and sugar.

Subsistence agriculture, including production of sorghum and other staples, remains the norm in many parts of the country. The South and the northern peripheries continue to be dependent on nomadic pastoralism and small-scale, rain-fed farming. These have only been partially displaced in some central and northern areas (especially Blue Nile state) by mechanized projects and huge irrigation schemes. Just as they were throughout much of the last century, these projects are deeply controversial. Many criticize the implications for workers' rights and smallholder land tenure. However, with the government seeking to diversify the economy away from oil through its 'Green Revolution' strategy, and Gulf Arab countries once again showing an interest in investing in schemes to secure their own food security, more mechanized projects are likely.

Despite the ongoing importance of agriculture, oil has become the main driver of the Sudanese economy. A series of recent discoveries has led to a significant increase in known reserves, which stood at an estimated 6.6 billion barrels in 2009 (although, for comparison, this was still only around one-fifth of reserves in Nigeria). As a result, output rose rapidly from a start-up level of 130,000 barrels per day following the opening, in August 1999, of the first oil export pipeline from the Unity and Heglig oilfields (in Concession blocks 1, 2, and 4, on the north–south border), to Port Sudan on the Red Sea coast. Oil production peaked at an average of almost 500,000 barrels per day in 2007, before falling back somewhat in 2008–09.

This steady increase resulted in economic growth averaging seven per cent a year in the decade to 2008, compared with an average of four per cent in the previous ten years. Moreover, growth was relatively stable and predictable, contrasting with the strong positive and negative swings associated with the former agricultural economy. It was boosted further in 2005–08 by the additional benefits of the peace agreement and the global oil price boom. Nevertheless, this improved growth has been from a very low base, and its geographical distribution has been extremely uneven, leading to a further concentration of wealth around a small urban elite. The precipitous drop in oil prices in late 2008 and

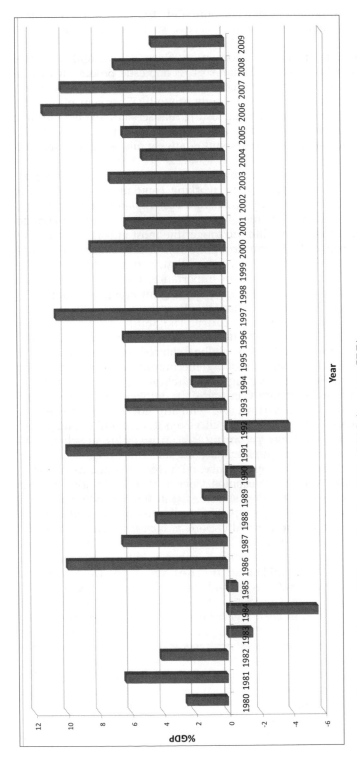

Figure 8.1 Sudan's GDP growth rates 1980–2009 (per cent GDP)

early 2009 also demonstrated Sudan's vulnerability to the global economic downturn, reducing economic growth sharply.

The knock-on of oil-driven growth on other economic sectors has been limited. Manufacturing, which long struggled owing to state domination and a lack of investment, has benefited in recent years from economic reforms, with the increased success of some food processing industries, notably sugar refining. Khartoum has seen a localized real-estate boom since 2005, driven in part by Arab investment. So also, to a lesser extent, has Juba, the southern capital. But there has been little expansion in construction elsewhere in Sudan.

Interest from the Gulf has also been behind some expansion in the services sector, especially in telecommunications and financial services. In the north of the country an Islamic financial system, which forbids the charging of interest, operates about 30 commercial banks. Most of these have prospered in recent years, despite some serious liquidity problems in 2006–07, in addition to their difficulties in accessing dollars as a result of US sanctions. In the south, by contrast, Islamic banks are not permitted, leaving the area with too few banks, as those from neighbouring African countries are not yet operating on a large scale.

Further Effects of the Oil Industry

The sudden rise in the importance of oil to the Sudanese economy makes it worth looking at the development and prospects of that industry in more detail. The original concession blocks (1, 2 and 4) in the Heglig Basin, are operated by the Greater Nile Petroleum Operating Company (GNPOC). GNPOC is a consortium between the China National Petroleum Corporation (CNPC), which holds 40 per cent of the company; the Malaysian state oil company, Petronas, with 30 per cent; ONGC, a state-owned Indian company, with 25 per cent; and the Sudanese state-owned firm, Sudapet, with five per cent. The crude oil from these fields, marketed as 'Nile Blend', has a low sulphur content, and fetches a good price on international markets. However, output has been in decline since 2005, as a number of the older oilfields mature, dropping from a peak of 265,000 barrels per day in the third quarter of 2006 to just 180,000 in the first half of 2009.

In April 2006, oil production began rather belatedly in blocks 3 and 7 in the Melut Basin, located deeper in Southern Sudan. This concession is operated by Petrodar, another consortium led by CNPC (41 per cent) and Petronas (40 per cent). Its first shipment, carried through a new pipeline to the export terminal at Port Sudan, was exported in September 2006. However, there were problems with the quality of the oil. One load was sold off for just US$2 a barrel, at a time when international prices were closer to US$60 a barrel. Although these difficulties were largely resolved in 2007, with output above 200,000 barrels per day in 2008–09, the 'Dar Blend' found in this area remains viscous and acidic, trading at a substantial discount to Nile Blend, especially when global demand is contracting, as in late 2008.

2006 was a significant year for Sudanese oil production, also marking the beginning of output from two other, less significant, concession blocks. Block 6, located in the north of the country, which is majority-owned and operated by CNPC, saw production rise, by 2008, to an estimated 40,000 barrels per day of 'Fula Blend'. This oil is very poor quality and is principally for domestic use, supplying the Al

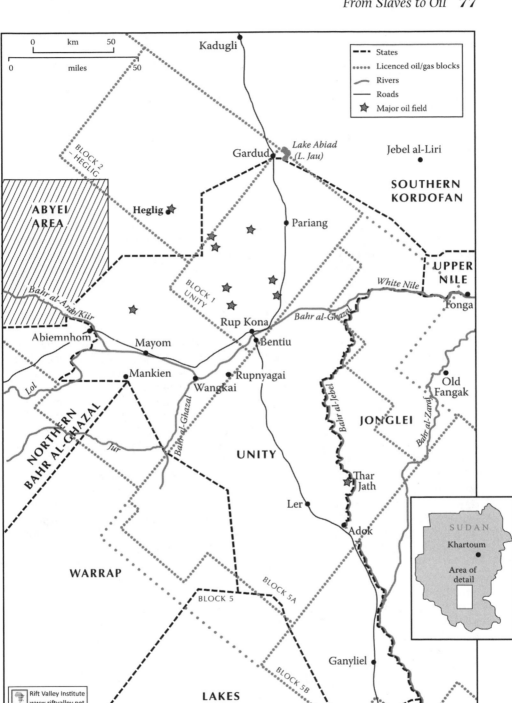

Map 8.2 Oil concessions

Jeili refinery in Khartoum. In addition, the Thar Jath oilfield in Block 5A, managed by the White Nile Petroleum Operating Company (WNPOC) – a consortium led by Petronas, with Lundin of Sweden, ONGC and Sudapet – began exporting just over 20,000 barrels per day of oil through the GNPOC pipeline.

There is further oil exploration continuing in various concession blocks across the country, and optimism has been voiced, at various times, about the prospects in Petronas' Block 8; the natural gas potential of offshore blocks 13 and 15, explored by CNPC; and the massive Block B, in southern Sudan, managed by Total. However, many of the other concessions have been taken up by relatively small firms, reflecting perceptions of a lower likelihood of discoveries. It is risky to look to the new blocks to reverse Sudan's existing oil production trend – which is downward. The ongoing fall in output from the Heglig Basin has not been offset by the hoped-for new output from other fields, owing in part to technical problems. As a result, the government's former forecast that Sudan would be producing a million barrels a day by 2009 has been revealed as no more than a pipe-dream – it would be lucky to rise back substantially above half a million.

The prospects for Sudan's future oil production, and thus for its future economic health, are also complicated by politics: in particular, by north–south relations. The 2005 Comprehensive Peace Agreement (CPA) stipulated that, at least until the 2011 referendum, 50 per cent of net government revenue from oil produced in the south should go to the semi-autonomous Government of Southern Sudan (GoSS), after two per cent has been allocated to the oil-producing states. However, this still leaves plenty of room for disagreement, not only because the delineation of the north–south border has not yet been agreed – with oil revenues from disputed areas such as Abyei up for debate – but also because of a general lack of transparency in the sector. The CPA therefore also provided that outstanding issues should be resolved by a new National Petroleum Commission (NPC), jointly chaired by the national and GoSS presidents, with an equal number of permanent members from north and south, and temporary members drawn from the relevant states.

There were substantial delays setting up the NPC, causing two years of paralysis in north–south oil sector quarrels. Although the Commission is now operational, there is ongoing potential for disagreements over a number of contentious issues. Certain concession blocks in the south have been disputed, with both the national government and southern militias awarding competing licences during the years of civil war. Although in theory these were resolved by the NPC, in practice there were ongoing competing claims – for example, in Block 5B, where Ascom of Moldova has been exploring under a GoSS licence, and in parts of Total's Block B.

A lack of transparency in the sector has been the subject of much criticism by politicians from the south. As well as disputing the allocations of oil reserves near the border, they have questioned the low prices received for some shipments of oil (especially Dar Blend). There have been claims that the full details of oil marketing contracts may not have been disclosed, and that the government is selling crude oil to traders at below market prices. These remain unproven. Accusations of corruption are extremely difficult to assess, given the variety of oil exploration and production-sharing agreements, the diversity of oil grades and prices, the problem of determining the proper shares of the federal, southern and state governments, the fact that some oil is exported while some is refined domestically, and the lack of clarity over ownership of the border reservoirs.

Finally, the economic prospects of Sudan's oil sector have been clouded by national and international political risk. US sanctions and a US-led divestment campaign against Sudan, motivated largely by the ongoing crisis in Darfur, have had some effect. They have kept many of the big Western firms out of the country – Marathon of the United States, for example, was forced to sell its stake in Block B. Some services and engineering companies have also withdrawn, such as Britain's Weir Group and Rolls Royce. Other firms have sought to remain in the country and deal with the divestment campaign by improving their record on corporate social responsibility. Nonetheless, the net effect has been less competition within the sector for contracts and concessions, which is likely to have reduced efficiency and cut into government profits.

On a local level, political instability also has the potential to disrupt oil production. Blocks 1, 2 and 4 include volatile north–south border areas, such as Abyei, the scene of serious fighting in mid-2008. Similarly, Block 6 has seen rebel attacks across the border from Darfur. Moreover, across the country, there is evidence that some local communities, resentful of the lack of benefits they receive from oil production, have begun to take action against the operators. In late 2008, for instance, nine Chinese oil workers were kidnapped in South Kordofan, and some were killed.

Although the oil companies operating in Sudan are unlikely to abandon their existing investments, security concerns could deter new investment and upgrading of existing oil infrastructure, especially in an environment of falling international oil prices. Uncertainty over the future of southern Sudan following the Referendum raises the possibility that renewed civil war could disrupt operations, that existing concessions might be called into question, and that – without access to the pipeline through the north to Port Sudan – the south might be unable to export its oil.

Balancing the Books

The government in Khartoum is officially committed to fiscal reform, and has implemented a series of IMF programmes since 1997 that helped to bring down triple-digit inflation. It has made efforts to improve revenue collection through a series of tax reforms. The finance ministry has also sought to impose improved discipline on line ministries, and to introduce a Treasury Single Account. In addition, there has been an ongoing attempt to reduce the size of the state, with a series of privatizations of state-owned firms. Nevertheless, the government is increasingly dependent on volatile oil earnings, which made up over 65 per cent of total revenue in 2008. Despite the fact that oil has dramatically boosted government revenue in recent years, rising demand for spending – driven in particular by the search for a 'peace dividend' and commitments to decentralization following the CPA in 2005 – has resulted in an ongoing struggle to balance the budget. This became very clear in 2009, when oil prices fell sharply.

The problems affecting the national government are even more marked in the case of the government of Southern Sudan, which, given the lack of a tax base and collection capacity, has almost no revenue apart from the oil transfers from the north. This is supplemented by international aid, but this failed to come through as quickly as expected following the CPA, as the multi-donor trust fund set up under the World Bank was slow to begin operations. At the same time,

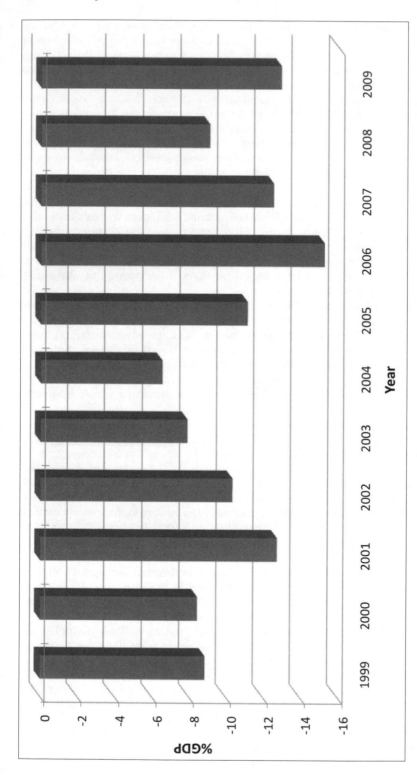

Figure 8.2 Sudan's fiscal deficits 1999–2009

spending has surged ahead, as the newly formed GoSS seeks to establish its control. Over half of spending goes on the public-sector wage bill, with much of that allocated to salaries for the Sudan People's Liberation Army. By contrast, infrastructure development has been disappointing, owing both to a lack of implementation capacity and to some well-publicized corruption scandals.

Half of the net revenue from oil produced in the south is supposed to be transferred to the GoSS. The central government also made specific undertakings to transfer funds to Darfur and to the east of the country as a result of separate peace agreements signed in 2006. Northern state governments have been receiving significant transfers through a decentralization process overseen by the Fiscal and Financial Allocation and Monitoring Commission. Even though not all of the promised transfers have been made, and the process itself has been deeply flawed and politicized, the increased earmarking has compromised efforts to control spending. Consequently, after showing small surpluses in 2003–04, the budget moved back into deficit from 2005, and domestic arrears began to increase.

As ministries were unable to pay their contractors, there was a knock-on impact on the banking sector, with a sharp rise in non-performing loans to well over 20 per cent in late 2006. These were concentrated in three large banks, particularly Omdurman National Bank, forcing the central bank to support the system by providing liquidity over some months. The result was to put pressure on the Sudanese currency, which had previously been appreciating against the US dollar, and the authorities' efforts to support it brought foreign-exchange reserves down to dangerously low levels in 2007. This pattern was also repeated in late 2008 and early 2009.

The increase in domestic public debt came in the context of a massive, mostly unserviced external public debt burden, much of which was originally built up, as outlined above, in failed 1970s development programmes. These arrears have cut off Sudan's access to mainstream concessional lending, although the government has still been able to arrange some loans from investing countries such as China, India and some Gulf states. This does nothing, however, to address the long-term problem of a public debt burden that was estimated at 70 per cent of GDP in 2009. In fact, the taking on of new commercial loans is yet another factor – together with rising oil revenue and, crucially, the government's management of the crisis in Darfur – that is making multilateral debt forgiveness under the Heavily Indebted Poor Countries Initiative extremely difficult to obtain.

The growth of the petroleum sector has had even more marked consequences for patterns of trade and investment. Oil in 2008 accounted for around 96 per cent of Sudan's total export revenue – sharply up from 20 per cent ten years previously. The next biggest single export-earner, sesame, by contrast, provided less than one per cent of total export revenue. The shift to oil has also affected Sudan's trading partners: 60 per cent of exports by value now go to China, according to IMF figures, while 30 per cent go to Japan.

However, import spending has more than kept pace with the sharp rise in export earnings. Sudan has been forced to buy many more capital goods for oil-related expansion and infrastructure. Government spending on imports has also risen, as the authorities have sought to fund both a series of conflicts and subsequent peace dividends. But an increasingly prosperous capital has boosted demand for consumer products as well. Around 38 per cent of import spending was on machinery in 2008, compared with 23 per cent on manufactured goods and 16 per cent on

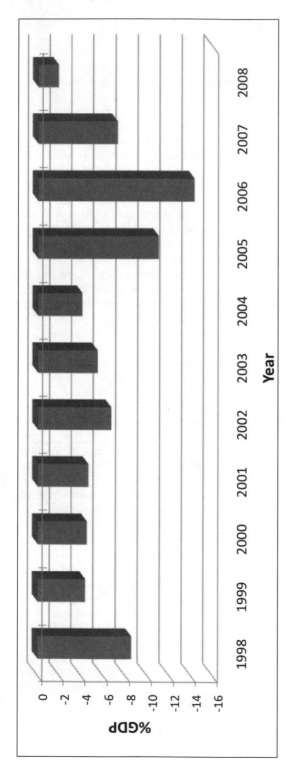

Figure 8.3   Sudan's current account deficit 1998–2008

transport equipment. A high proportion of these imports are from China – about 25 per cent in 2008, up from just three per cent fifteen years before. Saudi Arabia, India, Egypt and the United Arab Emirates are also important sources.

Oil development has therefore dramatically changed Sudan's current-account structure. Flows of money out of the country have increased, not only as a result of import spending, but also owing to rising repatriation of profits by foreign firms and increased spending on trade-related services. Until recently, these flows were only partly offset by oil export earnings and increased transfers home from the large Sudanese diaspora. As a result, the current-account deficit widened sharply, peaking at over 14 per cent of GDP in 2006. Although rising oil production and international prices finally began to contain the growth in Sudan's deficit growth in 2007–08, it is likely to have widened again in 2009 as a result of reduced inflows associated with the global economic downturn.

In order to finance this current-account deficit, Sudan has been forced to seek increased capital inflows, which have mostly come in the form of foreign direct investment. Although no detailed breakdown of this foreign investment is available, it is likely to have remained largely focused on the oil sector, although infrastructure, finance, transport, telecommunications and power have also attracted some interest. As a result, China will have remained the most important investor in Sudan, together with other Asian countries such as Malaysia and India, despite a sharp increase in interest from the Gulf Arab states.

Foreign direct investment in Sudan rose steadily until 2004, in line with oil-sector growth. There was a sharper increase in 2005–06, reflecting investment in a number of new oil projects, as well as infrastructure-building associated with the CPA and increased foreign interest in other sectors of Sudan's economy on the back of an oil price boom. Foreign direct investment dipped in 2007, however, sounding a warning signal, and it remained at a similar level in 2008, with a further decline likely as a result of the global financial crisis in 2009.

Conclusion

The increased dependence of Sudan's post-oil economy on the country's inter-national partners renders it vulnerable to a new set of domestic and international risks. The most pressing of these risks is uncertainty over future international oil prices. Oil prices are inherently volatile and – as Sudan discovered in its time as a cotton producer – dependence upon a single commodity always constitutes a major vulnerability. This is worsened by the fact that many of Sudan's major investors, notably the Gulf Arab states, also have oil-dependent economies.

Beyond the danger of a repeat of the oil price slump driven by the global economic downturn in 2009–10, there are specific factors that could bring oil revenues down for Sudan. Much of the oil, as we have seen, is relatively poor in quality, meaning that demand can suffer disproportionately if spare capacity in the market increases. In addition, there is a danger that rising production costs (driven up, for example, by the need for more security in the oil fields or expensive 'enhanced oil recovery' techniques) could cut into profits. Finally, there are even more serious risks of a hiatus in oil production as a result of conflict or, ultimately, lack of new discoveries.

When the oil runs out, Sudan will have to go through yet another uncomfort-able economic transition. The focus of its natural resource exploitation moved in the late nineteenth and early twentieth centuries from gold and slaves to agricultural projects. In the twenty-first century, a replacement will need to be found to replace oil and the solution is likely to be more agricultural projects. This would once again render Sudan vulnerable to risks from poor harvests, drought and falling international commodity prices. New large-scale agricultural projects, funded with capital from the Gulf, bring memories of the disasters of the 1970s. Critical voices in Sudan have portrayed them as a new form of colonialism. Distributional and human rights concerns are likely to re-emerge. There is a danger, in short, that the wheel could turn full circle, with indentured workers filling the roles played by slaves in the pre-modern era.

Recommended Reading

Sidahmed, Abdel Salam and Sidahmed, Alsir. *Sudan*. London: Routledge, 2005.
Yongo-Bure, Benaiah. *The Economic Development of Southern Sudan*. Lanham, MD: University Press of America, 2007.
Patey, Luke. *A Complex Reality: The Strategic Behaviour of Multinational Oil Corporations and the New Wars in Sudan*. Copenhagen: DIIS, 2006.
IMF, Sudan and the IMF: *Article IV consultations – Staff reports*, *IMF*, http://www.imf.org/external/country/sdn/index.htm.
The Economist Intelligence Unit's *Monthly Country Reports*, http://www.eiu.com.

9

Sudan's Fragile State, 1956–1989

PETER WOODWARD

Sudan's independence on 1 January 1956 was the outcome of a complex struggle with not one but two imperial powers, Britain and Egypt. Whereas most states in Africa attained independence through political negotiation with a single colonial master, and did so on terms that involved a degree of constitutional consideration and eventual agreement between them, Sudan had to free itself from two countries that, in theory, ruled it jointly as a condominium, but were in reality at odds with each other on key issues, including, notably, the fate of Sudan itself. Egypt felt it had a right of conquest which derived from the period between 1821 and 1885 when it had ruled most of Sudan: in the Egyptian view Britain's involvement in the campaign of 1898, while it made possible the defeat of the Mahdist forces, had allowed Britain to assert an unwelcome dominance over Sudanese affairs. The British view was that it would be contrary to Britain's interests to see Sudan united with Egypt, which was a prospect that remained a possibility right up to the eve of independence in 1955.

In consequence, Sudan's nationalists found that their attention in the 1940s and 1950s was focused on the manoeuvrings of the co-domini, Britain and Egypt, rather than on issues of a suitable constitution and other matters of governance. The system of self-government put in place in 1953 was referred to as an interim constitution: it was assumed that a permanent one would come later, when the question of the relationship with Egypt was settled. But after the decision to declare independence, Sudan's successive elected civilian governments were unable to agree on a new constitution. Instead they followed, in broad terms, that of 1953. It took later, military regimes to bring attempts at permanent constitutions.

Multi-party Democracy, 1953-1958

The shortcomings of the system were apparent even before independence. They intensified thereafter. From a constitutional perspective the interim arrangements were for a unitary state under a government chosen overwhelmingly on a constituency basis by first-past-the-post elections. Such a system was simple to understand and to operate, and reflected the style of one of the co-domini, Britain (the system being often referred to as a 'Westminster' constitution after the location of Britain's houses of parliament). Under its autocratic imperial rulers Sudan had always been formally a unitary state, though its administration had had a significant level of deconcentration, with the governors of provinces having a considerable degree of autonomy in day-to-day matters. With the coming of self-government and then independence the newly elected Sudanese government, presiding over a governmental machinery which had expanded rapidly since the early 1940s, sought to increase this central control.

British governors in the three southern provinces had predicted this turn of events in the lead up to self-government and had called for some form of special constitutional status for the region. Their calls had fallen on deaf ears. Even before independence there were growing signs of regional discontent which culminated in a mutiny of southern units of Sudan Defence Force in Torit in August 1955. The government indicated that if the southern MPs supported independence under the unitary constitution, a federal constitution would be considered down the line – but successive multi-party governments failed to deliver on this undertaking.

A Constitution is only one aspect of a political system. Party structures and political leadership are other significant aspects. Sudan has some relatively long-established political parties. The longest-established of these, one of the two parties which have dominated the politics of the multi-party periods, is the Umma Party, which was formed in 1945. The organization of the Umma Party has focused on the Mahdi family, the descendants of the nineteenth-century leader of Islamic revivalism, Muhammad Ahmad al-Mahdi. In the twentieth century his posthumous son Abd al-Rahman al-Mahdi set about transforming the followers of Mahdism, known collectively as the Ansar, into a proto-nationalist party. From the beginning the Umma party had a strongly anti-Egyptian character (the latter was to be expected since it was Abd al-Rahman's father who had overthrown Egyptian rule in 1885) and until 1953 it collaborated with Britain in its efforts to prevent union between Sudan and Egypt. The Umma party's wealth came largely from the family's estates where many Ansar worked for very little material reward, in the knowledge that they were serving the movement. Many came from the western and central areas of Sudan, where historical support for Mahdism translated into electoral support for the Umma Party.

The Umma Party's first rival, in the 1940s, was the Ashiqqa or Blood-Brothers. The Ashiqqa was initially a small group of intellectuals who took a pro-Egyptian position to win support in their struggle with the British. They soon linked themselves with one of Sudan's major Sufi orders, the Khatmiyya, led by Ali al-Mirghani, a longstanding rival of the Mahdist movement. From this alliance emerged the National Unionist Party (later Democratic Unionist Party) generally referred to simply as the Unionists. The Unionists were associated particularly with Sudan's merchant community, many of whom came from the northern and eastern regions of the country, and who formed prominent groups in many other urban centres throughout the country.

In northern Sudan at independence there were also smaller but disproportionately influential ideologically-based parties. The Sudan Communist Party relied on urban workers, especially in the railway centre of Atbara; while an offshoot of the Egyptian Muslim Brotherhood also took root in Sudan from the late 1940s, especially amongst students in schools and in the University of Khartoum.

The outlying regions of Sudan were less well represented in national politics. The Umma and the Unionists were able to dominate the vote of northern rural areas, but they showed comparatively little interest in regional development, while simultaneously stifling efforts to form regional parties. In southern Sudan there were no social equivalents of the Islamic networks in the north to support the emergence of party leaders of note. The very limited educational system of Condominium rule had produced only a tiny intelligentsia in the south, and few southerners made it to the country's only university in Khartoum. The result was a lack of representation in Sudan's centralized national politics, and a growing alienation from it; while politics within southern Sudan remained fragmented, with tiny political parties run by a very small cohort of men educated to secondary-school level. Sudan suffered from weaknesses in leadership of political parties, as well as weaknesses in the formation of the parties themselves. The heads of the Ansar and the Khatmiyya were spiritual leaders and placed themselves above the hurly-burly of parliamentary politics; they did not stand for election. Yet they were the major influences in the two largest parties, especially at election times when it was the spiritual movements that delivered the vote. Successive prime ministers were thus overshadowed by the patrons of the parties they represented. Such were the ingredients of what soon became a very centralized system in a huge and diverse country, one that suffered poor communications and great regional disparities in economic development.

The elections of late 1953 brought what is still the only outright victory by a political party in a properly contested multi-party election in Sudan. The NUP won a clear victory, and its leader Ismail al-Azhari became prime minister. But even before independence he suffered a defeat in parliament, reflecting the instability within his own party. Shortly after independence al-Azhari broadened his government to form a coalition with the Umma, with more southern participation. But that did not help him survive the machinations of factional politics and by July 1956, his own party had split. A rival group created the Popular Democratic Party (PDP), which went into coalition with the Umma Party under an Umma prime minister, Abdullah Khalil. That new government won the 1958 elections on a coalition ticket, but was subsequently embroiled in arguments over whether or not Sudan should accept a US aid package. A growing federalist movement in Parliament was also beginning to pose a threat to the dominance of the two main parties.

With the situation still unresolved and national politics in disarray Sudan suffered its first military takeover. In late 1958, the army - under the leadership of General Abboud - stepped in, apparently with the agreement of Prime Minister Khalil who felt that the political scene was descending towards chaos. The American aid package was accepted; and there was an initial sense of relief that a more decisive style of government would now be established,

The First Military Regime, 1958-1964

Abboud's regime was a classic military 'caretaker' regime. It was led by the country's most senior military figure and saw its task as a conservative restoration of order. Abboud's government achieved a level of acceptability on those grounds. It eventually included both Mahdist and Khatmiyya leaders. It also made efforts to restructure local and regional government as part of a new non-party system. There was a fresh impetus to economic development, including an agreement on the Nile waters with Egypt; extensions of the national railway network to the west and south; and expansion of the cotton growing Gezira scheme. In the early 1960s, however, the government began to run out of ideas, and from 1963 southern Sudan, no better represented under the military than it had been under the previous elected governments, saw the beginnings of civil war. The response of the military regime was violent repression, together with measures to encourage Islam in the region and restrict Christianity. Predictably these moves encountered further resistance and a cycle of rising violence ensued.

In 1964 a growing awareness in the north of what was happening in the south triggered a series of demonstrations in Khartoum and its environs that led to an uprising which became known as the 'October Revolution'. Tired and dispirited, with civil war growing in the south and doubts about the willingness of the forces to suppress the uprising, Abboud and his colleagues caved in with scarcely a shot being fired and a new transitional government was appointed. Briefly it appeared that there might be a new constitution, and a more radical approach to Sudan's endemic problems of political representation and disparity in economic development. There was also an attempt to end the civil war in the south with the calling of a Round-Table Conference, but this served only to deepen divisions, and conflict intensified. There were also new dissident voices from other geographically outlying areas, including the Beja Congress in the east and the Nuba Mountains Federation of the south-west. Hopes of radical change were finally dashed when the elections were held in 1965 on almost the same basis as the two previous ones – they were boycotted by the Southern Front, the largest southern party at the time – and the old parties with their old-established, predominantly rural support, regained their domination of the political scene.

Liberal Democracy Again, 1965-1969

If anything, parliamentary politics second time round was even more unstable than it had been in the first period. The elections of 1965, like those of 1958, delivered no clear majority. Abd al-Rahman al-Mahdi and his son, Siddiq, had both died and the Umma Party was led, as it has been until the present day, by the young Sadiq al-Mahdi, who was briefly prime minister but lacked the experience to steer the party or the government through the shoals of Sudanese political life. Meanwhile amongst the Unionists there was indiscipline and a continuation of the factional rivalry that has come to characterize the party. It was stirred especially by the former prime minister, al-Azhari, who had now managed to become president and used his position to influence developments within the parliament. With politics rapidly descending into farce, fresh elections were held in 1968. There was a stronger Southern presence in parliament, but the outcome was as indecisive as the two previous ones had been. Political life showed scarcely any improvement either and unstable and ineffective coalition government was renewed.

Unstable government might not have mattered so much if there had been improvement in the economy, but here too there was failure. The instability of the political elite was in part due to rivalry over access to economic opportunities that were controlled by government. These included new opportunities in mechanized agriculture in the rain-watered areas of the east and west of the country: 'suitcase' farming by neglectful absentee owners from the centre became a favourite new activity of the commercial sector, to the long term detriment of both the land and local communities.

At the same time, the state itself was expanding in size and decreasing in efficiency. Pressure for expansion was coming from the increasing numbers of school and college graduates who saw it as the major source of salaried employment. Sudan was becoming a classic parasitic or 'soft' state, absorbing resources while producing little if anything in the way of development. By the 1970s Sudan employed 120,000 in central government, provincial and local government had 130,000, over 50,000 were in the armed forces, with another 100,000 working in parastatals: in all approximately 400,000 in a population of less than 15 million. It was also losing control of more of the outlying areas of the country, especially the south. Following the Six-day War in 1967, Israel began supporting the rebels in the south, supplying them with weapons from 1969. Within months of the 1968 elections speculation grew about the possibility of another coup, and it was no great surprise when this came in May of the following year.

The Second Military Regime, 1969-1985

Military coups come in a variety of flavours, conservative, radical and simply predatory. The coup of 1969 in Sudan was significantly different to that of 1958. The 1958 coup, led by senior officers, had installed a conservative 'caretaker' regime. That of 1969 was an attempt to create a 'breakthrough' regime that would change the political organization of the country. It was carried out by middle-ranking officers inspired by Gamal Abdel Nasser and the Free Officers in Egypt in 1952; symptomatically, Sudan's new rulers dubbed themselves the Revolutionary Command Council (RCC).

But while some of the officers were Nasserists, others were more sympathetic to Sudan's Communist Party (SCP). The SCP was centred on the railway trade union, with its headquarters in Atbara north of Khartoum, and was considered one of the strongest communist parties in Africa and the Middle East. It offered, if not mass support for the new regime, at least a significant organizational base, especially in the urban centres of northern Sudan. The new regime embarked on radical policies, especially with regard to the economy where a programme of nationalization of banks and major businesses, especially foreign-owned businesses, was soon under way. However differences soon developed in the RCC between its SCP supporters and those closer to Nimeiri, who were depicted as pan-Arabists. One of the areas of disagreement was over Nimeiri's initial wish to take Sudan into a union with Egypt, as well as with Libya (where another young radical officer, Muamar Gaddafi, had seized power in 1969); Nasser was anathema to the SCP who recalled his repression of Egypt's communists. Nimeiri's aspirations for political reform were linked to an even more serious issue; he wished to create a mass single party movement of his own. That meant banning all Sudan's existing parties including the SCP, whose leader, Abd al-Khaliq Mahgoub, went underground.

In July 1971 pro-communist figures in the RCC staged their own coup. They were briefly successful, but Nimeiri escaped from detention and rallied sections of the army loyal to him and after bloody clashes in Khartoum managed to regain control. It was the first time since independence that the involvement of the military had brought violence on that scale to the capital itself. Nimeiri had survived and turned his wrath on the SCP. This was never to fully recover its position. But without the support of the SCP Nimeiri would need to look again at building some kind of organizational base of his own; particularly since it was apparent that the army itself could not be regarded as wholly reliable, and that further coup attempts were a real possibility. At the same time, the death of Nasser in 1970 had scuppered the support Nimeiri might have got from Egypt and ended any prospect of the planned three-way union. It was time to think again.

In the 1970s, bereft of the SCP, Nimeiri turned to a group of non-party figures who became known as 'technocrats'. They were central to a number of reforms intended to make a break with the country's experiences since independence. One of the first was peacemaking with the south. There had been hopes of that when Nimeiri first came to power, but the southern SCP leader, Joseph Garang, had linked the pursuit of peace to socialism, which alienated his fellow southerners, rather than providing a basis for reconciliation. After the attempted SCP coup of 1971 Garang was executed and Nimeiri turned to less overtly ideological southerners, most notably the respected lawyer Abel Alier. The southern Anyanya rebels had achieved sufficient unity for negotiation. Sudan's African neighbours, especially Uganda and Ethiopia, were supportive and the latter hosted the peace talks. With the defeat of the SCP there was also encouragement from Western countries with suggestions of potential aid projects. There were acceptable mediators in the form of the All Africa Council of Churches (AACC) supported by the World Council of Churches (WCC). The successful outcome was known as the Addis Ababa Agreement of 1972. It brought the establishment of a new regional government in the south. However early optimism encountered growing problems in the 1970s with growing ethnic tensions including complaints of 'Dinka domination' in the new government.

Another major reform was in the field of local government. Despite a series of experiments with local government since the 1940s, tribal leaders had maintained their role as the bottom tier of the state. Reformists had opposed this for some while, and following the October Revolution of 1964 the system came under sustained attack. 'Native Administration' had survived then, but in the early 1970s was to be swept away and replaced by a system of elected local councils. It seemed a progressive step, but with time questions were to be asked about the ability of the state to provide the human and financial resources to make a reality of the new system, while in rural areas in particular the informal influence of the tribal leaders was still felt and in time they were to make something of a comeback.

Both the regional settlement in the south and the new local government system were incorporated in a new Permanent Constitution proclaimed in 1973. At the centre of the new constitution was the creation of an executive presidency. Presented as a necessary reform to bring decisiveness to government, this was to provide Nimeiri with the means to establish what by the end of the decade was a classic example of increasingly despotic personal rule.

At the same time the populace were supposed to be empowered by the replacement of multi-party politics with a single party system, the Sudan Socialist Union (SSU). This was conceived as a pyramidal system with power flowing up from below, but it soon became clear that the SSU was a control mechanism in which Nimeiri loyalists and cheer-leaders predominated handing out presidential patronage, as in so many other single party systems.

The hopes of building stability through patronage were linked to what appeared to be new economic possibilities. One of these was in the area of agriculture, especially as the Gulf states, newly enriched by dramatic increases in oil revenues, provided loans for new investments in food production, amid talk of Sudan becoming the 'breadbasket' of the Arab world. Agricultural production did expand, but not as much as anticipated, while Sudan became heavily indebted in the process. The discovery of significant reserves of oil led to new hope that this debt could be managed. An American company, Chevron, began investing and seemed close to production. However the oil reserves were predominantly in the south, and Nimeiri began to interfere in the region's politics to try and ensure that his government would be the major beneficiary.

As Nimeiri attempted to break the mould of Sudanese politics, those he had ousted in turn sought his overthrow. The old parties and the new ideological movements tried repeatedly to bring him down, especially the Umma Party and the increasingly influential Muslim Brothers. In 1976 Umma supporters who had received arms and training from Libya infiltrated the capital, aiming to capture Nimeiri at the airport on his return from abroad. Nimeiri had another narrow escape as another battle raged for the capture of the capital. But unlike his 1971 escape, he decided this time that his opponents in northern Sudan could not be so easily repressed, and in the following year he announced a programme of National Reconciliation, and made peace with both Sadiq al-Mahdi, leader of the Umma Party, and Hassan al-Turabi, the head of the Muslim Brotherhood.

Those suspicious of the apparent ease with which the previously bitter enemies had come together were proved right; It was soon apparent that each party to the agreement was manoeuvring for advantage. First to fall out with Nimeiri was Sadiq al-Mahdi, who complained that alleged promises of reform were not being fulfilled and went into voluntary exile again in 1978. Hassan al-Turabi however saw the process as an opportunity to build up the Muslim Brotherhood within the state itself. He joined the SSU in a senior position and also became attorney general. At the same time he pressed repeatedly for the introduction of *sharia* (Islamic law), while his followers were encouraged to take up positions in all areas of the state. The extent and significance of this 'entryism' on the part of the Muslim Brotherhood was not to be fully realized for several years. For his part Nimeiri responded to the drift towards Islamism by publishing his own book entitled *The Islamic Way: Why?* In 1983 he introduced a version of Islamic law, which included the *hudud* punishments, with much public display and increased repression in the face of growing unrest. There were public executions and severings of limbs as a new Puritanism was imposed across the north of the country.

Nimeiri's new path in the north, coupled with his efforts to impose his will on the regional government in the south, resulted in growing opposition. In the south, his turn to National Reconciliation had sounded a warning in the context of economic developments. The south feared that the exploitation of newly-discovered oil deposits would rob the region of what rightfully belonged to it. At the same time, Nimeiri and Anwar al-Sadat, the president of Egypt, decided to begin construction of the long-discussed Jonglei Canal in southern Sudan to improve the flow of the White Nile by bypassing the swamps of the *sudd* and delivering more water for irrigation in northern Sudan and Egypt. Growing discontent in the south saw this as another downright robbery, for it would contribute little to the region and some argued would have damaging environmental effects.

These criticisms found a new strength in 1983 when, following a mutiny amongst southern troops at Bor deep in the south, John Garang, a Sudan army colonel and ex-Anyanya officer, announced the formation of the Sudan People's Liberation Army (SPLA). In the following year SPLA attacks forced Chevron to shut down its operations in the south and halted the work on the Jonglei Canal. It was a blow to Nimeiri, which also brought growing criticism within the army itself. These multiple dissatisfactions came together in another popular uprising, centred once more on Khartoum, in 1985 when Nimeiri was out of the country. The army could not be relied on to suppress the uprising and instead the military leaders backed down; Nimeiri, unable to return, went into exile in Cairo.

Nimeiri's downfall reflected not only discontent over the re-opening of civil war in the south and the imposition of harsh Islamic law in the north, but also judgement on the economic and social record of his years in power. Sudan's economy had largely failed to grow. The most lasting monument to Arab investment was the giant sugar scheme at Kenana, but even that was of arguable significance for the economy as a whole. Sudan was left mired in debt on a scale far greater than it had ever experienced before. Hopes of wealth from oil had been dashed by the renewal of civil war. Yet Nimeiri and those around him were widely believed to have made considerable personal gains, often by corrupt means. Thus the gap between rich and poor grew, a situation emphasized when famine struck the western regions of Kordofan and Darfur in the early 1980s. The government did little or nothing to alleviate the sufferings of Darfuris. Many died before international assistance arrived. At the same time Sudan's middle class was shrinking; many left the country especially for the Gulf states where their comparatively high educational level opened many doors.

Nimeiri's regime maintained the narrow base of Sudanese political life. He and many of his entourage were from families originally from the riverain areas north of Khartoum. Those from other parts continued to feel excluded. The re-division of the country into over twenty states was seen as an attempt, not to improve administration, but rather to break down the regional identities and potential solidarities of the nine provinces that had been inherited from the days of the Condominium. Meanwhile John Garang called for a 'New Sudan'. His vision for the country was one of empowerment for 'marginalized' peoples rather than separation for the south, as had been demanded by an earlier generation of southern rebels.

Return to Multi-party Democracy, 1986-1989

The overthrow of Nimeiri in 1985 was not the end of military involvement in government. Senior officers led by Siwar al-Dahab opted not to confront the popular uprising but to embrace it, creating a Transitional Military Council (TMC). The TMC's civilian partners in the National Alliance for Salvation were drawn mainly from the professional groups known as the 'modern forces', seen by many as representing radical and secularist aims. However it soon became clear that the TMC was the dominant force, and that there was little fresh thinking about addressing the country's deep seated problems. A meeting of representatives of the National Alliance with the SPLA at Koka Dam brought hopes of a settlement and a proposal did emerge, but had moved little further before elections were called. The hopes of change in the uprising of 1964 had been frustrated, and history was repeating itself in 1985-86. The old political parties were soon back on the scene and brought with them the old system of multi-party democracy with its accompanying marginalization of the radical leaders of the 1985 uprising.

As in the past, the elections of 1986 produced no clear majority and resulted in a coalition government under Umma Party leader Sadiq al-Mahdi. In the south the elections took place in only some areas. There was an unsuccessful meeting of the new prime minister with the SPLA leader, after which conflict in the south intensified. The issue of Islamic law remained unresolved. There were hopes that Nimeiri's 'September laws', as they had become known, would be repealed but this did not happen since al-Mahdi was concerned at the impact such a move might have on the weak coalitions he was forced to maintain. Meanwhile the economy remained largely stagnant. The tension produced by multiple failures contributed to the instability of successive coalitions. In an attempt to cut the Gordian knot in 1988 the Unionist Party made its own deal with the SPLA, and by the following year there were signs that Sadiq al-Mahdi was prepared to do likewise even if it meant ending Islamic law as demanded by the southerners. The Council of Ministers and the Assembly endorsed the DUP-SPLM accord in April 1989, Sadiq initialled a law suspending Islamic laws on 29 June, and the Council of Ministers endorsed it on 30 June.

However a new ingredient had been emerging in Sudanese politics in the shape of the National Islamic Front (NIF), as the party of the Muslim Brotherhood was now known. Its leader, Hassan al-Turabi, had been building up his movement since National Reconciliation in 1977 and although the NIF had won only 18.5 per cent of the popular vote, mainly in and around Khartoum, it organized astutely to win 23 of the 28 'graduate' seats. It was to be in and out of the succession of coalition governments thereafter, with its main concern centring always on defending and enhancing Islamic law. By 1989 the possibility that Islamic law might be ended by a deal with the SPLA encouraged army officers sympathetic to the NIF. Few had realized the extent to which NIF 'entryism' had penetrated not only the military but other areas of the state as well. This became apparent only after the coup.

Recommended Reading

El-Affendi, Abdelwahab. *Turabi's Revolution: Islam and Power in Sudan*. London: Grey Seal, 1991.

Alier, Abel. *Southern Sudan: Too Many Agreements Dishonoured*. Exeter: Ithaca Press, 1990.

Burr, J. Millard, and Collins, Robert O. *Requiem for Sudan: War, Drought and Disaster Relief, 1983-1993*. Boulder: Westview Press, 1994.

Niblock, Tim. *Class and Power in Sudan: The Dynamics of Sudanese Politics 1898-1985*. Albany: State University of New York Press, 1987.

Voll, John O. (ed.). *Sudan: State and Society in Crisis*. Bloomington: Indiana University Press, 1991.

Woodward, Peter. *Sudan 1898-1989: The Unstable State*. Boulder: Lynne Rienner, 1990 and London: Lester Crook Academic Publishing, 1990.

10
Islamism & the State
ABDEL SALAM SIDAHMED

Islamist groups are movements which work for the establishment of an Islamic order, a society where people live their lives in accordance with the teachings and regulations of Islam, and/or the establishment of an Islamic state – a state which applies *sharia* (Islamic law). In broad terms, one tendency – known as the educationalist tendency – sees the priority as working for the transformation and indoctrination of society as a prerequisite for the creation of an Islamic state. Another, the political tendency, regards the state as a vehicle of societal change and Islamization. The Sudanese Islamist movement belongs to the political tendency.

From the Muslim Brotherhood to the National Congress Party

The Islamist movement started in universities and high schools in the late 1940s under the influence of the Egyptian Muslim Brotherhood and in reaction to the leftist and communist trends that were prevalent in the student sector at the time. In 1954, a small number of Islamist groups came together and formed the Sudanese Muslim Brotherhood movement. The movement's influence remained confined to the student body throughout the 1950s and early 1960s. During the October 1964 uprising that toppled the first military regime of General Ibrahim Abboud, the Islamist movement formed the Islamic Charter Front (ICF) under the leadership of Hassan al-Turabi. During the 1960s, though the ICF's constituency remained narrow, it was the driving force behind the push to dissolve the Communist Party of Sudan in 1965 on charges of atheism. Likewise the ICF was able to push its call for the adoption of an Islamic constitution for the country onto the agenda of the mainstream, parties, the Umma Party and the Democratic Unionist Party (DUP).

Following the second military takeover led by Col. Jaafar Nimeiri in 1969, the Islamist movement initially adopted a hostile attitude toward the new regime, which began with leftist leanings. The Islamists joined the Umma and DUP to form the National Front opposition coalition. Armed opposition through the National Front gave some Islamist cadres the opportunity to receive military training. At the political level however, the movement remained primarily confined to the student sector, in which it has been the dominant force since the mid-1970s. In 1977, following Nimeiri's 'national reconciliation' with the National Front opposition, the Islamist movement under Turabi's leadership adopted a comprehensive strategy to transform the Islamist movement into a political force capable of assuming power in its own right. In practical terms this led to a strategic alliance with Nimeiri's regime which allowed the movement to expand its membership and strengthen its economic capabilities. Using its virtual control of the student body it sought to expand its influence in society at large, making use of petrodollars to set up new Islamic economic institutions that became the main vehicles of the economic empowerment of the Islamist movement and gave rise to an Islamist business class. There was a minor split led by a group of veterans who disagreed with Turabi's approach, but the overwhelming majority sided with Turabi. From then onwards, the breakaway group maintained the original name of the Muslim Brotherhood; Turabi's group on the other hand adopted the name of Islamic Movement (IM) for their organization.

Nimeiri's decision in 1983 to apply *sharia* – to which Turabi was not a party, even though he was Nimeiri's legal advisor at the time – came as a blessing to the Islamists. It provided a justification for their alliance with Nimeiri's regime, its corrupt character notwithstanding. The *sharia* experiment, however, and the excesses that characterized its application, alienated southern Sudanese politicians and widened opposition to Nimeiri across the political spectrum. Nimeiri's regime collapsed in April 1985 following a popular *intifada* or uprising and a military takeover. Just a few weeks before the collapse, Nimeiri had imprisoned the Islamist leadership, which, fortunately for them, enabled the movement to make a come-back to the political scene despite its rather long association with the defunct regime. Under a new umbrella organization, the National Islamic Front (NIF), the Islamist movement managed to capture 51 seats during the parliamentary election of 1986, thus becoming the third largest party in parliament after the Umma and DUP. The Umma and DUP joined together in a coalition government headed by Sadiq al-Mahdi, leader of the Umma party, as prime minister, and the NIF formed the official parliamentary opposition. The main concern of the NIF leaders during the parliamentary period was to secure the gains achieved during Nimeiri's years and to further expand their movement. To this end, they led an assault on the Umma-DUP government with the aim of either inheriting its largely Muslim constituencies or forcing it to give the NIF a share of power.

During the three year-long democratic episode (1986-89), the NIF first led the opposition to al-Mahdi's government, then joined the government coalition in mid-1988, then left the government in early 1989, as a result of extra-parliamentary pressure and the redrawing of government priorities. Whether in government or opposition the NIF proved to be very influential in setting the political agenda and successful in mobilizing public opinion in support of its own agenda. As far as issues of substance are concerned the NIF, among other things, emphasized preservation of Nimeiri's *sharia* laws, or their replacement with yet another 'Islamic alternative'; it also advocated a tough militarist stand toward the rebellion in the south which had broken out in 1983. The NIF aimed at discrediting the two mainstream parties, Umma and DUP, presenting itself as the only authentic custodian of the Arab-Islamic identity of the Sudanese nation.

The inclusion of the NIF in government demonstrated the extent to which it was determining the government's agenda even from the opposition benches; its exclusion from power in early 1989 seems to have prompted the Islamist coup of June 1989. The ability of the Islamists to stage a military coup was a result of a long-term strategy to infiltrate the army, a process which began after their reconciliation with Nimeiri in 1977. Utilizing their freedom of action and the cover of religious advocacy activities, the IM sought to penetrate the armed forces using various channels and techniques and the first cell of the Islamist officers appeared around 1980/81. Between 1981 and 1985 the cells of the Islamist officers grew considerably but not at the same pace as the Islamist movement at large. After the *intifada*, the IM intensified its efforts in officer recruitment, taking advantage of the relatively relaxed atmosphere of the parliamentary period, the growing politicization of the army, its tough militarist stand toward the war in the south, and its huge financial resources. By early 1989, the Islamist movement was ready to stage the coup.

On June 30, 1989, the Islamist officers in the army, led by Brigadier Omar Hassan al-Bashir and supported by about 200 members of the Islamic Movement's militia, succeeded in executing a bloodless military coup that toppled the government of Sadiq al-Mahdi and terminated the parliamentary regime. As a precaution, the new regime did not clearly declare its political or ideological affiliation on seizing power, but simply referred to itself as the Revolution of National Salvation (*thawrat al-inqaz al-watani*). Though the deception went as far as placing Turabi in detention alongside other political leaders, the politicized sectors of the Sudanese public quickly came to the conclusion that the new regime was closely connected to the Islamists. Henceforth, the regime installed in the June 30th coup became known, particularly among the opposition circles, as the NIF regime.

The military takeover of June 1989 presented the Islamists with the challenge of adjusting to the new realities of a movement in power. As pointed out above, prior to 1989 the political organ of the Islamists was the NIF, which was an umbrella organization built around the Islamic Movement core. In organizational terms the IM existed as a separate structure from the NIF, though its members, or most of them, were also NIF members. After the military coup of June 1989, the NIF was formally dissolved along with all other political parties. This decision was apparently endorsed by the NIF's *Shura* Council, which met and formally decided to disband itself and the organization to avoid causing 'an embarrassment to the government'. As regards the IM – which was not visible to the public – there was an initial uncertainty among the rank and file members as to the identity of the new power holders. Instructions were then given to members asking them to freeze all of the old partisan activity and to support the new regime.

Following Turabi's release from his staged detention, he initiated a process that culminated in the dissolution of the IM's structure and governing bodies. Turabi's vision was that the IM should be built anew as a broad and mass movement with a strong tendency towards expanding the ranks and attracting new membership (the formula was to adopt a ratio of 60 per cent new recruits in relation to 40 per cent from the old membership at all levels). During the first period after the coup, the IM's affairs were run by the same inner circle, which was also running the state (Turabi and his deputy, Ali Osman Taha, in addition to a few other associates including al-Bashir). Later on this group was gradually expanded to become an executive body of thirty members, and a wider *Shura* council of around 300 members, none of whom were elected.

The IM's membership became a reservoir from which ministers, top state officials, security officers and occupants of other essential positions were recruited. Likewise, IM members were brought in – by the top leadership – to run media organs, parastatal corporations, banks as well as institutions created by the new regime. IM members were also called on to provide grass roots support, becoming the backbone of the government militia, the Popular Defence Forces (PDF), and the Popular Neighbourhood Committees, and were generally mobilized to provide political support to the new regime as necessary. By the same token when trades unions and other professional bodies were reconstituted in 1992/93, IM members unsurprisingly became the leading figures of these syndicates.

Despite the fact that the IM emerged as the undisputed constituency of al-Bashir's regime, it did not operate openly. One explanation of this situation lies in the strategy of deception adopted by the Islamists who presented their power takeover as a national non-partisan revolution. As such it was not possible for the new regime to allow the IM as the only party that could operate openly and lawfully, when all the other parties had been banned. Another explanation was to be found in Turabi's pragmatic approach to politics and power: the IM had been primarily built for purposes of power control, now that power was safely secured, the Movement was redundant; membership energies were better utilized in the service of the state and its Islamic transformation programme.

In a nutshell, the Sudanese Islamist movement that emerged in the 1950s and grew to become one of the significant political forces in the country, ceased to exist as a coherent political group after it gained power in 1989. It was replaced by a structure that was visible only to its membership and acted primarily as a vehicle of mobilization in support of the new regime. Hence when the regime established the National Congress Party (NCP) to be its governing political organ, the reconstituted Islamic Movement became operative as a nucleus group within the NCP. This dual structure IM/NCP lasted for a limited period (roughly 1993-98), at the end of which Turabi, the Secretary-General of both structures, decided to abolish the IM and merge it with the NCP. In that respect, the NCP might be viewed as the latest manifestation of the Sudanese Islamist movement, similar to the experiments of the Islamic Charter Front of the 1960s and the National Islamic Front of the 1980s. There were, however, unique characteristics of the NCP which set it apart from those previous umbrella structures of the Islamist movement. Chief among these was that the NCP was set up under the shadow of power. At the outset, the body that later on became the NCP was established as the 'Congresses Systems', which was advocated as a non-partisan structure and a forum for popular participation and direct democracy. The formula of the Congresses System was however abandoned by Turabi and his aides around the mid-1990s, in favour of an ordinary political party. Thus, the NCP emerged as the ruling political party in 1996, and in February 1998, Turabi became the NCP secretary-general.

Turabi's election as secretary-general of the NCP was meant to signal the transition to a new stage in the evolution of the party, a stage in which the NCP would emerge as the leading party and the vehicle for the Islamic transformation of Sudanese society. At the beginning, however, the NCP – even with Turabi at the helm – did not have a lot of power or clear control over the affairs of the state. More crucially, it did not have a clear status vis-a-vis the state institutions despite the fact that the majority of the state officials and parliamentarians were

NCP members. As NCP secretary-general, Turabi tried to give the party some substance as a ruling party. In other words, he tried to impose the party's control over the state and its officials, including the president of the republic. Turabi, however, did not have his way; less than a year after his election as NCP secretary-general he was confronted with an internal revolt from his own inner circle of aides, many of whom were considered among his most loyal disciples. The revolt took the form of an internal memorandum submitted by ten senior figures within the party and the state to the NCP *Shura* council on 10 December 1998. The memo, which was adopted by the *Shura* council, proposed a reform package through which President al-Bashir was given effective leadership of the NCP as the party's chairman. On the other hand, the authority of the NCP secretary-general, Turabi, was radically curbed and reduced to administrative and secretarial tasks. The Memo of Ten – as it came to be known – triggered an internal dispute within the NCP that eventually led to the party's split in mid-2000.

Turabi, who was elected Speaker of the National Assembly in 1996, used that position as well as his influence within the Islamist constituency to launch a two-pronged attack aimed at regaining his influence in the party and state. At the level of the ruling party, Turabi and his loyalists launched a campaign of grass roots mobilization in preparation for the NCP 'constituent conference', which was eventually held in October 1999. Turabi and his loyalists carried the day. The conference revoked most of the Memo of Ten's reforms, adopted a new Statute for the NCP that restored control to the secretary-general, whose loyalists dominated the newly elected *Shura* Council, and relegated President al-Bashir to the position of a party chairman without any significant powers. And all the signatories of the Memo of Ten failed to get elected to a new 600-member *Shura* Council. At the National Assembly, Turabi designed a package of constitutional amendments aimed primarily at curbing President al-Bashir's powers through the creation of a new position of prime minister with executive powers, and direct popular election of state governors.

The constitutional package dominated the political scene throughout 1999. With his position consolidated in the party, Turabi launched what he probably thought would be the final onslaught on the president and his group by passing the constitutional amendments through the National Assembly. The Assembly, however, did not live to pass those amendments. On 12 December 1999, President al-Bashir declared a state of emergency throughout the country, dissolved the National Assembly, and suspended four articles in the constitution relating to the election and replacement of state governors. Turabi rejected the emergency measures as unconstitutional and filed a lawsuit to that effect to the Constitutional Court, but the Court affirmed the presidential measures.

Between January and April 2000 there were attempts at mediation by various Islamist personalities from Sudan and abroad, but the split proved to be irrevocable. In May 2000, al-Bashir – in his capacity as NCP chairman – called for a general meeting at the party headquarters to discuss the party's affairs. The meeting, which was boycotted by Turabi and his group, decided to suspend the secretary-general and his secretariat. Once again Turabi tried to seek legal remedies; he appealed to the Political Parties Registrar (a position created under the 1999 Political Associations Act) to revoke the NCP decision to suspend him and his secretariat. Unsurprisingly, the Parties Registrar did not consider Turabi's complaint, viewing this as an internal dispute within the NCP.

Finally, when Turabi felt that the tide was definitely turning against him, he decided to sever all links with his former disciples and current adversaries. Thus, on 27 June 2000, Turabi and some of his loyalists declared the formation of the National Popular Congress as a separate party – subsequently, Turabi's party was renamed simply the Popular Congress Party (PCP). As regards the NCP, its *Shura* Council met in July 2000 and adopted resolutions that endorsed the removal of Turabi as secretary-general and elected Ibrahim Ahmed Umar (one of the authors of the Memo of Ten) to act as interim secretary-general for the NCP. In later amendments of the NCP statutes, the post of secretary-general was abolished altogether and replaced by two vice-chairpersons. Initially, there was some competition between the NCP and PCP over the loyalty of the core Islamist constituency. In the course of time, however, the majority have come to support the NCP, either on grounds of a principled choice or on account of the NCP's control of the state. In the elections of 2010, the PCP was a rather insignificant opposition party.

Transformation of the State

The post-colonial Sudanese state inherited from the colonial state a two-tier administrative system (combining direct rule and native administration) and an economy dominated by the public sector. This structure remained intact with limited changes until the second military takeover of Jaafar Nimeiri in 1969. Under Nimeiri's regime (1969-85), the Sudanese state underwent significant structural changes. During its populist phase (1969-75), Nimeiri's regime proceeded to establish a one-party state and a presidential republic; local government was reformed by abolishing native administration and by the establishment of a pyramidal skeleton linking local structures with national decision making bodies. In the economic field, Nimeiri's regime, during its early years in power, took measures to nationalize foreign banks and companies, replacing them with public corporations. These measures, coupled with the ambitious development projects pursued by the regime, expanded the public sector and further enhanced the economic role of the state.

Nonetheless, the way the political system evolved under Nimeiri's regime – which degenerated into a 'one-man rule' – eventually weakened the state and led to the destruction of its institutions. The third parliamentary regime, which succeeded Nimeiri's, inherited a state structure damaged by the impact of a protracted dictatorial regime, a highly politicized army and civil service, and a weakened judiciary. Given the scale of problems confronting the elected civilian government and its failure to tackle them or to attend to reforming the state machinery at central or regional levels, the fragile state structure went into decline. The state became no more than a crisis management agency that barely coped with the rapidly deteriorating situation at all levels.

The poor performance of successive governments during the parliamentary period to address the range of problems facing the country, facilitated the military takeover of June 1989, which was widely anticipated. The new Islamist regime had to confront these same problems – civil, war, economy, security – but its more immediate challenge was to secure and consolidate its power. This challenge is better understood if placed within the context of the Sudanese political scene at the time of the Islamist takeover. The last government of Sadiq al-Mahdi – formed in March 1989 – included all of the main political parties with the exception of the NIF, two ministers from the trade unions' confederations, and a retired army general nominated by army commanders. As such, the Islamist coup of June 1989 appeared at odds with all other active forces in the country: all other political parties, trade unions, and the army establishment. It was no surprise, therefore, that all these forces joined together under an opposition umbrella, the National Democratic Alliance (NDA), which was formed in October 1989 with the aim of opposing the military regime and restoring national democracy.

To secure and consolidate its hold on power al-Bashir's regime resorted to an unprecedented and violent suppression of any form of opposition whether civilian or military. A physicians' strike in October 1989, which was regarded as heralding a general strike by the trade union movement to topple the regime, was violently put down: union leaders were imprisoned, one doctor tortured to death, and the secretary general of the Physicians' Federation sentenced to death. In April 1990, 28 army officers, and 54 rank-and-file soldiers, were summarily executed following an abortive coup attempt. These measures were followed by almost blanket purges in the army, security and civil services. During its first five years in power, the regime dismissed 11,000 military personnel, including 1,800 officers, and laid off 73,640 civil service employees from various state departments and corporations. These posts and positions were filled by Islamists.

Having consolidated its grip on power, the Islamist regime sought to establish a political system capable of realizing its political and ideological vision. The Revolutionary Command Council (RCC) was created. In the beginning, it assumed wide legislative and executive powers and, in the absence of a constitution or a popular mandate, resorted to rule by decree. The new power holders, however, knew that they would have to establish proper political and constitutional bodies and try to secure a measure of popular endorsement for those institutions and the regime as a whole. In the immediate period following the takeover, the new regime established what they called popular committees in urban neighbourhoods and villages to take care of local services and partially fill the vacuum resulting from the abolition of the local authority institutions. In theory, these popular committees were to be elected by the people in each neighbourhood or village. In practice, the process was tightly managed by the new regime; and the newly established popular committees were – unsurprisingly – dominated by Islamists.

In 1992, the RCC appointed a 'Transitional National Assembly' to act as a legislative authority until the establishment of an elected parliament. In 1993, the RCC dissolved itself and appointed Omar al-Bashir as President of the Republic. In August 1991, a 'political system consultative conference' was convened; it remained in session until April 1992, with between 800 and 2000 delegates attending. The conference resolved to adopt the 'Congresses System' formula as the governing political organization of the country. The process started in 1992 and was completed in 1995 with the establishment of the National Congress at the federal level. This process was accompanied by the reconstitution – again in a controlled manner – of trades unions, professional, women's and youth organizations, all of which had been dissolved after the coup. In December 1995, the president approved Constitutional Decree No. 13 which provided for the election of a National [federal] Assembly composed of 400 seats, two-thirds of which were to be directly elected from geographical constituencies, with the remaining third elected from the congresses in accordance with the statutes and internal regulations of the latter. Through the period 1993-1995, elections were held at the local, provincial and state levels to reconstitute local administration institutions and legislative authorities for the 25 states under the federal system. In March 1996, elections were held for the National Assembly, and so were presidential elections. Omar al-Bashir became the 'elected' president of the state and, as mentioned earlier, Hassan al-Turabi became the National Assembly Speaker.

The new 'elected' National assembly soon initiated measures to draft a permanent constitution for the Republic of Sudan. The process was completed in 1998 with the adoption of a new permanent constitution that came into effect on 1 July 1998. The constitution legitimized the existing presidential federal system, but adopted a rather moderate tone with regard to religion and state by being silent on the religion of the state, and placing Islamic *sharia* as a source of legislation on a par with custom and consensus. It also made citizenship the basis of all rights and duties regardless of religion or race. Among the most significant, and indeed controversial articles, was the adoption of a formula that allowed a measure of limited and controlled pluralism (*al-tawali al-siyasi*) that falls far short of outright multipartyism.

The 1998 constitution has apparently affected the concept and guiding principles of the governing political organ, the National Congress and its transformation into the National Congress Party. Initially, the NCP was projected not as a political party, but rather a political structure that provided a framework for popular participation and grassroots democracy. The formula of the Congresses' System rested on the gradual establishment of popular congresses at the local level – urban neighbourhoods or villages – to the provincial and state levels and finally the national/federal level which would become the National Congress and also include representatives of professional and mass organizations. By emphasising the non-partisan, non-ideological nature of the new political structure, the Islamist leadership was hoping to appeal to, and eventually attract the constituencies of the mainstream opposition parties, Umma and DUP. Turabi in particular, was convinced that the bulk of the DUP and Umma constituencies generally supported an Islamic orientation, but the leaderships of these parties – over the years – proved an obstacle to an Islamic transformation of the state and its policies. Now that the DUP and Umma leaderships had been sidelined as a result of the June 1989 power takeover, there was an opportunity to reach out directly to these Islamic-oriented constituencies to cultivate their support, and thereby broaden the popular base of the regime at the expense of the opposition parties. The Congresses' System was also designed to penetrate other traditional platforms such as tribal structures of the former Native Administration, and Sufi religious orders.

Despite this strategy the formula of the Congresses' System was abandoned in the mid-1990s, in favour of an ordinary political party, the NCP. The most obvious explanation is that the Congresses' System formula did not work, and was not taken seriously even by the regime's decision makers, let alone the public at large. On the other hand, both domestic political evolution of the regime and the pressure of international isolation seemed to have prompted the leadership to consider the adoption of limited pluralism in Sudan's political system. This choice was subsequently formalized in the 1998 constitution that adopted *al-tawali al-*

siyasi. Accordingly, the establishment of the NCP came in anticipation of 'political pluralism' in which the NCP would be expected to compete with other political forces in the country. Nonetheless, though the regime seemed to have abandoned its populist idea of direct participation and grassroots democracy, it had not given up on its plan of establishing hegemonic control over the political process in the country. Under the 1998 constitution, the regime sought to co-opt other political groups or breakaway factions from opposition parties, while maintaining a tight grip on power and the political process.

At the administrative level, al-Bashir's regime introduced a federal structure for the administration of the country. This measure seemingly came in response to a recommendation of the conference of 'National Dialogue' held in September 1989 on the prospects of peace in the country. The Islamist movement had already favoured a federal system, as was clear in the National Charter document issued by the NIF in 1987 outlining its vision for a peaceful settlement to the civil war and the future of Sudan's political system. In 1991 the RCC issued constitutional decree No. 4 which enacted federal rule in the country. After some experimentation with the federal structure, particularly with regard to the number and composition of states, the government settled for 25 states (15 in the north and 10 in the south). Further legislation was subsequently issued to organize administration at the district and local levels and, significantly, the reintroduction of Native Administration in rural areas. In theory the federal system, local government and Native Administration reforms were advocated as measures to empower people, ensure better and more direct participation, and improve delivery of services at the local and regional levels. On closer examination, however, it seems that the regime was more concerned with consolidation of its power than serving public interest. To start with, most of the bodies and executives at the state level continued to be appointed rather than elected (up until the elections of 2010, state governors continued to be appointed by the president). Furthermore, states on the whole suffered from lack of resources and remained dependent on grants from the federal government and whatever resources they could muster from taxes and other dues.

On the other hand, the regime seemed to have benefited from the federal system in a number of ways. The system allowed the regime to assert its control at all levels and – through decentralized organization of the state organs and committed officials – enhanced the regime's capacity to defend itself against counter attacks which would most likely target the centre of power in Khartoum. Additionally, the complex administrative structure of the federal system enabled the inner circle of the ruling elite to reward supporters, co-opt others and expand their patronage networks. On another level, by reintroducing Native Administration, the regime was trying to dismantle the constituencies of opposition parties such as the Umma party of former Prime Minister al-Mahdi which had maintained its stronghold in western Sudan during the last parliamentary elections of 1986. Likewise, Native Administration reforms were manipulated by the government and used as a vehicle to reward its allies and supporters and to penalize adversaries.

Two developments in the economic field have had important implications on the evolution of the Islamist regime: these were the economic liberalization and the drilling and export of oil. In 1992 the regime declared and carried out a comprehensive policy of economic liberalization under which the national currency was floated, subsidies on essential goods lifted, and most of the public sector corporations were either privatized or disbanded. Economically, liberalization freed the government from the burden of securing funds to finance subsidies and support mostly indebted and unproductive parastatals, as well as maintaining large number of public sector employees. At the political level, privatization enabled the regime to deal with the trade union movement. By reducing the workforce in various institutions and reducing the role of the state as the main employer, the regime could neutralize the impact of potential strikes on government operations and service. Privatization also allowed the regime to pursue an undeclared policy of transfer and redistribution of wealth for the benefit of its own Islamist business class. On its part, the rise of the oil industry with the commencement of production and export of oil in 1999 enhanced the resources at the disposal of the regime and had far reaching political implications.

War and Peace

When the Islamist regime assumed power in mid-1989, the rebel movement, SPLM/A occupied around 80 per cent of the countryside of the southern region, some parts of the Nuba Mountains, and parts of the southern Blue Nile. The regime approached the civil war in the south with a view to turning the challenge posed by the conflict into an asset. Through its tough militarist approach it sought to use the war as a tool in its control mechanism. In ideological terms the regime presented the civil war as a problem that threatened the very survival of the Sudanese nation; every citizen was therefore expected to contribute to the government's war effort, its *jihad* against the enemies of Islam and the nation. Within this framework, it set up the Popular Defence Forces (PDF) as a government militia to support the armed forces in the war zone. The PDF mobilization, the mandatory military service for youth and students, and the intensive religiously-inspired propaganda associated with this mobilization, were all meant to keep younger generations within the orbit of the Islamist regime and prevent the opposition forces from attracting a following among them. At another level, the regime imposed mandatory military service among government employees (those who escaped the dismissal axe) as a manifestation of loyalty. By and large, the civil war and the government's approach to it seemed to have strengthened the oppressive dimension of the regime as many human rights violations were committed within the context of the war and/or under its pretext.

Peace on the other hand produced new dynamics and triggered a process that could have significantly transformed the regime and opened the way for the rise of a new and more participatory political system. The 2005 Comprehensive Peace Agreement (CPA) created a constitutional and political framework that was geared towards democratic transformation. Yet, when elections were finally held in April 2010, they were hardly a manifestation of the democratic transformation envisaged by the CPA. Rather, elections simply returned the ruling NCP-SPLM coalition brought about by the CPA, and paved the way for the 2011 referendum on self-determination for southern Sudan.

While the CPA process has been under way, the Darfur conflict has caused a realignment of factions within the inner circle of the ruling NCP in favour of the 'militarist' tendency within the regime, which in its turn led to the government's intransigence and complicated the prospect of a political settlement to the crisis.

The Authoritarian State and the Clientelist State

The Islamist regime came with the ideological vision of radical transformation and restructuring of the state on Islamic grounds (known as *al-mashru' al-hadari* – which literally means 'civilizational scheme', but could also be translated as 'cultural authenticity scheme'). As alluded to earlier, the first phase – geared towards consolidation of Islamist control of the state – witnessed extreme repression and a heavy-handed approach directed against all other political forces and was accompanied by systematic layoffs of civil and military personnel. The Islamist regime sought to replace the secular state structure with an ideologically committed apparatus that could be trusted to pursue the movement's vision of change. In the process, force was used first to assume power and then to consolidate it. It looks as if the Islamist leadership believed that because their objectives were indeed noble – establishment of the Islamic order – any method used to attain power or preserve it was therefore justifiable. Yet, the manner in which the Islamist movement handled the question of power and the way it managed state–society relations have greatly influenced the type of state that emerged under Islamist rule. Thus, rather than the establishment of an Islamic state that represent an embodiment of the will of the Muslim society – Turabi's stated goal – two inter-related manifestations of the state emerged under the Islamist regime: a security-authoritarian state and a clientelist state. The security-authoritarian state roughly corresponded to the 1989-99 period, and was characterized first by the creation and consolidation of organs of repression, and second by the pursuit of repressive practices against opposition and the general terrorization of the society at large. All these measures and policies correspond to the rise of a security state. The second step was the setting up of political and constitutional bodies geared towards the establishment of a political system that ensured the Islamist control of the state and its hegemony over society; hence the rise of an authoritarian state. By its very nature an authoritarian state had to rely extensively on coercion – the security arm – rather than persuasion to establish its hegemony. It should be noted in passing here, that the authoritarian state that emerged under the Islamist regime was not necessarily a totalitarian state, despite being an ideologically driven venture. This is a result of the complex political and ideological map of the country. Ideologically, there are several Islamic groups – some politically active, others concerned mostly with religious advocacy – which were tolerated and allowed to carry on their activities (as long as they did not make any bid for power). On the political level, the regime started a process of limited accommodation of smaller political groups. This process started with the signature of the Khartoum Peace Agreement in 1997 with some southern groups (mostly breakaway factions from the SPLM/A), and culminated with the adoption of the 1998 constitution with its controlled pluralism. Though the state remained authoritarian, that phase witnessed the genesis of the clientelist state.

The split of 1999/2000 and departure of Turabi and his group effectively led to the decline of the authoritarian state. A divided ruling elite cannot maintain an authoritarian state unless one faction subdues the other. Subsequent political developments such as the negotiation and signing up of the CPA, and other peace agreements brought other players on the scene, chief among which is the SPLM which became a partner in government alongside the NCP. Nonetheless, the Islamist ruling group maintained its hegemony over state and society; it also maintained its security arm and the will to deploy that force as it deemed necessary. With the inflow of oil revenue from 1999, the inner circle of the regime found it more effective to build and utilize its patronage networks, and so the clientelist state emerged.

The clientelist state rested on a new patronage system, the result of the concentration of power and wealth in the hands of the Islamists and under the custody of their regime. Opportunities, goods and services became virtually inaccessible to the public without the support or approval of a state official at some level. This situation was compounded by the absence of meaningful political participation, a lack of accountability among state officials, and the almost total destruction of independent civil society forums. With no means to articulate their demands or assert their rights, members of the public have no other option but to seek help from those in power. Unlike conventional patronage patterns where patrons are made up of local notables, patrons of the Islamist regime are either local or provincial officials, or those tribal/religious leaders who pledged loyalty to the regime. The availability of oil revenues since 1999 has enhanced the capacity of the regime to sustain its patronage system through rewards, co-option and penalties.

The Islamization Scheme and its Dynamics

According to Islamist movements in general, Islam is both a religion and a way of life, and therefore is as relevant in the public domain as in the private sphere. Within this framework, the Sudanese Islamist movement set for itself the task of advocating what it regarded as a genuine commitment to Islam and the realization of a social reform on religious grounds – an Islamic transformation of society. In strategic terms this has justified a policy of attaining political power – through whatever means – in order to utilize the authority of the state in its endeavour of Islamic transformation. Thus after the success of its coup and consolidation of its power, the Islamist regime embarked on a process geared towards implementation of its Islamic transformation of society.

In 1991, the regime issued a new penal code based on *sharia*, Criminal Act (CA), 1991. By itself the Criminal Act was not a radical move since *sharia*- based legislation had already been in place since its enactment by president Nimeiri in 1983. Rather, since the issue of the *sharia* was the basis of heated dispute throughout the parliamentary period, its enforcement by the new regime was meant to give an indication of its orientation. Other legal measures in this regard included the revision of civil transactions to incorporate usury-free Islamic banking systems, and the introduction of mandatory *zakat* (alms-in-tax) in 1990. In 1996, the Khartoum state introduced a public order law which was said to be inspired by Islam, with a special police force and a special court setup to enforce it.

These legal procedures were accompanied by certain policy measures apparently carried out with the aim of enhancing religious commitment, or ensuring that religious morality was upheld. Examples of these measures included the extensive building of mosques and prayer places in all government buildings, educational institutions, and any other building used by the public; the expansion of religious educational institutions (such as Quran university); and the intensification of media programmes geared towards religious indoctrination. There were also some 'directives' (officially or unofficially enforced) regarding women's modesty and dress code, so that although in legal terms there was no official policy of *hijab* it gradually became the official norm that women should be dressed in particular ways (head covered, long, loose clothing, etc).

In 1993, the regime had established the Ministry of Social Planning which was entrusted with overseeing the ambitious vision of Islamic transformation of Sudanese society within a ten-year comprehensive strategy. The new ministry brought under its jurisdiction various state departments concerned with social policy such as social welfare, youth, sports, religious endowments, and *zakat*. Thus the new ministry was almost a mini-government, set up with the goal of achieving a coordinated policy geared towards realization of the Islamist vision of social transformation. In a related development, the regime adopted what was called the Comprehensive Islamic Call (or Advocacy) Programme, with the objective of indoctrination and expansion of Islamization in accordance with the Islamist movement's ideology.

By the onset of the second decade of Islamist rule, the cultural authenticity project was, however, showing signs of failure. To start with, the government itself reconsidered some of the steps taken in its pursuit of the Islamic trans-formation programme during the 1990s, chief among which was the downsizing of the social planning ministry in 2001 to a conventional social affairs ministry. Additionally, the public order special court was abolished in the year 2000 following numerous complaints and criticisms voiced against this law even from within the establishment itself (the law, however remained on the books). In tandem with these reconsiderations, there was less vigilance by the regime in enforcement of its religious oriented programmes and legislation and, signifi-cantly, almost no more talk about *al-mashru' alhadhari*. Despite all of this, Islamism was sustained as an ideological cover and a source of the regime's legitimacy, particularly in the eyes of its own constituency. In reality, however, with the ousting of the veteran Islamist leader and ideologue Hassan al-Turabi in 1999/2000, the Islamic credentials of the regime became at best questionable. That said, it may be argued that there is more of a public visibility of religious adherence among the Sudanese Muslims than before: mosques are full, there is more strict observance of fasting, pilgrimage, and other rituals; there is also better religious education especially among young people. All these are valid observations; the question, however, is whether this *ritualistic* Islamization with its medieval jurisprudence was the main objective of the Islamist movement when it decided to take power by force.

In conclusion, the Islamist movement pursued a putschist policy in seizing power; a policy which was justified on grounds of an overall commitment to use power to create an improved society grounded on Islamic values and regulations. The manner through which the Islamist movement secured power, and the measures it undertook to consolidate that power, generated an authoritarian, coercive state that was primarily preoccupied with maintaining its control over society. Power itself, however, soon became a bone of contention within the inner circle of the Islamist regime and the ensuing dispute led to the split within the Islamist movement. In the wake of this split, the faction which retained power, while not relinquishing authoritarianism, came to rely also on clientelist politics made possible partially by oil revenues. Likewise while they overtly main-tained committed to the visible – mostly ritualistic – aspects of an Islamization programme, they became less concerned with the dream of 'civilizing' society through their *cultural authenticity project* that was heavily publicized during their first years in power.

Recommended Reading

El-Affendi, Abdel Wahab. *Turabi's Revolution: Islam and Power in Sudan*. London: Grey Seal, 1990.

Fluer-Lobban, Carolyn. *Shari'a and Islamism in Sudan: Conflict, Law and Social Transformation*. International Library of African Studies Series. London: IB Tauris, 2011.

Gallab, Abdullahi. *The First Islamic Republic: Development and Disintegration of Islamism in the Sudan*. Burlington: Ashgate, 2008.

Hale, Sondra. *Gender and Politics in Sudan: Islamism, Socialism, and the State*. Boulder: Westview Press, 1997.

Sidahmed, Abdel Salam. *Politics and Islam in Contemporary Sudan*. Richmond: Curzon Press, 1997.

Sidahmed, Abdel Salam & Sidahmed, Alsir. *Sudan*. The Contemporary Middle East Series. London: Routledge Curzon, 2005.

Warburg, Gabriel. *Islam, Sectarianism and Politics in Sudan since the Mahdiyya*. London: Hurst, 2003.

11

Traditional Authority, Local Government & Justice

CHERRY LEONARDI
& MUSA ABDUL JALIL

In a small town in southern Sudan, a young man is sitting in the shade on the root of a mango tree. He has just emerged from a squat brick building in which he has shouted and elbowed his way to the attention of two clerks, who demand over a hundred US dollars from him, in return for a scrap of paper with a rubber stamp on it. The young man, John, now waits patiently, perhaps returning daily before eventually his name or number is called, and then he enters a small square office adjacent to the chaos of the clerks' office.

Here, before the high desk of the county judge, he faces the relatives of Paul. Five years ago a female cousin of John's gave birth to Paul's child, but Paul has not yet given any kind of marriage payment or bridewealth to her family. John is around 30 years old and as yet unmarried; the cattle his cousin should have earned the family through her marriage are vital for John's own marriage. His family had tried to settle the problem privately and peacefully with Paul and his relatives, but the dispute had escalated. To avoid potentially deadly fighting, John's uncles had taken the case to a series of chiefs' courts and town courts. None had been able to enforce the payment of the customary minimum of 36 cattle from Paul and his father, a powerful military officer, and so John had decided to approach the county judge. This was a costly step to take, but John was convinced that the dollars he was investing would bring access to the power of the police to enforce a favourable decision from the judge.

For John, the only distinction between the court to which he is now appealing and the courts that had previously heard his case lie in its higher cost and its closer link to the organs of state power. The county judge himself is from a prominent local family of paramount chiefs. He had gone to school in the days when the British still ruled Sudan, and became a minor government official. In the 1980s the SPLA ordered him to become a 'chief' on one of the appeal courts they established in the area. More recently he had been given paralegal training and was appointed as county judge. His court applies statutory laws and procedures, but the great majority of cases are settled by customary compensation payments.

John's case is one example of the myriad, complex disputes that arise across Sudan. Cultures and customs vary, but there is a common need for arenas in which grievances may be addressed and resources claimed. Many people in Sudan rely primarily on access to land and water for farming and grazing, and on the resources of marriage exchanges. If a neighbour encroaches on cultivable

108

land, or another group of herders deny access to a water-source or a grazing route, or a daughter falls pregnant, or a marriage is breaking down, there is usually some attempt to deal with the problem privately, and a strong culture against rushing too hastily to outside authorities. But when the immediate parties are unable to come to terms, they must inevitably turn either to violence or to mediation.

Mediation in disputes is a function played by numerous different actors; across Sudan, family and community elders are nearly always the first and preferred source of mediation. Successive governments have, however, sought to institutionalize certain official avenues of dispute resolution. Often couched in terms of empowering traditional authority, or protecting local custom, this has really been an attempt to increase government control over local society. Yet, while the resulting institutions of local government or Native Administration are seen by government as a channel for regulating and monitoring local communities, they have nevertheless tended to function as a two-way conduit. People have long recognized the value of appealing to a mediator who can back up a favourable decision with the sanction of government force, as illustrated by John's faith in the county court. Other kinds of sanction may be equally or more powerful, such as that of religious and spiritual authorities. The state-recognized local judicial institutions are only ever one among a number of potential sources of dispute resolution. But the fact that they have become an accepted one demonstrates the way in which people have come to engage with the state as manifested in its local forms, despite its alien, colonial origins and continuing questionable legitimacy. State weakness or even failure, often attributed to Sudan's postcolonial history, does not therefore preclude engagement with the state at the local level. And the most widespread motive for such engagement has been the search for justice and for rights to land and other resources.

The Hakuma

John's county court is a brick building that forms part of the *merkaz*, the offices of the district or county government, located in the centre of the town since the early colonial period. Often these government centres were located on the sites of former stations of the Turco-Egyptian government and of the traders who had travelled southwards from the mid-nineteenth century in search of ivory and slaves. To the north, provincial towns had already formed under precolonial states or under the Turkiyya or Mahdiyya. For local people, towns *were* the government, the *hakuma*, as the Sudanese state is widely known. And in many areas, the towns and government were also associated with the military. Some southern languages, for example, use words for government that also relate to the army and military officers, or refer to officials – whether British or Sudanese – as 'Turks'. Across Sudan, the military associations of government are underlined by the style of uniforms worn by local government officers. The alien origins of the *hakuma* and its specific urban loci have contributed to the historical sense of distance between rural communities and the state.

Local people have, however, long been drawn into the *merkaz*, as military or police recruits, government employees, traders, or even prisoners. Throughout much of the colonial period, the district-level government was headed by a British district commissioner, who in turn reported to a British governor of one of the nine or so large provinces. For the majority of Sudanese, it was the provincial or district government that was the *hakuma*, with perhaps only a vague sense of a distant capital 'on the river', as Darfuris put it. Over the twentieth century increasing numbers would visit or move to Khartoum, but for rural communities the local town has remained the seat of government.

Since independence, local government offices have been staffed by Sudanese civil servants, yet they have retained something of the alien origins of their predecessors as far as local society is concerned. There is something about entering government employment, military service or even urban life that is seen to remove a person from their original community and transform them into the bureaucratic, uniformed representatives of the *hakuma*. This is less stark if the government officer at least comes from the area in which they are employed, but in many periods it was government policy to deliberately locate them outside their home areas. In the 1950s, Equatorian chiefs complained that new southern local government officers were being transferred too rapidly, before they had a chance to get to know a district as their British predecessors had. Unsurprisingly, there is a widespread belief that local interests and cultural particularities can only be understood by those originating in that locality, or at least by those who have lived there for many years.

The principles of detached neutrality and institutional hierarchy that underpin bureaucratic government have always been at odds to some extent with the moral and social principles that govern local communities across Sudan. Many Sudanese have become adept at operating under both sets of principles. Yet government employment is still seen to alienate individuals from local society, restricting the authority and effectiveness of local government officers. At the same time rulers and politicians have sought to create institutions that are more easily controlled by patronage and political manipulation than professional bureaucrats might be (and which offer a cheaper means of administration than salaried graduates). Local communities, meanwhile, have needed effective negotiators and spokesmen who could defend them from government demands and depredations. Out of these partially complementary, partially conflicting needs emerged the role of 'traditional' leaders.

Understanding Traditional Authority

The term 'traditional authority' is a problematic one because it is often taken to indicate an age-old and untouched indigenous custom. It is important to realize that traditional leaders across Sudan in fact reflect a far more modern – and uneasy – accommodation between government and society. When British officers arrived from 1899, they sought to overcome the limitations of their resources through alliances with Sudanese leaders. Yet the individuals and families identified as useful colonial allies had often gained their prominence relatively recently, through prior alliances with the Turco-Egyptian or Mahdist governments. In many other cases, especially in southern and eastern Sudan, British officers encountered a bewildering multiplicity of local authority, and, by their own admission, had to construct new kinds of leadership altogether. Even where the *nazir, omda* or *sheikh* came from a historically important family, the nature of their authority would be changed by the demands of mediating with the colonial government. Much of the variation in the legitimacy and effectiveness of traditional leadership in Sudan today arises from the contingency of its origins, and the variable success of individual leaders in maintaining their authority within their community, at the same time as (or despite) also working with government.

A uniform hierarchy was established in most areas, from sheikh up to *nazir* or *sultan* (or from headman up to chief in the south). In the area where John, the plaintiff in our court case lives, the chiefs are known in the local language as 'chiefs of the cloth' (a reference to their original colonial uniforms or sashes) to distinguish them from other chiefs such as the spearmasters, who perform vital sacrifices, and whose spiritual power is often seen to be incompatible with 'government' work. The emergence of the traditional leaders in the Condominium period was further complicated by their relationship to religious authority. Sufi sheikhs or holy men, and indigenous spiritual leaders like rain-makers, spearmasters or prophets often had the greatest degree of inherent authority. But colonial officers also saw them as a potential source of resistance or revolt; their power base was too independent of government. In some cases, governments were able to overcome this by tying such leaders more closely into government patronage networks; the most powerful northern sectarian leaders were entrenched in their privileged economic and political positions quite deliberately by the Condominium government.

At a more local level, British officers preferred to appoint secular leaders as sheikhs or chiefs. But even then, many of these leaders retained close connections to the prominent local religious authorities, whose support would be vital to maintaining their position. Since at least the time of the Funj and Fur sultanates, Islamic and political forms of authority have been mutually dependent in northern Sudan. Nowadays all across Sudan, chiefs, sheikhs, *omdas* and *nazirs* are often related to the leading religious or spiritual families in their areas, or maintain close relations of patronage and allegiance; their different forms of authority tend to be complementary and interdependent rather than competitive.

It was the judicial role of the government-recognized sheikhs and chiefs that was first formally legalized in the 1920s and 1930s through a series of ordinances, culminating in the southern Chiefs Courts Ordinance and northern Native Courts Ordinance of 1931–32. This legislation conveyed administrative as well as judicial power: the courts were used not only to settle disputes and maintain order but also to punish disobedience towards the sheikh or the government. The chiefs and sheikhs were also playing a key role in tax collection, and this would gradually be expanded to include tax assessment and a limited degree of accounting, particularly as their staff of clerks and retainers expanded. Chiefs and sheikhs were made responsible for a range of local government functions, including conscripting labour for roads and construction, overseeing markets and 'native' quarters of towns, controlling borders, and enforcing agricultural or grazing orders. The hierarchies were formalized as the system of *idara ahliya*, or Native Administration as the British termed it, (a translation that continues to be employed in northern Sudan, despite its colonial connotations; in southern Sudan the usual term now is Traditional Authorities).

However much the judicial powers of the Native Administration were related to their government work, the resulting courts nevertheless came to be utilized by people in their quest to win local disputes. In John's area, colonial officials noted that local people quickly realized that the new courts kept written records and that they were more likely to be able to make future claims or call in debts if the original transaction or case had been recorded by the chiefs. Across Sudan, the Native Administration courts drew on the backing of state force in ways that were far from traditional, though there was some precedent in precolonial states such as the Darfur Sultanate. But this backing could also make them more effective and swift at enforcing their decisions, and so they gradually became established and accepted, operating alongside other forms of dispute resolution such as councils of elders or the mediation of spiritual leaders. In southern Sudan, the chiefs' courts amalgamated local judicial principles with those of the colonial government to produce hybrid legal systems. Across northern Sudan, customary justice was further complicated by Islamic *sharia* law. The 1902 Mohammedan Law Courts Ordinance recognized the pre-eminence of *shari'a* in matters of family and marital law, including inheritance. Yet civil courts and the Native Administration courts have also applied *sharia* law in such cases, provided they have a learned or semi-learned *alim* or religious sheikh as a court member.

The fusion of judicial and administrative powers in the Native Administration has long been a source of complaint. Another enduring and contentious aspect of British policy was the direct relation of administrative structures to territory and land rights. In much of northern Sudan, communal land rights were entrenched as a system of tribal homelands or *dars*, each of which also defined the jurisdiction of a paramount chief, usually called a *nazir* or *sultan*. So the larger tribes gained control of territory and the privilege of a powerful head, recognized by the government. Yet the neat tribal patchwork that British officers envisaged never materialized, because territories were not ethnically homogenous. Smaller ethnic groups and individual immigrants found themselves in an inferior position to the large *dar*-owning tribes, both in terms of rights to land (and water), and in terms of representation in the higher levels of local administration and justice, and later political arenas. The ensuing tensions have only been exacerbated by the alienation of land for mechanized agriculture and oil production, leading to growing pressure for grazing and for fertile farming land. The quest for rights to land and water are therefore commonly pursued through demands to have a *nazir*. The British also rewarded the loyalty of prominent religious or tribal leaders by awarding them land, a policy continued by subsequent governments. The association of land with the Native Administration was reversed under Nimeiri's government in 1970–71, when the accelerating demand for land for agricultural production was combined with a gradual drive since the 1950s to abolish Native Administration altogether. The resulting Unregistered Lands Act of 1970 established government ownership of all land not privately owned and registered, that is, all the communal land governed primarily under customary systems. The following year, Native Administration was abolished formally through the People's Local Government Act. These two measures undermined the previously clear demarcation of tribal rights and responsibilities for land and natural resources, opening up confusion, uncertainty and conflict, which remain largely unresolved even today.

Traditional vs. Modern Government

The 1971 Local Government Act has been seen as the culmination of efforts by members of the nationalist *effendiya* to attack the Native Administration as colonial collaborators and relics of backward rural life, whose stranglehold over rural communities was hindering development and political participation. Yet the idea of a deep enmity between Sudanese graduates and the Native Administration is in many ways misleading. Many traditional leaders have themselves also been highly educated and had prior experience of government-related employment, a tendency encouraged by colonial administrators. The political parties of the nationalist era utilized traditional networks for their popular support; indeed it was the success of the sectarian parties in gaining rural support through their religious orders and the Native Administration that partly prompted criticism of the system from those also opposed to these parties. Relatives of the Native Administration leaders have often had greater access to education and pursued political, military, international or other professional careers. Many leading Sudanese politicians have originated from chiefly families. At the local or regional level, powerful patronage networks have formed, headed by the Native Administration, religious leaders, merchants and wealthy landowners and farmers. In the town where John's case was heard, both the county judge and the county commissioner, as well as a number of officials in the county or state government, come from the two or three leading families of chiefs. Such local or regional elites have formed and cemented over the last century or more, and have provided greater political continuity than have the changing governments and varying administrative policies.

The strength of these local elites, and the overlaps between *effendiya* and Native Administration, was particularly apparent in the lead-up to and aftermath of the 1971 Local Government Act. The professional administrative officers serving in local government campaigned against the abolition of Native Administration from the mid-1960s, convinced that the traditional leadership was vital to the preservation of basic order and security, and the collection of taxes. Even after the removal of former Native Administration leaders from the new councils and courts, local government officers continued to turn to them for advice and assistance in resolving disputes, especially as the local governments struggled with the perennial problems of understaffing and lack of resources. It was in fact these administrative officers who by the 1980s began to call for a reinstatement of Native Administration in Darfur and eastern Sudan, in order to deal with escalating conflicts over grazing and other resource issues.

There may be, then, less of a traditional–modern dichotomy in local government and more of a tension between administrators – both Native Administration and civil servants – and politicians or military leaders. Reforms of local government have inevitably been driven by political agendas, which both the civil service and the Native Administration have to some extent resisted. The earliest reforms came in 1937 with the development of councils as the basis for a new system of local government to replace the Native Administration. In 1951 this was further advanced, with the attempt to replace tribal units of administration with territorial ones, and to gradually replace Native Administration with representative local government councils. In reality, however, the prominent or dominant role of the traditional leaders on these councils ensured a significant degree of continuity. Even after 1971, the traditional leaders and other powerful local 'Big Men' were able to exercise continuing control over the new councils, through their extensive patronage networks. In southern Sudan the 1970–71 legislation was never put into effect, and the chiefs continued to perform both judicial and administrative functions.

The 1971 Act also stipulated for the first time an explicitly political role for local government officers, and the local councils were tightly linked to Nimeiri's

Sudan Socialist Union. The control exercised by the ruling regime over local government was further enhanced by its appointment of provincial commissioners, whose extensive power over all government departments within the territorial unit of the province has been described by John Howell as a 'prefectoral' system of decentralized government. The provincial government not only gained supervisory power over the local councils, but also gained direct control of the police and security forces within the province. In many ways the local government reforms thus saw not greater devolution but increased central control, through the appointment of powerful provincial commissioners, and the politicization of the administration.

The importance of the judicial role of the traditional leaders was made particularly apparent by the abolition of Native Administration. The benches of magistrates that replaced Native Administration courts provoked vastly increased numbers of appeals to higher courts, and the judges were unable to handle the volume of dissatisfied litigants. As early as 1976, the benches were therefore replaced with courts made up overwhelmingly of former Native Administration leaders. Throughout the 1980s there was discussion of a wider reinstatement of Native Administration, but it would be the National Salvation government that would finally see this to fruition in the 1990s. Nowadays the role of the Native Administration no longer involves tax collection, and varies across northern Sudan: it is strongest in Darfur, Kordofan, Red Sea and Kassala; it plays a limited role, particularly among pastoralists and in land disputes, in the riverain and eastern areas; and it is largely irrelevant in Gezira and Khartoum states, except in terms of the displaced community leaders appointed by the government.

Some have seen the revival of and intervention in the Native Administration by the current *Ingaz* government as a deliberately divisive and regressive step, calculated to foment inter-ethnic competition and conflict. Certainly some of the interventions have had this effect. But the reinstatement of Native Administration in the 1990s was also both a culmination of the gradual recognition of the post-1971 failings of local administration and justice, and a characteristically pragmatic attempt to gain popular support for the Islamist Revolution, particularly from the rural areas. Where the Nimeiri regime had sought to destroy local elites, the NIF and NCP has tried instead to co-opt and reshape them. It appears to have been particularly successful in rivalling and weakening the old patronage networks of the traditional sectarian parties. But the regime's programme of social engineering in the 1990s went further than pragmatism in seeking to train the Native Administration to proselytize the Islamist revolution and mobilize *mujahidin* to fight in the south, as well as reviving the political and security functions of Native Administration.

The NIF government also replaced the old structure of provinces and districts with a new federal system of twenty-six states, divided into localities. Each state (*wilaya*) is headed by a governor (*wali*) and each locality (*mahaliya*) by a commissioner (*mutamad*), with councils and popular committees at both levels. The commitment to federalism and state autonomy was further reinforced in the 2005 Comprehensive Peace Agreement (CPA), but has not been realized on the ground. State governors have tended to be preoccupied with security and relations with the central government; the latter maintains federal immunities allowing overlapping control over aspects of state government. States have assemblies and ministers, but the governors wield the greatest power through their links to the ruling party and its security agencies. In many southern states, there have been bitter struggles between state assemblies and the governors, who have been accused of continuing the kind of autocratic style of government they practised previously as military rulers. Through the continued appointment of governors and commissioners, both the Government of National Unity (GoNU) and the Government of Southern Sudan (GoSS) thus exercised direct control over the state governments, which in turn devolved little real power to local government. State and local governments have also been hamstrung by limited resources, most of which are swallowed up by government salaries (and corruption). It remains to be seen whether the newly elected state governors will exercise greater autonomy than their appointed predecessors.

In the south, the SPLA had relied heavily on chiefs during the war to organize provisions and recruitment or conscription of young men and boys into its forces: this was a difficult role for chiefs, who often suffered personally from physical abuse by the soldiers, and yet also risked losing popular legitimacy. Since around 2004, the SPLM has made more concerted efforts to acknowledge and come to better terms with the chiefs, often aided by international organizations hoping that traditional authority and customary law might answer some of the governance dilemmas in the south. Accordingly, a major role for Traditional Authorities and customary law has been stipulated in the GoSS Local Government Act (2009). The CPA extended the federal structure of states to southern Sudan, underneath which the SPLM local government units of county, *payam* and *boma* have been retained. The Local Government Act envisages councils at each of these levels, together with Traditional Authorities and a corresponding hierarchy of customary courts and councils. Local government has so far centred on the chiefs, supervised by county governments under county commissioners, who are in turn appointed by the GoSS.

On the one hand, throughout the last century, decentralization has largely existed on paper only: a series of administrative reforms have seen continued or increased centralized control over local government, and councils have at best enjoyed deconcentrated rather than devolved powers. Crucially, government resources rarely reach the province/state level, and certainly never go below it. But on the other hand, local government institutions have provided arenas, like the councils, through which more people can engage with the state and the cultures of bureaucratic, representative government, which has created both a sense of participation and of frustration. It is no coincidence that the leaders of the earliest southern political parties had mostly been low-level administrative officers under the British, who found their ambitions frustrated by the appointment of northern officers to the higher positions. Local councils have also helped to form and cement the local political elites that have been so powerful within local society. Conflicts and political strategies have, however, generated greater attempts than ever before to harness or replace those local elites since the 1990s.

Divide and Rule?

Opinion – whether Sudanese or international – remains divided on the desirability and legitimacy of Native Administration or traditional authority. Some point to the resilience of traditional leaders as indicative of their fundamental legitimacy, and view them as defenders of cultural particularity against a centralizing, autocratic state, and as providers of restorative justice and communal harmony. Critics claim instead that the system of Native Administration provides only for privilege and abuse, that it is undemocratic, exclusionary and regressive, and/or that it has been corrupted beyond redemption by the political manipulation of recent years.

This variance in opinion is shaped by individual position, age and stance, but also by the particular area of Sudan being discussed. On the whole, younger, urbanized and educated Sudanese are more likely to criticize the failings of Native Administration, with its widespread association with heredity and gerontocracy. But there is also immense variation across Sudan and among the traditional leaders themselves. Some have succeeded – perhaps over generations – in retaining the respect and even affection of their people, largely through maintaining the delicate balance by which they keep government satisfied whilst still appearing to defend the interests of the local communities. The means by which they accomplish this may sometimes be surprising, including resorting to armed struggle either for or against the government, so long as they can convince people that they are acting in their interests. Apparent political malleability can therefore be a tactical strategy by traditional leaders to maintain good community relations with successive governments. On the other hand, many enjoy only limited popular support, largely because they are seen to have placed government or their own interests above the good of the chiefdom. It is not seen as particularly shocking to profit from one's position, but traditional leaders quickly lose authority if they are seen to act against the interests of the majority or the most powerful groups within their administration.

If we abandon romantic visions of traditional tribal leadership, it is apparent that it is the link between communal resources and Native Administration that is most critical to the importance of the latter. As we have seen, no effective alternative has yet been found for the settlement of inter-communal disputes over natural resources. Conversely some traditional leaders in eastern Sudan and elsewhere have lost authority by reportedly selling communal land to government or private investors. In northern Sudan, the tribal *dar* territories have been partially re-recognized by the NIF/NCP governments, reviving their association with the Native Administration unit of a *nazarah*. Tribal units that were formerly placed under *dar*-owning tribes have long struggled for independent political recognition and an accompanying territory. Such struggles offer opportunities for governments and politicians to intervene to gain support and manipulate divisions. Even in Southern Sudan, where *dars* have never been formally created, land rights are bound up with the system of traditional administration. Chiefs do not own the land, but their legitimacy in some areas rests heavily on their ability to defend communal land rights against the new pressures of displacement and urbanization.

The search for land rights has contributed to the association of ethnic or kin groups with a particular unit of local administration. In turn, governments have sought or rewarded loyalty by creating new administrative units for groups, and encouraged the perception that rights and resources can only be guaranteed by each group having a corresponding traditional leadership position. The result has been a proliferation of ever smaller administrative units, and vigorous struggles to create or promote new positions in Native Administration, which conveniently ensures that people are preoccupied with local power struggles rather than national politics. Local government reforms since the colonial period intended to replace so-called tribal units with territorial ones; instead, the two have fused, so that ethnic or sectional units seek recognition as territorial units, leading to ever greater fragmentation.

In northern regions of Sudan, the NIF/NCP has intervened very significantly in local administration to foment conflict or to shore up support. This has been particularly apparent in the case of Darfur, where a division of the old province into three states transformed the former majority Fur into a minority in each state, and a new title of amir was inserted in the higher levels of Native Administration (especially in west Darfur state) to enable greater manipulation of appointments. Certain groups have been rewarded with newly independent units in the Native Administration and titles for their support of the government or in order to undermine other groups and their leaders. The government has intervened comprehensively in the selection of individual leaders, particularly in Darfur; the hereditary tradition is respected but governors and commissioners appoint their chosen member of the chiefly family rather than the popular or family choice. No wonder that Darfuri rebel movements have deliberately targeted some of the government-appointed leaders since 2003.

This political interference has, however, largely been confined to the higher levels of the Native Administration. Village sheikhs have retained much greater credibility and have continued to play a key role in dispute resolution at the local level; they have also moved with their people, including into the Darfur camps for the internally displaced. Like the southern chiefs, their position was never abolished, even in 1971. The intermediate level of *omda* has also retained potential legitimacy, but here there is greater individual variation in terms of links to government. Sheikhs are appointed by *omdas*, and *omdas* are themselves elected and appointed internally by *nazirs*, rather than directly by governors or commissioners (who retain the powers of approval). The *omdas* and the higher-level leaders, like *nazirs*, also play an important role in managing access to natural resources, and this can create attachment even to an unpopular *nazir*, if he is seen as a means by which to defend communal interests.

The perceived politicization of the higher levels of traditional leadership has contributed to vocal criticism in many regions, and usually predominantly among younger generations and urban populations. Critics also point to the incompetence of traditional leaders, particularly in relation to accessing the resources of relief and development. In eastern Sudan, for example, the Native Administration leaders have been criticized for allowing (or profiting from) the alienation of communal land for mechanized schemes, and for failing to access relief and development effectively, particularly during floods or droughts. But such criticisms are also contributing to ongoing change in the personnel of the Native Administration across Sudan, as communities and families seek to choose leaders with greater education and the kind of experience that will enable them to access aid and development resources more reliably. In the south, international organizations have relied heavily on chiefs to assist the implementation of relief or development projects, and some recently selected chiefs have prior experience of leadership in the refugee or IDP camps.

Such camps, whether inside or outside Sudan, are very revealing of the fragile legitimacy of traditional authorities. Frequently they have offered leadership opportunities to new, younger or more literate or multilingual individuals, who might have seized upon the disruptions of displacement in order to challenge the established authorities. Yet in many cases even these new camp leaders have some connection to the traditional families, and in other cases the traditional leaders have retained their authority within the camps. What is often most apparent is the preservation, if not of the individual personnel, then of the *institutions* of the traditional leadership. And even among those critical of Native Administration, underlying systems of customary dispute resolution have tended to retain legitimacy.

Local Justice

Despite the widespread criticisms of the politicization, corruption or incompetence of traditional authorities, people continue to approach them to settle disputes and cases, as we saw at the outset. Even in regions devastated by war, people have needed mediation in their disputes. Yet, perhaps in recognition of the relatively autonomous dynamics of local recourse to justice and mediation, governments have also sought to control and regulate local courts. Native or chiefs' courts are thus governed by clear limits on their sentencing powers and form defined levels in the overall judicial hierarchy, rather than existing as a separate system. At the same time people have sought out the force of government backing in the courts to ensure that favourable judgements are executed: however implicitly, 'customary' justice actually relies on its recognition by the state for its authority. In John's area, chiefs continued to settle disputes during the decades of war from 1983; when people wanted to appeal against the chiefs' decisions, they were sometimes willing even to approach the military authorities for settlement of their cases. The hope of a favourable settlement has long been the primary reason for people to interact with the state, however arbitrary and militarized it appears.

John's decision to approach the county court, however, is indicative of an increasing tendency, even in this cattle-keeping area of southern Sudan, to approach the government courts or police directly. In his case this was a progression from previous hearings in the chiefs' courts, but more widely chiefs complain that they are being by-passed and the old hierarchy of traditional courts undermined. In part this is the result of the disruptions of war and military rule, in which a multitude of military, security and police officers have intervened in disputes. But it also reflects a wider change across Sudan, namely the process of urbanization. The massive growth of Khartoum and smaller expansion of regional towns since Sudan's independence has radically increased the number of people who live within close reach of government institutions. In the towns and cities, people are as or more likely to interact with the police and the statutory law courts, which also administer *sharia* matters nowadays, than with a chief or sheikh. On the one hand, urban populations are more subject to state control, including by the powerful agencies of national security. On the other hand, beyond criminal and political or security matters, town dwellers often have a degree of choice as to in which court to open their case. There is a kind of marketplace of arenas of dispute resolution, which is also to some extent responsive to popular demand and evaluation of individual judges.

In this context, the customary courts are often quite flexible in terms of the basis of the law that they apply. In southern towns, the chiefs' courts apply an ad hoc mixture of customary principles and compensation, and statutory (or even international) legal codes and penalties. Customary law has never been fixed and rigid; each court decision is the product of its immediate context and lengthy processes of negotiation. The resulting dynamism is particularly apparent in urban courts, where migrants, returnees and younger generations gradually push for change as they argue their case in the public arenas of the courts, even if the latter are dominated by elder men. The system is clearly weighted against women and youth, but this does not preclude the latter sometimes finding ways to use the courts to their own advantage. There is tremendous social and cultural change going on in Sudan, and it is reflected in the courts.

Even where the Native Administration has declined in legitimacy or popularity, systems of customary dispute resolution remain deeply important. Disputes over customary land tenure continue to be dealt with exclusively by the native courts in rural areas. In eastern Sudan, Beja youth in the towns criticize their leaders, but uphold the Beja system of customary dispute resolution, or *silif*. In Darfur and elsewhere, the collective mediation of elders, the *ajawid*, remains a key means of conflict resolution, known as *judiyya*. The Native Administration leaders may play a role in these processes, but the underlying moral values are seen to be much deeper than this recent form of authority.

Resolution of serious conflicts has also been a key function of the traditional leadership, and one which is said to have been undermined, with serious consequences, by government policies. It follows naturally from the judicial role of the traditional leaders and from their position as the custodians of communal rights in land, water or migratory access. The success of conflict resolution initiatives, however, depends on a fragile combination of indigenous legitimacy and government support. However deep the resolution achieved by traditional mechanisms, peace agreements tend to fall apart without the vested interest of powerful political and military forces in the region. On the other hand, governments have sought to manipulate 'traditional' peacemaking for their own ends: in Darfur this has tended to involve agreements made by politically-appointed leaders, which lack popular support or trust. In general, grassroots peace initiatives only succeed where there is a successful combination of local legitimacy and effective government backing and follow-through. The problem is that current governments have a vested interest in maintaining rather than solving conflicts on the peripheries.

Conclusion

John's case was eventually heard by the county judge, who told him that really a family matter like this should be settled at home, or by a chief. John insisted that the case should be heard, but Paul failed to respond to the summons. Disgusted, John declared that the courts were useless nowadays; it was no wonder that so many young men were dying in sectional fighting. The inability of local courts, even the official county courts with their paralegal judges, to enforce their authority against the power of the military and government officers belies the growing rhetoric of empowering traditional or local authorities in Southern Sudan. Yet, conversely, the recurring abuses and enduring remoteness of military and government cultures also ensures that people across the country continue to rely upon the more accessible and debatably more legitimate institutions of traditional leadership. On the one hand, the military and security priorities of government have undermined the effectiveness of local government and native administration. But on the other hand, as long as these remain the priorities, the need for trusted intermediaries with government is only reinforced.

Even in a region like Darfur, where there has been extensive central government interference in Native Administration, there are still traditional leaders who are seen to have withstood political manipulation, or are judged to have acted in the interests of their own people. It is perhaps impossible to give a verdict on the legitimacy of Sudanese Native Administration as a whole, when there are so many variables that shape the authority of any individual leader. It is clear, though, that the common desire for locally-originating leadership has been magnified by divisive government policies, so that people are frequently convinced of the need for a position in the system in order to defend their particular group and its economic interests.

In the early 1970s, the architect of the abolition of the Native Administration, Gaafar Bakheit, looked back at the struggles over this proposal before 1969:

> No man in authority was able to contemplate the rural areas being void of *nazirs* and *sheikhs*. These were the pillars of authority in a country where authority was so fragmented that it often tended to lose effect and gradually die. Thus as long as native administration was capable of exerting political influence in the rural areas, political parties, out of sheer self-interest, would not try to eradicate it.

He was looking back, but 40 years on from the May Revolution, his words have a prophetic rather than retrospective truth.

Local Sudanese judgements of their leaders are inevitably more pragmatic and rooted in the constraints of the local and wider context than are those of external observers. Understanding the nature of traditional authority and the bargains that it rests upon requires stepping into that local context and looking at the surroundings from there. The *legitimacy* of traditional leadership is fragile and unstable, demanding individual ability to balance the demands of government and diverse, changing societies. Native Administration has not survived because it represents some kind of ideal, much-loved or age-old authority, but because it is entrenched in local power structures that have been more enduring than national ones. These local elites have manipulated their alliances with national governments and political parties as well as vice versa. But their greater resilience reflects the enduring importance of the local to the majority of Sudanese people, and their limited attachment to any central agendas. The latter have tended to ride roughshod over local interests and livelihoods, and to prioritize political mobilization and security enforcement over local development.

Sudanese are not intrinsically parochial but their historical experience has taught that local political structures, including Native Administration, offer more chance of stability, however corrupt or incompetent they may be. Of course many feel excluded from these structures and so contest them, often through appeals to national political forces or even nowadays to international languages of rights and reform. The ensuing debates ensure that even local structures are gradually changing, particularly as new avenues to employment and accumulation open up. It remains to be seen what the ongoing effects of militarization, displacement, economic migration and urbanization will be on local political and judicial structures. But it is important to understand that what might be labelled 'conservatism' or 'traditionalism' is often a pragmatic tolerance of structures of privilege and power that have nevertheless offered the best chance of stable governance, dispute and conflict resolution, and, above all, defence of communal economic rights and livelihoods in the face of extractive government and private interests.

Recommended Reading

Abdul-Jalil, Musa A., Mohammed, Adam Azzain and Yousuf, Ahmed A. 'Native administration and local governance in Darfur: past and future', in *War in Darfur and the Search for Peace*, edited by Alex de Waal. Cambridge MA: Harvard University Press, 2007: 39-47.

El Amin, Khalid Ali, 'Eastern Sudan indigenous conflict prevention, management and resolution mechanisms: effectiveness, continuity and change', *African Security Review* 13, 2 (2004): pp. 1-20.

Bradbury, Mark et. al. *Local Peace Processes in Sudan: A Baseline Study.* Rift Valley Institute, (2006),

Branch, Adam & Mampilly, Zachariah Cherian. 'Winning the war but losing the peace? The dilemma of SPLM/A civil administration and the tasks ahead', *Journal of Modern African Studies* 43, 1 (2005): pp. 1-20.

Howell, John, ed. *Local Government and Politics in the Sudan.* Khartoum: Khartoum University Press, 1974.

Leonardi, Cherry et. al. *Local Justice in Southern Sudan.* Rift Valley Institute and United States Institute of Peace (2010), http://www.riftvalley.net/publications.

Mading Deng, Francis. *Customary Law in the Modern World: the Crossfire of Sudan's War of Identities.* Abingdon UK/New York: Routledge, 2009.

Miller, Catherine, ed. *Land, Ethnicity and Political Legitimacy in Eastern Sudan.* Kassala & Gedaref States. Cairo: CEDEJ/DSRC, 2005.

12

Twentieth-Century Civil Wars

DOUGLAS H. JOHNSON

The civil war in southern Sudan has often been represented as Africa's longest civil war, starting in August 1955, before the country gained independence. Like all characterizations this simplifies the truth. This chapter will give a streamlined account of the Sudan's civil wars, but in doing so it will attempt to highlight the complexities of the conflicts.

The Sudan's pre-independence past is a history of colonialisms that were imposed on a succession of conquest states. This had a marked effect not only on the way the Sudan was governed, but on the way the Sudanese peoples responded to government. 'To understand native feelings,' the anthropologist Evans-Pritchard told a group of administrators attending the Oxford University Summer School on Colonial Administration in 1938, 'we have to bear in mind that the southern Sudan was conquered by force and is ruled by force, the threat of force, and the memory of force. Natives do not pay taxes nor make roads from a sense of moral obligation', he went on to say, 'but because they are afraid of retaliation. The moral relations between natives and Government provide the most fundamental of administrative problems, for the natives have to integrate into their social system a political organization that has no moral value for them.'

While Evans-Pritchard was speaking specifically about the south, his observation could have applied to many other parts of the Sudan. By the end of the Condominium period administration may have taken on a more benign aspect, and the application of force may have declined, but both the threat of force and the memory of force remained. The administration still conducted periodic 'flag marches' where detachments of soldiers visited areas 'to show the flag', often burning down the huts of individual tax-defaulters or other offenders; thus demonstrating the threat of force and reinforcing the memory of force.

The nature of co-dominal rivalry was such that much of the time Britain was trying to balance or curb the power of Egypt in the Sudan, and no more so than at the end of the Condominium. At this point Britain's objective was not to hold on to the Sudan against a rising nationalist tide, but to prevent Egypt from taking over when Britain left. This had a direct impact on the control of force the government was able to exert, and with Sudanisation of the civil administration, the police and the army in 1954, that control was loosened.

122

The 1955 Southern Disturbances

To the southern Sudanese, the process of 'Sudanisation', a requirement agreed between Britain and Egypt before the Sudan could exercise self-determination, looked less like national liberation and more like re-colonization. The vast majority of new administrators, police and army officers who came into the south to replace British officials were northern Sudanese with no previous experience in the south, no knowledge of local languages (unlike most of the British they replaced), and little knowledge of the people they were supposed to govern.

The tension this sudden changeover caused throughout the southern Sudan, the lack of any real stake in the new government that most southerners had, and the uncertainties of the future created an explosive situation in many parts of the south, especially in the rapidly developing towns of Nzara and Yambio in western Equatoria and in the main garrisons of the Equatorial Corps of the Sudan Defence Force, whose headquarters were in Torit, in eastern Equatoria.

The mutiny that broke out in Torit in August 1955 was part of a local conspiracy among some of the soldiers, but there was very little planning for a general rising. There were other mutinies within the army, police and prison service – in Kapoeta, Juba, Terekeka, Yei, Meridi, Yambio, Nzara and Malakal – but these outbreaks were more in response to the news from Torit than a co-ordinated rebellion. The mutineers had no clear objective: some wanted to delay the departure of the British, others proclaimed an intention to unite with Egypt. There were no strong demands for southern independence at this point. While there was widespread anxiety in the south, the lack of organization and clear objectives of the mutiny meant it could not mobilize general popular support. In Wau the northern administrators agreed to leave the province administration in the hands of their southern junior colleagues, among them police inspector Gordon Muortat Mayen, who later, as president of the Nile Provisional Government in the 1960s, become a leading advocate for southern independence. But in 1955 he helped to keep the province quiet, and the mutiny soon subsided after the arrival of reinforcements from the north and the majority of mutineers fled either to Uganda or the bush.

One unintended consequence of the mutiny was that it accelerated Britain's departure from the Sudan before a constitutional arrangement could be put in place. Shocked by the scale of the outbreak of violence in the south, concerned that continuing unrest would offer the Egyptians an opportunity to increase their military presence in the Sudan, and conscious of their lingering responsibility without authority, Britain urged the Sudanese government of prime minister Ismail al-Azhari to circumvent the self-determination plebiscite and opt for a declaration of independence through parliament. Southern members at first balked at this extra-constitutional measure, but were persuaded to vote for independence on the promise that a federal constitution would be 'considered'. So on 1 January 1956, a year earlier than expected, without a permanent constitution, and through a vote in a parliament that had exceeded its mandate, the Sudan became independent.

Failure of the Federal Option

One reason why it is incorrect to date the start of the civil war to the Torit Mutiny is that aside from the activities of a few dispersed mutineers, there was very little fighting in the south for the rest of the decade. Southern political leaders instead focused on the promise of a federal solution for the country. When the northern majority in parliament decided that they had 'considered' federalism and had decided against it, southern parliamentarians organized themselves around the federal issue in the first post-independence elections in early 1958. Not only was a large majority of pro-federalist southern MPs returned, but a number of other MPs from other marginal areas – the east, the Nuba Mountains, Darfur – began to warm to the idea. This is one of the reasons why the military seized power in 1958, to save the country from 'falling apart'.

The First Civil War

It was under the first military government of General Ibrahim Abboud that the policy of building national unity around the twin principles of Arabism and Islam was actively pursued. This affected not only the former parliamentarians, but southern civil servants and students, who were the most visible targets of Arabization and proselytization. Southern leaders were arrested or went into exile, schools were closed and students, too, faced the choice of arrest or flight. Many went into exile into neighbouring countries following widespread school strikes in the south in 1962, while others moved into the bush and joined up with the remnants of the 1955 mutineers. The exiles included former parliamentarians Joseph Oduho and Fr. Saturnino Lohure, and the civil administrator William Deng, who became prominent leaders in the political and armed struggle.

1962 saw the formation of the first exile political movement, the Sudan African Closed District National Union (which later dropped the 'Closed District' and became SANU), and 1963 saw the first organized military activity of guerrilla units answering to the name of 'Anyanya' (poison, or snake venom). It is from this time (1962-3) that the first civil war can be said to have begun.

SANU petitioned both the UN and the fledgling OAU, putting forward the case for self-determination for the south and warning the OAU, in particular, against giving legitimacy to military dictatorships like Abboud's. With no external political support and no source of supply, guerrilla units in the field tended to operate independently of each other. The overthrow of the military government in 1964 paradoxically gave the Anyanya their first real access to arms. The civilian government in Khartoum chose to support the Simba rebels in the Congo, but arms intended for the Simba fell into the hands of the Anyanya, making them a far more potent military force than they had previously been.

An attempt was made to reach a political solution for the 'Southern Problem' at the 1965 round table conference in Khartoum where all the major northern parties were represented, along with the newly formed Southern Front. SANU, too, was persuaded to attend. But the conference got no further than each party stating its position and no real compromise was reached. One result was that SANU split. William Deng chose to stay inside the country and work through the parliamentary system, while Joseph Oduho and Aggrey Jaden went back into exile. Fr. Saturnino Lohure continued his work seeking arms and supplies for the Anyanya.

Factionalism thus beset the southern guerrilla movements from the outset. Over the next few years there were several attempts at forming 'provisional governments' in the bush: the Azania Liberation Front, the Anyidi Liberation Front, the Nile Provisional Government, the Nile Republic, even a Sueh River

Republic under Samuel Abujohn in Zandeland. Very often fighting in the field was between these different groups.

The early civil war took place mainly along the south's international borders (where the guerrillas had their bases) and especially in Equatoria. This limited territorial range was one of the movement's weaknesses, and only gradually did the civil war expand outside these areas and begin to overcome these factional differences.

Those killed in factional fighting were not the main casualties. In 1965 the army carried out a series of massacres, the largest of which took place in Juba and Wau in which a large number of educated southerners were killed. Fr. Saturnino, one of the key figures, was killed through collusion between the Sudanese and Ugandan armies as he crossed into Uganda in 1967, and William Deng was assassinated by the army in 1968.

With the 1967 Arab-Israeli War and the 1969 left-wing coup that brought in a second military government under Jaafar Nimeiri the Sudan entered the Cold War on the side of the Arab bloc and the socialist states. This had a direct effect on the conduct of the war in the south. Egypt and Libya assisted the Sudan with weapons and trained personnel (especially pilots), and the Sudanese army was substantially rearmed by the Soviet bloc. Israel, for its part, now took an interest in the Anyanya, and was assisted in its support by Idi Amin, first as commander of the Ugandan army, and then as military dictator of Uganda itself.

Just as the Anyanya were finding a new unity through Israeli support, Khartoum was afflicted by its own Cold War factionalism. The attempted communist coup against Nimeiri in 1971 weakened his position and gave him a strong incentive to seek an end to the civil war through negotiation. Joseph Lagu received Israel's backing, and as the conduit for military supplies was able to bring the other Anyanya units under his command and supplant the exile politicians as leader of the movement (now renamed the Southern Sudanese Liberation Movement, or SSLM).

The Addis Ababa Agreement and the Lessons of Peace

It was from this position of relative weakness and strength that Nimeiri's government and Lagu's SSLM were able to negotiate an end to the war in 1972. The Addis Ababa Agreement gave the south less than the self-determination that the many guerrilla groups had claimed they were fighting for, and the semi-autonomous Southern Region established with its capital in Juba was far less than the federal solution the southern leaders of the 1950s had advocated. Its survival was based on an alliance between Nimeiri and the south against Nimeiri's northern opponents – especially those parties such as the Umma, the DUP and the Islamic Charter Front (later to transform into the National Islamic Front) who were committed to a unitary Islamic state in one form or another.

This alliance lasted through the two most serious coup attempts in Khartoum in 1975 and 1976, but began to break apart in 1977 with 'National Reconciliation', when Nimeiri offered his strongest northern opponents, including Sadiq al-Mahdi (the leader of the 1976 coup attempt) and Hassan al-Turabi, places in the government. This brought hard-line opponents of the Addis Ababa Agreement into the central government and began the process of the Islamic reform of the Sudan's laws.

The confirmation in 1979 of the discovery of large oil deposits within the north-south borderlands of Upper Nile and Kordofan, while offering the Sudan the prospect of finally escaping its underdevelopment and indebtedness, paradoxically further undermined the stability initially brought by the Addis Ababa Agreement. The attempt in 1980 by Hassan al-Turabi, then Attorney-General in Khartoum, to have the National Assembly redraw the Southern Region's borders to include the oil fields in Kordofan, though unsuccessful in the face of united southern opposition, was a warning to the south that there were those in Khartoum who were determined to keep the development of the oil fields firmly under central, rather than regional, control.

Nimeiri increasingly intervened in the politics of the Southern Region, dissolving governments, appointing caretaker governments, calling for new elections, and supporting the idea of re-dividing the Southern Region into its original three provinces. This idea was first proposed by Joseph Lagu, resentful of the influence of leaders from Upper Nile and Bahr al-Ghazal in the Regional Government, in order to promote Equatorian particularism, but it failed to get the backing of a majority in the south, and even had considerable opposition in Equatoria. Nimeiri overrode this opposition when he unilaterally abrogated the Addis Ababa Agreement in May 1983 and divided the south into three weaker regions. The removal of the constitutional provisions embodied in the Addis Ababa Agreement enabled Nimeiri to introduce *sharia* law through the National Assembly in September. By this time the civil war in the south had already begun.

There were a number of lessons that the future SPLM/A leadership learned from the way the first civil war ended and from the failure of the Addis Ababa Agreement to bring lasting peace. These lessons had a lasting impact on the way the SPLM/A was organized and ultimately on its negotiating strategy. The first lesson was the danger of factionalism within the exile movement and the guerrilla army. At the outset, therefore, the SPLA subordinated the political to the military wing and resolutely rejected the idea of forming 'fake governments' in exile. Any signs of factionalism in the military were rigorously, and ruthlessly, suppressed. A second lesson was that the Anyanya movement's goal of independence for the South had left it without allies in other parts of the Sudan. And a third was that the constitutional guarantees for the Southern Region and the powers allocated to it in the Addis Ababa Agreement were too vaguely described and had been easily overridden. A fourth lesson was that the total absorption of the Anyanya into the armed forces had left the south without protection when its constitutional position within the nation was under threat.

The Outbreak of the Second Civil War

The political events in the Southern Region were shadowed by a rising military resistance among the former Anyanya forces. Some Anyanya, in particular some politicians in exile, were disappointed that the Addis Ababa Agreement fell short of self-determination for the south and rejected it outright. There was discontent among other Anyanya units during the process of their integration into the Sudan Armed Forces. There were serious mutinies in Akobo in 1975, Wau in 1976 and Juba in 1977. Those mutineers who were neither captured nor killed escaped into the bush, and many found their way to Ethiopia, where the Derg regime that had overthrown Haile Selassie in 1974 gave them support, in retaliation for Nimeiri's support for Eritrean guerrillas and other anti-Derg forces.

The mutineers began calling themselves 'Anyanya II'. It was a loose organization, but in 1980 it began making hit-and-run attacks inside the Sudan from its bases in Ethiopia. It was broadly separatist in its aims, and it linked up with other disaffected groups inside the country. One such was the Abyei Liberation Front, formed in Abyei, in Southern Kordofan, in response to attacks on the Ngok Dinka by Misseriya Arabs supported by members of the army and police.

From 1980 through 1983 the Anyanya II attracted deserters from the army and police, but also secondary school students and other civilians. These new recruits were channelled back to training camps in Ethiopia. There were growing contacts between the Anyanya II and former Anyanya officers in the army. As political tensions rose in the Southern Region over Nimeiri's move toward abrogating the Addis Ababa Agreement and imposing *sharia* law, the links between the ex-Anyanya in the army and the new Anyanya II became stronger.

The flash point came at Bor, where the garrison was composed entirely of ex-Anyanya soldiers in Battalion 105. A confrontation between the battalion and the army began in January 1983 when the battalion refused orders to be transferred north. When the garrison was finally attacked by other units of the Sudanese army on 16 May it repulsed its attackers and then withdrew into the bush where, by pre-arrangement, it met up with Anyanya II and headed for Ethiopia. Other mutinies soon followed in other parts of the south and desertions accelerated.

The Sudan People's Liberation Movement/Army (SPLM/A) was founded in July out of the amalgamation of the Anyanya II and the new mutineers in Ethiopia. There was an immediate conflict over leadership, and more senior officers, veterans of the first Anyanya, such as Samuel Gai Tut and Akuot Atem, were pushed aside by a group of younger Anyanya veterans that included John Garang, Kerubino Kuanyin Bol, Salva Kiir Mayardit and William Nyuon Bany. This split was exacerbated by a disagreement over the movement's aims: the old guard wanted independence for the south, while the Young Turks advocated a more revolutionary transformation for the whole Sudan. This latter goal was supported (some say instigated) by the Ethiopian government, which was fighting its own secessionists in Eritrea, and the creation of a 'New Sudan' became the official platform of the SPLM/A.

This split at the foundation of the SPLA had two broad consequences. The first was that it failed to create a united southern movement, and fighting broke out between the main camp of the SPLA and the mainly Nuer adherents of Samuel Gai Tut. The SPLA was never, as some suggested, simply a Dinka army, but the proximity of the Nuer to the Ethiopian border meant that fighting quickly degenerated into a fight between the frontier Nuer and the SPLA, and this gave Khartoum the opportunity to support the disaffected Anyanya II remnants and transform them into the first of the tribal militias it deployed to counter the SPLA's infiltration of the rural areas. A strange collaboration began, whereby the Government in Khartoum supported the supposedly separatist Anyanya II against the anti-separatist SPLA.

The SPLA's objective of a 'New Sudan' enabled it to reach beyond the bounds of the south to make both political and military alliances with other disaffected regions of the Sudan. By 1986 it had carried the war outside of the south into the adjacent areas of the Blue Nile and Nuba Mountains. It was no longer just a north-south civil war, nor a Muslim-Christian war, nor even an Arab-African war.

Table 12.1 *Anyana and SPLM/A: a Comparison*

Anyanya	SPLM/SPLA
BEGINNING OF ANYANYA WAR	BEGINNING OF SPLA WAR
1954-8: Southerners lobby for federal state	*1975-6*: 'Anyanya II' formed in Ethiopia
– 1954 Juba Conference confirms support for federalism	*1980-3*: Increased Anyanya II activity
1955: Torit Mutiny and southern Disturbances (August)	– 'Abyei Liberation Front' active
1957: National elections return large federalist bloc of southern MPs to parliament	*1983*: Beginning of war
1958-64: First military government	– Bor Mutiny (16 May)
– 1960-4 Policy of Arabization	– Abolition of Southern Region (24 May)
– 1962 school strikes throughout south	– Amalgamation of Anyanya II and mutineers with formation of SPLM/SPLA in Ethiopia (July)
– Refugee movements into neighbouring countries	– Introduction of 'September Laws'
1962: SANU exile movement formed	
1963: Emergence of Anyanya as organized guerilla force	
ANYANYA RECRUITMENT	SPLA RECRUITMENT
– Mutineers	– Mutineers
– Civil servants	– Civil servants
– Students	– Students and young people
– Largely local recruits serving in local units	– Organized recruiting throughout 'liberated areas'
ANYANYA MILITARY STRUCTURE	SPLA MILITARY STRUCTURE
– Mainly organized by provinces	– Organized along orthodox military lines (battalions, brigades)
– No external training camps or supply centres	– External training camps and bases for first eight years
– Inter-provincial co-operation improved towards end	– Large internal bases
– Loose hierarchy of military command	– Hierarchy of military command
ANYANYA EXTERNAL SUPPORT	SPLM/SPLA EXTERNAL SUPPORT
– Church organizations	– Ethiopia: Derg regime 1983-91; current regime after 1995
– Unreliable neighbours (Obote hostile, Amin favourable)	– Lonrho up until 1991
– No support from OAU	– Uganda under Museveni
– Israel after 1967	– Kenya (passive?)
	– Eritrea in the 1990s
	– Southern African liberation movements in 1990s (through SPLM Harare office)

Anyanya	SPLM/SPLA
ANYANYA SOURCE OF ARMS – Stolen/captured government weapons – Weapons captured from 'Simba' in 1965 – Weapons supplied by external supporters towards the end of war (Uganda, Israel)	SPLA SOURCE OF ARMS – Captured weapons – Weapons supplied by Ethiopia – Weapons obtained from sympathetic movements (SWAPO, ANC) – Arms purchases
ANYANYA THEATRE OF OPERATIONS – Confined to rural areas of southern Sudan – No towns taken	SPLA THEATRE OF OPERATIONS – Extensive control of southern Sudan – Several towns taken and held, including a number of province capitals – Expanded fighting outside southern Sudan (Nuba Mountains, southern Blue Nile, Eastern Sudan)
ANYANYA FORM OF ADMINISTRATION – Rudimentary civil structures – 'Shadow' administration of chiefs in rural areas – No relief wing	SPLA FORM OF ADMINISTRATION – Military-civil administrators – Co-optation and subordination of chiefs courts – Boma/Payam/County structure created in 1990s – Organized relief wing
ANYANYA ORGANIZATIONAL CHALLENGES – Guerrilla factionalism at beginning – Exile political wings often divorced from armed wings – Unified command with external support at end – Political wing subordinated to military command at end	SPLA ORGANIZATIONAL CHALLENGES – Unified command with external support from the beginning – Political wing subordinated to military command (no paper cabinets) – Factionalism emerges with loss of external support – Partial re-unification achieved at end

ANYANYA OBJECTIVES & ACHIEVEMENTS
Aims:
– Self-determination
Achievement:
– Semi-autonomous Southern Region
	SPLM OBJECTIVES & ACHIEVEMENTS
	Aims:
	– 'New Sudan'
	Achievement:
	– CPA
	  – Stronger southern government
	  – Ministerial positions in national government
	  – Self-determination

ANYANYA UNDER PEACE AGREEMENT – Absorbed into regular army, police, prisons, game wardens – Many soldiers rotated out of south to northern garrisons – Senior officers gradually retired and weeded out of army	SPLA UNDER PEACE AGREEMENT – Separate army retained in south – Demobilization and/or absorption of militias – JIU's formed from SPLA and SAF as separate units

In its initial stages the war was seasonal. The SPLA advanced in the rainy season, and receded in the dry season as the Sudanese army fanned out from its garrisons. The SPLA measured its progress by the high water mark the army reached at the end of each dry season, and there was a steady erosion of the scale of the army's advances. A truce between the SPLA and the Anyanya II in 1987 was followed by incorporation of most of the Anyanya II into the SPLA in 1988. This left most of the rural areas of the south under SPLA control in the dry season as well as the rains. (Only a few Anyanya II commanders, like Paulino Matip in Western Upper Nile, remained aloof because of personal hostility towards John Garang). By early 1989 the SPLA had taken control of many of the major towns of the region as well.

Peace was very nearly achieved in 1989 when the government of Sadiq al-Mahdi finally agreed to negotiate with the SPLM very largely on the SPLM's terms of a secular state. There was no mention of self-determination for the south at this stage. Negotiations were forestalled by the NIF-backed coup of Omar al-Bashir on 30 June 1989, and fighting was to continue for another fifteen years.

The Split in the SPLA, 1991-2000

In the early years of the 'Salvation Revolution' government of Bashir the SPLA maintained its military momentum, seizing control of all the government's garrisons in Western Equatoria by early 1991. The SPLM's commitment to a united Sudan (albeit a secular state) meant that it was able to form a common political front with the main northern Sudanese parties, now in exile and opposition and gathered together under the umbrella of the National Democratic Alliance (NDA).

But the civil wars in Ethiopia were also intensifying at this time. Khartoum (with US support) backed the Eritrean People's Liberation Front, Tigray People's Liberation Front, Oromo Liberation Front and other anti-Mengistu forces, while the SPLA became increasingly involved in giving armed support to its patron, much to its cost, both militarily and politically.

The military position was delicately poised by the beginning of 1991. The SPLA looked as if it was about to take control of most of the south, including Juba. But the fall of Mengistu in May deprived the SPLA of its bases, its supplies and its support and left it vulnerable to a flanking attack through Ethiopia by the Sudanese army, who had backed the winning side.

The SPLA's policy of suppressing political dissent within the movement also had the opposite effect to that intended, and weakened its cohesion. A challenge to Garang's leadership was launched by two commanders in Nasir, now left vulnerable by the collapse of their former Ethiopian ally. In August 1991 Riek Machar and Lam Akol declared over the BBC World Service that Garang was overthrown and that the movement would henceforth fight for the total independence of the south.

Garang, based some hundreds of miles away in Torit, was far from overthrown, but the split was serious. The Nasir faction had the surreptitious support of Khartoum, who arranged an apparent transfer of allegiance of their remaining Anyanya II militias. Over the next year some very prominent SPLA commanders who had also fallen out with Garang went over to the Nasir side. Fighting broke out in areas the SPLA had previously secured, and Garang was spooked into desperate actions of his own: he attempted to open a second front in Darfur, which failed, and he launched a premature attack on Juba, which came near to success, but also failed. Between 1993 and 1995 Khartoum was able to press the SPLA severely in Eastern Equatoria and the area between Juba and the Uganda border.

But Khartoum's own momentum began to fade by 1995. Internationally it was now isolated as its former allies, Ethiopia and Eritrea, became alarmed about its political intentions in the region, and Uganda was also hostile to Khartoum's support of the LRA. From 1996 to 1999 the SPLA made significant advances in the south, the Nuba Mountains, Blue Nile and, in alliance with the NDA, the Eastern Sudan.

The Nasir faction failed to create a cohesive movement. Personal opposition to Garang was not enough to unite the different commanders. The movement had difficulty even deciding on a name, calling itself in succession SPLA-Nasir Faction, SPLA-United, and the South Sudan Independence Movement/Army (SSIM/A). The underlying contradiction of claiming to be fighting for the total independence of the south while collaborating more or less openly with Khartoum against the SPLA could not be resolved. The movement fractured and many of its commanders went back to the SPLA. In desperation Riek Machar, now virtually deserted by his army, signed a 'Peace Charter' with Khartoum in 1996, which was followed by the Khartoum Agreement of 1997, ostensibly committing Khartoum to allowing the south to vote, at some undetermined date in the future, on unity or independence.

The Khartoum Agreement did not stop the factionalism within the anti-Garang southern forces, and in fact that factionalism intensified as Riek and Paulino Matip fought for control of the Western Upper Nile oil fields. Khartoum's clear preference for Matip eventually led to Riek Machar rejoining the SPLM in 2002.

But Khartoum was able to use these splinter groups to open up the oil fields for exploitation. From 1999 the oil revenues that now came on stream gave Khartoum a new edge and increased its war capability. The Sudan Armed Forces (SAF) developed a new strategy in the oil fields by combining air power with regular army units and militias in operations designed to depopulate strategic areas. This strategy was adapted to other theatres as well, notably northern Bahr al-Ghazal and the Nuba Mountains. The SPLA responded by trying to intensify activities along other fronts, most notably eastern Sudan.

Escalation of Fighting during the Peace Negotiations

Peace negotiations under the auspices of the regional Inter-Governmental Authority on Development (IGAD) were started in 1993 but had been moribund for many years. Following the 9/11 attacks in 2001 the Bush administration in the US brought a new commitment to supporting the IGAD talks, and in 2002 a ceasefire was established in the Nuba Mountains and peace talks were restarted in earnest at Machakos in Kenya. The Machakos Protocol, signed on 20 July 2002, established the framework of the future peace agreement, committing both sides to the unity of the country, but granting the south the option of an independence referendum after an interim period. But the agreement was between the government and the SPLM only. Neither the NDA nor any other opposition group in any other part of the Sudan was included. A number of

Darfur leaders petitioned IGAD to be included in the peace talks late in 2002, but their request was declined. This was to have a significant impact on events in Darfur in 2003.

More than two years passed before the outline agreed at Machakos produced the Comprehensive Peace Agreement, signed in January 2005. During that time fighting intensified in many areas, despite agreements to the cessation of hostilities and the protection of civilians. Khartoum continued to clear civilian populations out of the oil fields area and, when Lam Akol finally rejoined the SPLM, sent the militias and army in a sweep through the Shilluk kingdom as well. When fighting in Darfur escalated in early 2003, it transferred its oil fields strategy to Darfur, co-ordinating attacks on civilian targets by militias supported by the air force, and followed up by the army. It manipulated the cease fire agreements it signed to shift troops from one theatre to another: moving troops out of the Nuba Mountains into the adjacent oil fields in 2002, and moving troops out of the south into Darfur after 2003. Despite the presence of a US State Department-funded Civilian Protection Monitoring Team, its continued attacks on civilians in the south brought no sanctions, no international retribution, no public condemnation, establishing a precedent that Khartoum took note of as it expanded its war effort in Darfur.

The SPLA learned at least one lesson from the Addis Ababa Agreement, and it has not been absorbed into the SAF. The regular army has been largely withdrawn from the south, and the southern militias have been absorbed into either the SPLA or SAF. The SPLA and the SAF have formed Joint Integrated Units (JIUs) for deployment in Abyei, the Nuba Mountains, Blue Nile and parts of the south. These JIUs have been characterized as neither joint nor integrated and are often the focus of violent tensions, as the fighting in Malakal in 2006 and 2009 has shown. The 10,000 strong UNMIS force who are supposed to monitor the cease-fire have found their movements and activities restricted by both sides. The security situation in Southern Sudan remains fragile.

Recommended Reading

Albino, Oliver. *The Sudan: A Southern Viewpoint*. London: Oxford University Press, 1970.

Beshir, Mohamed Omer. *The Southern Sudan: Background to Conflict*. London: C. Hurst and Co, 1968.

Johnson, Douglas H. *The Root Causes of Sudan's Civil Wars*. Oxford: James Currey Publishers, 2003 & revised edition, 2011.

Lagu, Joseph. *Sudan Odyssey through a State: From Ruin to Hope*. Omdurman: MOB Centre for Sudanese Studies, 2006.

Nyaba, Peter Adwok. *The Politics of Liberation in South Sudan: An Insider's View*. Kampala: Fountain Publishers, 1997 & 2000.

Wawa, Yosa. *Southern Sudanese Pursuits of Self-Determination: Documents in Political History*. Kisubi: Marianum Press, 2005.

13

The War in the West

JEROME TUBIANA

Our problem is not between farmers and herders. Lies, useless, useless!
You're blind, open your eyes, our problem is ethnic cleansing.

Brejing is the largest Sudanese refugee camp in Chad, a tent city that shelters almost 30,000 people from Darfur, most of whom are Masalit, one of the main non-Arab groups in the region. Abdallah Idris, who is singing this song, is one of them. Around him are several musicians with makeshift instruments: a five-stringed lute with a metal plate for a sound box, a blue jerry-can disguised as a drum, empty Pepsi bottles painted in the colours of the Sudanese flag. The group calls itself *Firkha Sabha Darfur al-Hurri*, the orchestra of the dawn of free Darfur. Abdallah Idris sings both in his mother tongue and in Arabic. As he sings, men shout war cries and women ululate: the crowd approves each verse of his song. Shaded from the afternoon sun by a single tree, the circle around him grows: men, women and children cross the bed of white sand of the wadi, the dry riverbed that separates us from the tents in Brejing. This is the song they hear:

If you wake up and Darfur has been destroyed, it's too late.
We are Darfurian army, *inshallah, inshallah,* Darfur army.
Darfur liberated, even the flies in the sky are free.
The *shebab* have become lions, you can't, no you can't!
If they see you [Abbala], they will cut your throat
without saying *bismillahi* [in the name of God], you can't, no you can't!

The *shebab,* the young people of fighting age that the song talks about, who are today dressed in fashionable jeans, begin to jump as high as possible, taking it in turns or two at a time, spraying the audience with sand. The Masalit are famous for these jumping dances. But the song they sing incorporates a litany of other ethnic groups from Darfur, Arab and non-Arab alike:

I'm Masalit, I'm Fur, I'm Zaghawa, I'm Dajo,
I'm Jebel, I'm Erenga, I'm Berti, I'm Tunjur,
I'm Goran, I'm Gimir, I'm Rizeigat, I'm Habbaniya,
We won't go back to Omar Bashir!

'The aim of my poetry is to unify the people of Darfur,' explains Abdallah Idris 'because they have the same problems. The tribe is not the goal, unity is the sole

133

objective.' 'All Darfurians,' he adds, 'must unite and fight the government of Khartoum.'

In conversation, he recalls the brief period – he was not 20 years old – when Ahmed Ibrahim Diraige was governor of Darfur, from 1981 to 1983. This was the first time since the pre-colonial period that a member of Darfur's majority ethnic group, the Fur, had been at the head of the local government. 'At the time, there was peace everywhere, you could travel from Nyala to Ed-Daein [the main towns in South Darfur] without any trouble. But the National Congress Party injected tribalism into the whole country. It segregated people in the form of tribes: Arab, Fur, Masalit. I ask, on the contrary, that we unite as we did during the Diraige rule.'

Fluid Identities

Although the name Darfur means 'land of the Fur' in Arabic, the region, today as big as France (500,000 square kilometres) is populated by numerous ethnic groups besides the Fur. These include non-Arab peoples and Arab groups, the latter also divided into many branches, such as the Rizeigat and the Habbaniya mentioned in Abdallah's song. Historically Darfurian identity transcended ethnic boundaries. Before the present conflict, non-Arab groups did not refer to themselves as 'indigenous' or 'African' in the way they do today, drawing a line between themselves and the Arabs that, in reality, has always been fluid.

Coverage of Darfur in Western media and in the publications of activists working to bring attention to the war, though it may have brought world attention to the problems of Darfur, has rarely shown prudence when identifying – and naming – those involved in the conflict. Thus we read of 'black', 'African' victims and 'Arab' perpetrators, a Manichaean vision that only acts to worsen the unprecedented split that the war has produced between the groups claiming to have an 'Arab' identity and the rest – the Fur, the Zaghawa and the Masalit, and a dozen or more smaller groups.

But it is not only the Western media which deals in ethnic categories. All sides in the war have seized on ethnic difference as a source of support. Despite the inclusive rhetoric of Abdallah Idris' song, the rebel movements in Darfur recruit primarily amongst non-Arab groups. They denounce the monopoly of power in Khartoum since the independence of Sudan by elites drawn from the three main Arab (or 'arabized') tribes of the central Nile Valley, but probably represent less than five per cent of the Sudanese population. For Darfurians the government in Khartoum appears to be dominated by these groups, all from outside their region: the Jaaliyin (in the person, notably, of the President, Omar Hassan al-Bashir), the Shaigiya (Vice-president Ali Osman Mohamed Taha) and the Danagla (the former Defense Minister Bakri Hassan Saleh). In return, the regime has invoked Arab solidarity to recruit allies in Darfur, creating proxy forces known as 'janjawid', a Darfuri term previously used for armed bandits. Beginning in 2003, after the first rebel victories the *janjawid* were given *carte blanche* to attack non-Arab communities accused of supporting the rebellion. The government's policy of ethnic mobilization helps explain the polarizing description of the conflict as a massacre of 'African', 'black', or even ' indigenous' civilians by Arab government forces, even though there are Arabs and non-Arabs on both sides.

Some non-Arab groups (like the Gimir, the Tama, the Fellata) have in fact sided mostly with the government, while others have remained neutral. As the war has progressed, an increasing number have joined opposition movements. But in Darfur the very definition of who is and who is not and Arab is problematic. Arabs in Darfur often claim lineages which stretch back to Arabia, over hundreds of years and hundreds of miles. And in recent years, even before the war in Darfur, Arab identity has been reinforced by Pan-Arabism, particularly the Libyan version. But local Arabs often have skin that is as dark as that of their neighbours who claim to be of different origin. Attempts at Arabization have often been denounced in the countries of the Sahel; they mask the profound Africanization of those Arabs that live there.

This is not a question of religion: almost all Darfurians are Muslims, and the historic Islamization of the region owes less to the nomadic Arabs than to the non-Arab marabouts and wandering scholars who adhered to Sufism imported from West Africa. Language is not necessarily a good criterion either: certain non-Arab groups (the Berti and the Birgid for example) adopted Arabic some time ago as their mother tongue, while those who claim a notional Arab identity, like some of the Misseriya Jebel and Fellata, yet still speak other languages.

In the past, the Arabs of Darfur were mostly nomadic pastoralists, whereas most of the farming communities were non-Arab. Here, as in other parts of the Muslim world, the word 'Arab' was often used specifically to mean nomads that still lived in the same way that their mythic ancestors had done on the other side of the Red Sea before the great expansion from the Arabian peninsula in the middle ages. Such differences in modes of production and ways of life can play a more important part in conflict over resources than ethnicity as such. And this, consequently, is another area where the Arab/non-Arab distinction in Darfur breaks down. Some Arab groups have long farmed the land; and some non-Arab groups (such as the Zaghawa and the Meidob) have been primarily pastoralists and stockraisers. During the course of the last few decades, moreover, Arabs have settled more and more and converted to farming, blurring further the boundaries between groups.

From the Centre to the Margin

Like many conflicts in the Horn of Africa, the Darfur rebellion can be seen primarily as a revolt by the inhabitants of a formerly powerful historic centre which has become marginalized. From the seventeenth to the early twentieth century, the sultanate of Darfur lay at the centre of trade routes running north and south, and pilgrimage routes from west to east. For a time its sultans ruled Kordofan; and it was only briefly conquered by the Turkiyya in the 1870s. The sultans re-established their independence as the Mahdist state crumbled; it was only the Anglo-Egyptian conquest in 1916 which reduced Darfur to a subordinate status on the periphery of Sudan. Under the Condominium, power and wealth became concentrated in the Nile valley. Since that time, Darfur's inhabitants have consistently felt that they are contributing to the country's wealth without benefiting from it in return. The greatest symbol of this has been the project to build an asphalt road from Khartoum to El-Fasher, an undertaking made by the National Islamic Front, for which Darfurians paid a sugar surtax in the early 1990s, increasing the price of this vital commodity threefold. The money disappeared and the road still has not been built.

Quite apart from the symbolic asphalt, provision of government services in Darfur – and the west in general – has been marked by clear geographical inequalities. In 2003, the state of West Darfur only had 26 doctors, or less than one doctor per 75,000 inhabitants (a record in northern Sudan), compared to one doctor per thousand inhabitants in Khartoum. It had 11,000 inhabitants per water point, compared with 2,000 per water point in Northern State, on the Nile north of Khartoum.

Beyond economic underdevelopment, the term 'marginalization' – omnipresent in the discourse of Darfur rebel movements – encapsulates a strong feeling of discrimination. In the Nile valley, Darfurians were and still are *gharbawin*, 'the people of the West', migrants in search of work, mainly in the Gezira cotton fields. For a time, they themselves were ambivalent about their culture. From the 1960s, there was a widespread tendency to seek an escape from marginalization by imitating the Arabs from the Nile Valley, copying their clothes, their cuisine – even their way of speaking. Often educated in Khartoum, members of the Darfurian elite considered the culture of the capital as the model to be followed on the road to development. This process was described as 'Sudanisation': it was about becoming full-fledged Sudanese citizens. Among Darfurians today the urge to acculturate is much less strong than it once was; instead the sense of being discriminated against is strengthening a claim to distinctive Darfurian identity. This is combined with a nostalgia for past glory and an increasing consciousness of the importance of local history and culture. 'Teaching Masalit history is forbidden by the government', explains the singer Abdallah Idris, who is also a teacher. 'As well as the Masalit language. This has to change. Our language should be on television, the radio, in the media.'

The sense of cultural exclusion, persistent since independence, became more acute from the mid-1980s. The government of Sadiq Al-Mahdi from 1986 to 1989, then the National Islamic Front of Omar al-Bashir and his Islamist mentor, Hassan Al-Turabi – have been particularly disappointing for Darfurians. Many placed their hopes in the Islamist project, which promised an expansion of the governing elites under the auspices of religious renewal. In 1999 Al-Turabi's exclusion from power signified the regime's retreat to their old ethnic base: that of the Arabs of the Nile Valley.

In 2000, some of the Turabi's Darfuri supporters wrote and secretly disseminated the *Black Book*. This was a compilation of statistics detailing the over-representation in government and national administration of northern riverain elites. It showed that since 1954, irrespective of the government in power, the proportion of ministers from the north and central states had oscillated between 47.7 per cent (under Sadiq Al-Mahdi between 1986 and 1989) and 79.5 per cent (at the time of independence). West Darfur provided between 0 per cent and 22 per cent of ministers (the highest percentage was during the period 1986-9) and southern Sudan between 7.8 per cent and 17 per cent. Some of the authors of the *Black Book* went on to found the Justice and Equality Movement (JEM), one of the original two Darfuri rebel groups that has retained Turabi's revolutionary radicalism rather than his religious ideology.

Wider political changes soon accentuated the feeling of the marginalization of Darfur. In 2002 talks started in Kenya, between the government and the Sudan People's Liberation Movement with the aim of putting an end to almost twenty years of fighting in the south and the Nuba mountains. Darfuris had no voice in these negotiations. In April 2003 during a key moment of the talks in

Naivasha, when security questions were being addressed, Darfur rebels carried out their first major operation: an attack on the El-Fasher airport which destroyed several government aircraft. This marked the beginning of open conflict in Darfur.

Two months before the attack on El-Fasher, the recently-formed Darfur Liberation Movement, which had been carrying out sporadic attacks on government targets for about a year, changed its name to the Sudan Liberation Army/ Movement. The name was clearly inspired by the SPLM and it is impossible not to remark on the similarity in the political programmes of the two organizations. The SLA embraced the concept of a unified 'New Sudan' first articulated by John Garang, the leader of the SPLM/A. In contrast to the programme of the JEM, the other Darfur rebel movement, the SLA manifesto was resolutely secular. The SLA also imitated the SPLA at the strategic level; aiming to administer rural areas of Darfur where the government controlled only small garrison towns, largely deserted by their civilian population. And it tried to draw international aid and attention of the international community to these 'liberated areas', as the SPLA had done.

The SPLA had made some previous, ineffectual attempts to encourage an insurgency in Darfur, and as the conflict developed they offered some limited support to the SLA. Advisors from the south, and Darfurians from the ranks of the SPLA, joined the new front. But links quickly disintegrated after the CPA was signed and John Garang died. 'His death is a loss for all of Sudan', said Adam Yaqub, a Zaghawa commander from the SLA who had previously spent five years in the SPLA. 'But peace in Darfur would not have come from him. Peace will come from us, by weapons and talks.'

Land and Identity

Darfuris' sense of marginalization may have laid the basis for conflict, but it does not in itself explain the militarization of thousands of civilians. Whether they chose to join the rebels or the *janjawid*, Darfurians entered into war against each other for local reasons, which go back for the most part to the 1970's and '80's. Nimeiri's regime, initially Nasserite and Marxist, suppressed two important legacies of the sultanate: the traditional leaders incorporated by the British into the Native Administration and the land tenure system. Historically, Darfur was divided into territories ruled over by chiefs from different ethnic groups who distributed land to those who needed it, regardless of their ethnicity. This was a system that the British maintained, and which seems to have given Darfur a certain stability up to that point. Today, the land tenure system in Darfur is often understood as a division of the region into tribal territories. However, the historic reality is somewhat more complex.

Historically, the land tenure system had two aspects. The first was the *dar* system. The sultanate was almost entirely divided into *dar* (territories), at the head of which the sultans placed or recognized traditional, hereditary chiefs from different ethnic groups (called *shartay*, or sometimes *melik*). They were not chief of one tribe, but of an area: they had to welcome and treat members of diverse ethnic groups living in or passing through their *dar* equally. This was, therefore, more of an administrative system than one of land tenure. However, by giving land to a dynasty belonging to a particular group, the system could be interpreted as one of collective land ownership by ethnic groups. Historically, this ownership may have been largely symbolic, but today it is the basis for claims for tribal territories. As a Fur intellectual put it, 'the land belongs to the community which the *shartay* belongs to. Traditionally, the *shartay* is responsible for the land, but the land belongs to the community.'

The second element of the land tenure system is the *hawakir* (singular *hakura*). In modern language, in Darfur as in Chad, the term designates private property of small proportion: a field, a courtyard in a house. In legal documents of which the oldest date back to the end of the seventeenth century, the *hakura* designates land, generally smaller than a *dar* and included inside a *dar,* that the sultans distributed to individuals at their leisure: traditional leaders, noblemen, religious men and traders from elsewhere, of all origins. This gave the owner rights to the wealth of the *hakura* and to its inhabitants, notably the collection of taxes. Unlike the *dar*, rights in the *hakura* were clearly individual or familial rights.

Oral tradition and written documents make a distinction between the owners of *hakura* and the traditional chiefs in charge of a *dar*. It seems that the first were considered to be well and truly land owners, which is implied in the terms that designate them, such as *sahib-al-hakura* (master of the *hakura*) or *sid-al-ard* (master of the land). On the contrary, the traditional chief of a dar is above all *sheikh-al-rijal* (leader of the people), administrating the people rather than the land, or *sid-al-seif* (master of the sword) which underlines his political and military power. Confusingly Darfurians today do not always make this distinction. They conflate the two functions, using the term *hakura* for *dar*. Those, notably amongst the rebels, who call for the restoration of the '*hakura* system' are in fact talking about the *dar* system. They confuse the *hawakir* system with the traditional system which has more or less been preserved in the *idara ahliya* (Native Admininstration).

The system did not – and does not – allow for an equal sharing of land between tribes: certain groups have *dar* and others smaller *hawakir* inside these *dar*, and others have neither *dar* nor *hakura*. But in the past communities without *dar* or *hakura* were not deprived of access to land. It seems that it was impossible for those in authority to forbid anyone who asked peacefully to live on his land. True nomads such as the Abbala (camel-owning) Arabs did not possess any land, but they could circulate freely throughout Darfur, as long as they respected farmers' fields.

A land tenure map of Darfur as it was when the British took over administration reflected particular moments in history, the influence of certain groups, families or individuals, as well as good relationships with sultans. The system was not egalitarian nor fair, but it was stable and flexible. 'Stability', 'balance' and even 'harmony' are words, albeit somewhat idealistically, that Darfurians use today to refer to the land tenure system of the sultanate, which in some respects continued into the Condominium. Crucially, the system was stable because, with all its injustices, it allowed everyone to have access to land.

Up until the present conflict, Arab and non-Arab communities were also systematically joined together through marriage. In El-Fasher, a Kaytinga (Zaghawa of Fur ancestry) *shartay* remarked: 'before the war we married Arab women as a way of resolving disputes. Perhaps that's the answer: for us all to take Arab wives.' One old white-bearded Zaghawa among his guests looked him straight in the eye and responded 'Oh no! If you do that I'll kill you.' Later the old man told me that he himself married an Arab woman in the 1970s, but that he did not believe such a thing would be possible nowadays. 'If I did that today my family would never want to see me again. Three weeks ago a Zaghawa girl married an Arab. She did it against her parents' will, and her family disowned her.'

'Since this war began', the *shartay* told me, 'the communities that were perfectly integrated with the Tunjur, like the Tarjem and Sahanin, have demanded an Arab identity. It's only since the conflict started that they say: 'we are Arabs'. All to have favours from the government. After the rebels' first successes, the government realized that the army was weak and asked for help from the Arabs. Some of them had been waiting for this opportunity for a long time. As soon as it presented itself they joined the *janjawid*. We have never forbidden them from cultivating land, from taking their animals to pasture. We didn't refuse them anything, but what they want is for that land to be their own. I'm not afraid and, if it comes to it, we'll die for this land.'

A fundamental distinction should be made between two aspects of the land tenure question. One is a question of economic resources, of access to grazing, water and cultivable land; the other is a matter of political symbolism, the ownership of land as a mark of power. Both contribute to the current conflict. But the fact that the communities deprived of land tenure rights (essentially the camel-owning Abbala Arabs) are calling into question the traditional system is above all political and symbolic: for Darfurians, the land ownership rights are intrinsically linked to the prestige of leadership.

The Wars before the War

Between 1987 and 1989, an armed conflict pitted the Fur against Arab groups in Darfur. The war united many Arab groups who had previously mostly fought against one another. Four hundred Fur villages were burned, and 3,000 people were killed, mostly Fur. Then, in the 1990s, the Abbala, the camel-owning Arabs, extended the war to the Masalit and the Zaghawa.

Despite the fact that they were relatively poorly armed, Masalit traditional militias were initially able to gain the upper hand and chase a large part of the Arabs from Dar Masalit. The Fur, Masalit and Zaghawa militias became the basis for the rebel groups that appeared in 2003, just as, on the other side, the Arab militias became for the most part government auxiliary troops. The government convinced the Arabs that the rebels were a danger to them; and non-Arab political leaders like Abdel Wahid Mohamed Ahmed al-Nur attempted to transform grievances against the nomadic Arabs into political grievances on a national level.

The war in Darfur is often seen by Darfuris as the result of multiple previous conflicts. Everyone in Darfur, according to their ethnic origin, where they are from, their history and their relationship with those in power, has his own version of the origins of the conflict. Zaghawa, for example, often mention a dispute with Arab pastoralists in 1968 over a lake called Jinek that was an important stage in the nomadic route to rainy season grazing grounds. It started with a quarrel over a gun (something rare at this time) owned by Mahamat 'Bired-el-Fasil' (he who loves division), a well-known Zaghawa militia leader and camel thief (it was not uncommon to be both). The government solved the conflict by imprisoning twelve Zaghawa and twelve Arabs for ten years, including Bired-el-Fasil. Forty years later, he explained: 'At that time, the government was fair, whether we were Arab or Zaghawa, they treated us in the same way, judged us in the same way. Not like today. I was freed after five years, and I have not bought a rifle since. But the peace talks did not really solve any problems. From then on, we and the Arabs started to live like snakes and mice.'

In 1968, the main concern was access to water and firearms. In the conflicts of the 1990s power and land were at stake. As these conflicts multiplied, Khartoum's response was at best one of indifference; and in many cases the government actively fanned the flames. The language of marginalization was used by both sides. At the beginning of the conflict, Mahamat Ibrahim Izzat, a government official in North Darfur and a Rizeigat Mahariya whose father was killed by the Fur in 1988, justified the Abbala Arabs' hunger for land: 'Before, many Arabs wanted to continue their nomadic lifestyle at all costs. This war has given them the desire to settle. The nomads do not have politicians, they have an illiteracy rate of up to 90 per cent, and until now they had not even thought of participating in government. They simply look for pastures and only a few of them think about going to school. Other groups, such as the Zaghawa, have been settled for a long time, they have stability and are better educated. Our people are so far behind that they do not have the leaders capable of becoming ministers, or president. We can share with the rebels the idea that Darfur is underdeveloped. They say that Darfur is marginalized, but we, the Arabs, are further away. We are beyond the margins.' This kind of complaint on the part of the Abbala Arabs, which has led them to cleave to the government, has been increasingly recognized by the rebel movements, allowing them to recruit more and more Abbala, starting with Mahamat Ibrahim Izzat's brother, Yusuf.

Climate War?

Inspired by Marxism or Islamism, successive regimes in Khartoum saw the fighting in Darfur during the 1980s and 90s from the same viewpoint: tribal rivalries from a bygone age, the last vestiges of a feudal system that had to disappear. But the new violence was less a resurgence of ancestral vendettas than the result of rapid social change, of identities and ideologies from outside, and an unprecedented level of population growth, from less than 1.5 million inhabitants in 1956, to more than 6 million today. Population movement was also driven by an increasingly unreliable climate. During the last forty years, the region has experienced intense waves of drought, rainfall that became increasingly variable and a general reduction in the length of the rainy seasons. In Darfur, temperatures rose by 0.7°C between 1990 and 2005, whilst rainfall fell by between 16 per cent and 30 per cent in forty years. The decline in rainfall in the region coincides with a rise in the temperature of the Indian Ocean.

These factors converged in 1983-5 in a famine of unprecedented severity which drew international attention to Darfur for the first time. Abubakar Mahmoud, a Zaghawa teacher in a refugee camp in Eastern Chad, was only four years old in 1985, but he remembers his parents going to El-Fasher and queuing for three or four days to get what they called the 'sorghum of Reagan', which was delivered by plane. 100,000 people died; that the number was not greater was a result not so much of the Reagan *durra*, but of the resilience of the population. Abubakar's family also ate wild plants, in particular *mokhet*, the berries from the tree *Boscia senegalensis;* 'It is very bitter. It has to be dried on the soil and cleaned, then put in water at least three times, the water poured from time to time and the taste can become acceptable.' The inhabitants of Darfur, notably the Zaghawa in the far north, knew how to survive by eating wild fruits and cereals during difficult periods.

The drought drove people south in search of less arid land. Already in the 1970s, at the behest of members of their educated elite, and anticipating the coming droughts, thousands of Zaghawa moved to the far south of Darfur. During the 1980s, other communities from North Darfur, in particular Abbala Arabs, took the same path. Today the Arabs' camels graze on the green flanks of the volcanic Jebel Marra mountain range, which is more than 3,000 metres high and lies at the centre of the Fur heartland. A small community of Rizeigat Arabs from the Jalul branch, that of Musa Hilal, the most notorious of the leaders of the *janjawid*. has put its tents made of palm leaves to the south of the mountain. Its head is the Sheikh Abdallah Abubakar, who was born 88 years ago in Um Sayala, a settlement in north Darfur which has now become a *janjawid* base.'All the north has become a desert, there is no more water. That's the reason why we settled here', he explains. In accordance with custom, he went to ask his Fur counterparts, who own the Jebel Marra lands, if he could move there. The region was much less inhabited than today, and they had no trouble finding an area 'where there was no-one, only forest, lions and leopards'. The Sheikh Abdallah had to 'open the land', as Darfurians say, which means cutting down trees and driving away wild animals, to farm, to feed the livestock and the people.

More and more Arab nomads have become sedentarized. In the regions where they have settled, the Arabs or Zaghawa newcomers have adapted well. Farmers have enjoyed bigger harvests than they had previously in their homelands, and herders have benefited from the tse-tse fly retreat to the south, also triggered by climate change. However, their arrival has brought conflict with earlier residents – for increasingly rare natural resources, land ownership, control of trade and political power. The Abbala generally side with the government and the Zaghawa with the rebels, but these two groups are both detested by most of their Arab and non-Arab neighbours. The communities of the *dars* where they have settled fear that they will use their military power to seize the land. For the Zaghawa, this idea is substantiated by the signing of the Abuja Agreement in May 2006 by a single faction of the SLA, that of the Zaghawa rebel chief Mini Arkoy Menawi, who has since become Senior Assistant to President Bashir. With regard to the Abbala, their large presence at the heart of the government's auxiliary troops means that they are widely considered no better than criminals.

Unsimplifiying Darfur

Most of the Abbala men living in Sheikh Abdallah Abubakar's camp wear military clothes. The Jalul admit that some of them have been recruited as government auxiliary troops, and have even become part of official army units such as the *Haras-al-Hodud* (Border guard). But they regret that their neighbours now call them '*janjawid*', whether they are civilians or soldiers. In the local Arab dialect '*janjawid*' means 'horsemen with G3' – a G3 being the German assault rifle often carried by the militias. Later the word was altered to '*jinjawad*', or 'devil-horsemen'. For the Jalul, this is a term that applies only to livestock thieves.

In recent years, tired of being considered by all – the other Arabs as well as non-Arabs – as criminals, the Jalul of Sheikh Abdallah Abubakar have slowly turned against the government, becoming closer to the Fur rebels of the SLA faction led by Abelwahid Mohamed Ahmed al-Nur, their neighbours living higher up in the mountains. Many other Arabs also changed sides after the Abuja agreement of 2006. Absent from the peace talks in Abuja, in Nigeria, the Abbala felt that they had been let down by the government on questions as important as land and disarmament.

The Abuja agreement did not bring peace, but it changed the structure of the conflict. Arab groups that had been supported by the government but who were less worried about obeying it than confirming their own land conquests, started fighting amongst themselves. The bloodiest fighting in Darfur in recent years has not been between Arabs and non-Arabs, but between well-armed Arab groups. On the other side, rebel factions, sometimes fighting against one another, have become more and more numerous. This fragmentation has been caused by the government, ready to sponsor groups, as well as by the international community, which is now more flexible than at Abuja and ready to acknowledge any war leader or even to create them.

The international community, Darfur civil society and many rebel leaders have made the unification of the rebel groups a priority. But attempts at unification or reunification have generally been short-lived. In 2006, soon after Abuja, the JEM and the Zaghawa factions of the SLA formed the NRF (National Redemption Front). The new front enjoyed significant victories against Mini Menawi's pro-government forces, then against government troops. But the JEM became involved in civil war in Chad fighting on the side of the President of Chad, Idriss Déby, himself a Zaghawa, against Chadian rebels backed by Khartoum. And the SLA, already divided, kept splintering along ethnic lines: the 'unity conference' which took place in April 2007 in Ammaray, North Darfur, was boycotted by the Fur and gave birth only to a purely Zaghawa faction, ironically called SLA-Unity.

The founder of the SLA, Abdel Wahid Mohamed al-Nur, lives in exile in Paris, relying on his once strong but slowly eroding reputation amongst hundreds of thousands of Fur IDPs to maintain a role as a key actor in Darfur. The JEM makes up for its limited popularity and its narrow ethnic base in a few Zaghawa clans by more enterprising military exploits. In May 2008, the movement launched a lightning raid on Khartoum from the Chadian border. Recalling a similar attempt in the 1970s by Sadiq al-Mahdi to depose Jaafar Nimeiri in an attack mounted from Libya, the JEM attack was a military failure but a success in political and media terms. By bringing the war to the centre of the country, the JEM gained national standing. After the raid it rallied a number of factions, mostly from the SLA. The 'new JEM', which is supposed to have shelved any traces of Islamist ideology, has enlarged its base considerably and had in its ranks not only Zaghawa from all clans, but also Masalit and Arabs from Darfur and Kordofan, some of whom are former *janjawid*. In late 2009 and early 2010, though, there was a sudden rapprochement between the governments of Chad and Sudan. JEM was deprived of its rear-bases and its main source of vehicles, arms and money, its troops had to go back to Darfur and its leader, Dr Khalil Ibrahim, was expelled to Libya. Nevertheless JEM remains the most prominent rebel movement in Darfur.

The war in Darfur is an evolving conflict. It has given rise to mass killing and displacement on a vast scale, but the intensity of the killing, culminating between mid-2003 and mid-2004, has considerably decreased since then. Mortality statistics have been the subject of dispute. In October 2004, the United Nations released a figure of 70,000 deaths from hunger and disease between March and September 2004. It was based on mortality studies carried out by the World Health Organization in a few IDP camps during a three-month period (June to August 2004), and a survey conducted by the Coalition for International Justice of around a thousand refugees in Chad at the same time. By relying on these somewhat limited studies, the WHO arrived at average mortality figure of 10,000 deaths per month. In March 2005, the United Nations Office for the Coordination of Humanitarian Affairs (OCHA) used this average to estimate a total of 180,000 deaths since September 2003, a figure obtained simply by re-multiplying these 10,000 deaths per month by eighteen months of conflict. Aware that this estimate did not take into account violent deaths and that the war had begun before September 2003, others produced an extrapolated figure of around 400,000 conflict-related casualties between February 2003 and April 2005. This oft-cited figure is problematic, however, as levels of violence were not constant during that period. The US Department of State estimated the number of deaths between March 2003 and January 2005 at somewhere between 63,000 to 146,000. This data covers the period from April 2003 to mid-2004 when most of the government's army and *janjawid* attacks took place By contrast, figures from the United Nations and the African Union indicate that there were 370 violent deaths per month in 2006, 250 in 2007, and less than 150 in 2008.

The emergence of Darfur as an international cause célèbre owes less to levels of mortality than to a growing global awareness of preventable violence, particularly in Africa. The first year of counterinsurgency in Darfur passed unnoticed. It was the tenth anniversary of the Rwandan genocide in 2004 and the memory of international inaction in Rwanda that triggered attention to the death toll in Darfur on the part of United Nations officials, human rights activists and journalists. By analogy with Rwanda, the killings in Darfur were labelled by some, particularly in the United States, as a 'genocide'. The US-based Darfur campaign embraced the term and, along with it, the simplistic dichotomy between 'Africans' and 'Arabs'; this was perpetuated in the language of the 2009 indictment against Omar al-Bashir prepared by the Prosecutor of the International Criminal Court (ICC). The prosecutor argued that the Sudan government had sought to 'end the history of the Fur, Masalit and Zaghawa people'. The President's 'alibi was a counterinsurgency, his intent was genocide'. The prosecutor also alleged that 5,000 people were still dying each month in Darfur, and that genocide was still ongoing in the IDP camps in Darfur.

This simplistic western discourse has now entered into the rhetoric both of the rebels and of the increasingly politicized inhabitants of displaced camps in Darfur and refugee camps in Chad. Interviewed in July 2009, the SLA leader Abdel Wahid Mohamed al-Nur compared the IDP camps to 'concentration camps'. Rebels and displaced civilians alike are increasingly presenting themselves as 'Africans' and stigmatizing their enemies as 'genocidaires'. The internationalization of the war may have produced irreversible changes of political consciousness among Darfuris. The complexities and accommodations between different groups that characterized an earlier era of Darfuri life may now be irrecoverable. Back in Brejing refugee camp on the Chadian border, the 'Orchestra of the Dawn of Free Darfur' is still performing. Someone in the crowd brandishes a portrait of Omar al-Bashir, superimposed on the body of a hyena. The crowd jeers. And Abdallah Idris sings:

Omar Bashir has armed the *janjawid* who have killed our wives,
He's a butcher of human beings,
He has brought the horseriders, the *janjawid*.
The guys riding horses, your father will go to The Hague!
Our revolution says: all criminals should go to justice.
Darfur file is in the Hague, now. Be patient, don't escape, no escape!
Omar Bashir, you're blind, you opened your eyes when the issue arrived at the International Criminal Court.
Our problem is ethnic cleansing and genocide.

Recommended Reading

Daly, Martin. *Darfur's Sorrow: A History of Destruction and Genocide*. Cambridge: University Press, 2007.
De Waal, Alex (ed.). *War in Darfur and the Search for Peace*, Global Equity Initiative. Cambridge: Harvard University Press, 2007.
Doornbos, Paul. 'On becoming Sudanese', in *Sudan: State, Capital and Transformation*, edited by Barnett, Tony and Abdelkarim, Abbas. London: Croom Helm, 1988: 99-120.
Flint, Julie and de Waal, Alex. *Darfur: A New History of a Long War*. London: Zed Books, 2008.
O'Fahey, Rex Sean. *The Darfur Sultanate*. London: Hurst and Co, 2008.
Prunier, Gérard. *Darfur: An Ambiguous Genocide*. London: Hurst and Co, 2005.
Tubiana, Jérôme, 'Learning from Darfur', *Dispatches: Out of Poverty*, 4 (2009): 195-218.
Tubiana, Jérôme. *Chroniques du Darfour*. Paris: Glénat, 2010.

14

A Short History of Sudanese Popular Music

AHMAD SIKAINGA

In the literature on the rise of modern Sudan, there is a dominance of political analysis and a comparative absence of social and cultural history. Topics such as popular culture, music, dance and clothing have received scant attention from historians. These subjects have mostly been left to anthropologists and others whose research has been in rural areas. Yet such activities are central to the emergence of a common popular culture in the urban centres of the country. This is a culture that springs from the lives of marginal groups, of manual workers, peasants, slaves and women, and from the merging of a great diversity of indigenous and external influences.

This chapter examines the role of distinct styles of music, singing, and dance in the shaping of contemporary Sudanese urban cultural expression. Hybridized and cosmopolitan, the popular arts that have developed in the cities of Sudan challenge the binary terms conventionally used to describe Sudanese national culture: the idea of an Arab Muslim north versus an African and Christian or non-Muslim south. As the recent wars in Darfur and in Eastern Sudan have clearly shown, the north is not a monolithic entity, but a complex region inhabited by a multitude of ethnic and linguistic groups, with different cultural traditions. The popular culture that is still emerging from the meeting of these groups is central to the ongoing debate on Sudanese identity and the question of the future of that identity.

The musical traditions of modern Sudan are the product of a long history of migration, intermarriage, miscegenation and cultural hybridization. To the indigenous cultures of Nubian peoples in the north, the Beja in the east , the Fur in the west and the Nuba in central Sudan have been added, successively, the influence of migrants from the Middle East, from North (and later West) Africa, and from the societies of southern Sudan. Uniting them all, one way or another, is the long history of slavery and the slave trade.

For several centuries, the Arabic-speaking northern Sudanese obtained slaves from non-Arab, non-Muslim communities in southern Sudan and adjacent territories. Slavery and the slave trade reached a peak under Turco-Egyptian rule in the nineteenth century, and the institution of slavery continued to thrive under the Mahdist state (1885-1898). Although the majority of Sudanese slaves were exported to Mediterranean and Middle Eastern markets, many remained in the northern part of the Sudan. Here they became domestic servants, soldiers,

145

labourers, or concubines. Following the Anglo-Egyptian conquest of the Mahdist state, slavery, though not the slave trade, persisted until the late 1930s. Finally a combination of international pressure, the logic of the colonial economy and the actions of the slaves themselves led to the demise of slavery as a legal institution. But the ideology of slavery did not disappear: former slaves and their descendants remained socially and culturally marginalized in Sudanese society and have done to this day.

Like their counterparts in other parts of the world, Sudanese slaves brought with them cultural traditions from their home regions in southern Sudan and the borderlands. Their cultural practices had a profound impact on social life in the northern Sudan and on all forms of artistic expressions. One of the most important groups in the dissemination of these traditions were the slave soldiers who formed the backbone of the Turco-Egyptian, Mahdist, and the Anglo-Egyptian armies.

Music and Religion

From the sixteenth century onwards, as a result of the growing dominance of Islam and the Arabic language, distinct musical styles began to emerge. The most prominent of those was called *madeih*, a religious chanting that praised the Prophet Muhammad and local holy men. With the spread of the mystical practices of Sufism, religious chanting, or *zikr*, became a central feature of religious practice. *Zikr* is a ritual through which the participants endeavour to reach a state of perfection through uninterrupted meditation and the chanting of the divine attributes of God. It has remained one of the most popular religious activities in the Sudan, visible in public devotions such as the large-scale ceremonies that take place in Omdurman. With its fast tempo and the colourful performances, the *zikr* clearly reflects the blending of Islam with indigenous cultural tradition. Another genre of singing, which is common among some rural communities in the central parts of the Sudan is called the *dobait*, vocalized singing in which a romantic theme or praise is communicated.

An important religious practice in the north, originating in practices that predate Islam, is the *zar*. *Zar* is both a category of spirits and a possession cult, largely in the hands of women. Possession by *zar* spirits can cause problems such as illness, sometimes interpreted as a form of mental illness, and many of the rituals of the *zar* ceremonies are directed at controlling such disorders. Healing is enacted through possession trances. Participants become actively possessed; while in this state they act out the characteristics of the possessing spirit in behaviour, dress, movement, and sometimes speech. Healing from the illness involves extended singing, drumming, and dancing. These performances allow women to transgress everyday social norms through dramatic enactments, including drinking and smoking.

The Growth of the Three Cities

Urbanization in the modern period in Sudan dates from Turco-Egyptian rule. As the capital of the Turkish regime, Khartoum metamorphosed from a small fishing village into a major commercial and administrative centre. The expansion of trade into the Upper Nile regions in the early 1840s had a significant impact on the growth of the city. With its strategic location on major land routes and waterways, Khartoum became the economic hub of the Sudan, a cosmopolitan city with vibrant commercial markets and bazaars where local and imported Middle Eastern and European goods were bought and sold. Its population grew from an estimated 40,000 in 1860 to about 70,000 in the early 1880s. Residents included Arabic-speaking Jaaliyin and Shaigiya, and Mahas and Danagla who migrated from Nubia, in the far north and found employment as boat builders and sailors, accompanying ivory and slave raiding expeditions to the White Nile. There were also West African immigrants such as Hausa, Fulani, and Borno, most of whom came as pilgrims en route to Mecca. Some of these pilgrims were stranded in the Sudan either on their way to Mecca or on their return, establishing a bridgehead for later, more extensive migration from West Africa.

Khartoum was also the home of a large number of foreigners from the Middle East, North Africa, and Europe. The largest of these groups were the Egyptians, most of whom were soldiers, traders or employees of the government. The Egyptian community included Coptic Christians who were traders, accountants and bookkeepers. Numbering about five hundred families, the Copts established their own school and church and became a well-established community in the Sudan. Even after the collapse of the Turco-Egyptian regime in 1884, many Copts were employed as clerks and bookkeepers during the Mahdiyya (1884-98).

To vary daily routine in the inhospitable climate, Khartoum's foreign residents engaged in a wide range of leisure activities that reflected their diverse ethnic and cultural backgrounds. Leisure activities in Khartoum also reflected its social and class distinctions. Turco-Egyptian officials held lavish parties in their homes where Middle Eastern singers performed and young female slaves danced. The leisure activities of local Sudanese, including slaves themselves, involved the reproduction of cultural practices from the Sudanese hinterland and adjacent regions such as Abyssinia and Ubangi-Chari. Pellegrino Matteucci, the Italian explorer who lived in the Sudan in the late 1870s, described at some length a slave carnival in Khartoum. He relates that one day each year the slaves would cease work and gather at the Muqran, then a poor neighborhood at the confluence of the Blue and the White Niles. They dressed in the style of their home areas, played music, and danced. They elected a 'king of the slaves' and staged satires on the behaviour of their masters. Slaves, liberated slaves, and the urban poor pursued their leisure activities in the streets and the *anadi* (local bars). These sites created unmonitored social spaces for these communities to live out the heritage of their home areas.

Khartoum was destroyed by the Khalifa Abdallahi, the Mahdi's successor, and Omdurman became the capital of the Mahdist state (1885-1898). Many of Khartoum's residents moved to the new capital. The Khalifa's policy of bringing his kinsmen and supporters from Kordofan and Darfur, led to a high concentration of people from these regions in the city. Following the Anglo-Egyptian conquest of the Mahdist state, Khartoum was revived and became the headquarters of the new regime. Together with Omdurman and Khartoum North it became the political and the economic hub of the country once again. In the three towns of Greater Khartoum a vibrant urban popular culture and new styles of singing emerged, setting the standard for the rest of the country.

One of the regular social activities in Khartoum and Omdurman in the early years of the twentieth century was called *zafa*, a festival that was held twice a year to celebrate *eid al-fitr* (at the end of Ramadan) and the *mawlid al-Nabi*, the Prophet Muhammad's birthday. The *zafa* became a popular occasion in which various segments of the urban population participated. It involved a parade that included leaders of the various Sufi orders, government officials, senior police and army officers, and other dignitaries. Each Sufi order carried its own banner and chanted religious songs.

Military Bands and Brass Instruments

The first introduction of Middle Eastern and Western instruments in the Sudan was by soldiers who served in the military bands of the Egyptian army. One of most significant institutions of Turco-Egyptian rule was military slavery. During the first two decades of Turkish rule, thousands of Sudanese from the non-Muslim communities in southern and the western Sudan and the Blue Nile region were drafted into Muhammad Ali's army. Military bands were an integral part of the Turco-Egyptian army, and many of these soldiers were trained in brass instruments. The best known bands were al-Musiqa al-Bahariyya (Naval Band), Musiqa al-Balky (Police Band) and Beringi and Kingi Musiqa. Following the British conquest of Egypt in 1882, the old Egyptian army was disbanded and a new one was established, which included six Sudanese units. Before the occupation, Sudanese military bands were trained by an Italian instructor named Boba Bey. After the British re-conquest, Boba was replaced by a British instructor, and two schools of music were established in Cairo.

In 1897 the British established the first purely Sudanese bands. Two infantry staff bands were sent from Wadi Halfa and Suakin to Cairo to receive instruction. The British felt that the members of these units were too old, and so discharged them; thirty-eight young Sudanese boys were sent from the Sudan to Cairo instead. These boys formed what came to be known as the Sudanese Frontier Band. They were trained in brass instruments, and within one year they were able to play several of these. Sudanese bands continued to receive training in Cairo until 1912 when a school of music was established in Omdurman.

Sudanese units of the Egyptian army played a major role in the Anglo-Egyptian campaign against the Mahdist State in the late 1890s. After the establishment of British rule in the Sudan these units remained an integral part of the Egyptian army until the 1924 uprising, which led to the evacuation of the Egyptian army from the Sudan and the disbandment of the units. The British continued the recruitment policies of their predecessors by targeting particular ethnic groups from non-Arab and non-Muslim and non-Arab communities in the south and the west, resulting in a concentration of people from the same ethnic group in each unit. Each unit performed a march based on musical tunes or songs from its home area. This led to the emergence, for example, of a Shilluk March, a Banda March, a Binga March, a Baggara March, and so forth. This interaction between local and European musical traditions had major effects on Sudanese music. Sudanese members of military bands can be regarded as the first professional musicians, taking the lead in the process of modernization and indigenization.

After their discharge from the army, former soldiers were settled by the British colonial authorities in specific quarters, known as the Radif, Malakiyya and Abbasiyya (the last named after Abbas Pasha, the khedive of Egypt), in towns such as Kosti, Wad Medani, Omdurman and El-Obeid. This was intended to give colonial authorities a degree of control over the soldiers after their discharge. About twenty three settlements were established between 1900 and 1922, distributed among White Nile, Kordofan, Kassala, Funj, Upper Nile and Dar Fur Provinces. In addition to the Radif and Malakiyya quarters, ex-service men, former slaves, and other marginal groups established their own neighbourhoods in the three towns, such as Hayy al-Dubbat ('The Officers' Quarter') in Omdurman and the Deims in Khartoum. The settlements attracted a multitude of people, including liberated slaves, runaways, West Africans, and migrant workers from other parts of the Sudan. In these quarters new forms of musical and dancing styles emerged, blending folk tradition and martial music. Former members of military bands taught music classes and formed the backbone of the orchestras that came to dominate the performing arts in many Sudanese towns after World War II. The Radif quarter in Kosti, for example, produced performers such as Abd Allah wad al-Radif and a group called the Tomat, the first female performers in Kosti.

The Haqiba Era

As the headquarters of the Anglo-Egyptian government, Khartoum was an 'official' town. Many residents were foreigners, traders or government employees. Omdurman, on the other hand, maintained its original Mahdist character. It became the cultural hub of the country, a microcosm of the Sudan. *Nas* Omdurman (people of Omdurman), as they preferred to call themselves, developed a strong sense of nationalism. The provision of formal education under colonial rule led to the emergence of a small educated class who read foreign newspapers and magazines, established literary associations and organized cultural activities involving poetry reading, singing, and so forth. It was in this environment that a new style of singing called *haqiba* emerged in the 1920s.

The *haqiba* incorporated the *madeih* style and was performed by individual vocalists accompanied by a chorus. The main musical instrument was the tambourine. However, in this particular form of singing the main emphasis was on the lyrics rather than the tunes. At the beginning, *haqiba* singers performed mainly at weddings and other social occasions. With the arrival of the record industry, *haqiba* songs were recorded and circulated. The first commercial recording in the Sudan appeared as early as 1921, when an Egyptian record company opened a branch in Omdurman. A few years later, two other companies – Audion and Misiyan – established branches in Omdurman. The production of phonograph records played a major role in popularizing *haqiba* songs, as did the political climate of the early 1920s. Slogans of the White Flag League and pro-Egyptian groups – such as 'Unity of the Nile Valley' became major themes. Among the pioneers of *haqiba* were Muhammad Ahmad Sarour and Khalil Farah, a Nubian.

The 1930s saw the instrumental repertoire expanded with the mandolin, violin, accordion, trumpet, and piano, replacing the vocal chorus. Pioneers of this new style included Ibrahim al-Kashif, Hassan Atiyya, Ahmad al-Mustafa, Hassan Sulayman. The Omdurman radio station, established in 1941, began to play a major role in the dissemination of music and the *haqiba* began to lose grounds to new styles.

Music from the Margins: The Emergence of *tum tum*

The *haqiba* was decidedly a male domain, but several singing styles emerged among Sudanese women. One was *saira* or praise singing, performed during wedding ceremonies and sometimes to urge men on to fight in battles. Accompanied by *daluka* (drum) beats, the *saira* praised male courage, chivalry, generosity, and other masculine virtues. In the 1930s in the urban centres of the north, a distinctive style of women's singing called *tum tum* emerged. The pioneers of the *tum tum* were two sisters, Um Bashayer and Um Gabayer, from the Radif quarters in Kosti, on the White Nile south of Khartoum. Among the most important elements that distinguished the *tum tum* were its simple lyrics and its danceable rhythm. The lyrics expressed romantic themes that illuminated the plight of women in Sudanese society. Among the most popular *tum tum* singers in the capital were Rabha Al-Tum Tum and Fatima Khamis. Pioneered by ex-slaves and beer brewers in the Radif and Malakiyya neighbourhoods, *tum tum* was embraced by young women across the social spectrum and became the dominant form of music in the urban centres.

One of the most celebrated female singers of this era was Aisha Al-Fallatiya, a Sudanese of West African origin who gained fame during World War II when she joined several male singers and toured the camps of the Sudan Defence Force in East and North Africa. Aisha paved the way for a new generation of women singers. They included the highly celebrated al-Balabil, three sisters who became the most popular singers in the Sudan in the 1970s and the 1980s. The decade of the 1980s also witnessed a distinctive style of women's dance known as *kashif* (revealing), en erotic dance, which took place in wedding and private gatherings. The *kashif* was disapproved of by the conservative forces in Sudanese society, particularly Islamists, which led to the harassment and persecution of the performers.

The Golden Era, 1950s-1970s

The 1950s and 1960s were the heyday of Sudanese popular music. Based on the *haqiba* and *tum tum* traditions, the music of this era reflected local innovation as well as foreign influences such as rumba and samba. This era produced a steady stream of highly gifted Sudanese singers, whose music has not been surpassed until today. They included Ibrahim Awad, the first Sudanese singer to dance on stage, Muhammad Wardi, Sayyid Khalifa, Osman al-Shafi, Osman Hussein, al-Taj Mustafa and Ramadan Hassan. During this period, the Sudanese public was also exposed to African-American jazz and rhythm and blues singers such as Ray Charles, Harry Belafonte and James Brown and the reggae star, Jimmy Cliff. Their influences led to the emergence of so-called jazz bands in the Sudan, which relied heavily on electric instruments, particularly the guitar, which came to northern Sudan from Congo, via southern Sudan. Jazz bands introduced a new, important element in Sudanese music, namely stage dancing and the participation of audiences. One of the pioneers of this style was Sharhabil Ahmad, who is considered today as the doyen of 'Sudanese jazz'. His successors included the members of Firqat Jazz al-Dium, which was founded in the Khartoum Deims by

Omar Abdu, a Sudanese of West African origin, and his siblings, who sang in both local Sudanese Arabic and Hausa language.

Southern Sudanese musicians sang in either local languages or in 'Juba Arabic', a distinctive Arabic spoken in the southern capital and elsewhere in southern Sudan. One of the most famous southern artists whose songs became popular in northern Sudan was the late Yusuf Fetaki. There was also a saxophone player named Aballa Deng, a man of Dinka origin who was a member of the Sudan Railways Police, stationed in Atbara, and who later joined the radio and television orchestra.

An institution that played a vital role in the development of the Sudanese music was the Institute of Music and Drama, established in the late 1960s. The institute provided hundreds of students with a post-secondary training in music, drama and folklore. The institute also made considerable efforts to shed light on the musical traditions of various Sudanese communities in the rural areas. Radio Omdurman had played a key role in popularizing Sudanese urban music in the rural areas; the 1970s saw an opposite trend – the introduction of music from the rural areas into the capital. This period saw an explosion of in what came to be known as 'Kordofanian music', thanks to the efforts of such performers as Abdel Qadir Salim, Ibrahim Musa Abba, and Saidiq Abbas. A similar role was played in recent years by Omar Ihsas, who introduced musical styles from Darfur into the capital.

Recent Trends

Sudan's recent history of war and famine has had its impact on music and other aspects of urban popular culture. Huge numbers of displaced people and immigrants from southern and western Sudan now live in Greater Khartoum, most of them non-Arabs. They have developed new musical tastes; Reggae, Hip Hop and Congolese music have become a feature of social life in neighbourhoods such as Mayo, Angola, and Mandela, where the majority of southern and western Sudanese congregated. But the most important development in recent years has been negative. The rise of Islamism has produced an assault on popular culture, beginning with Numeiri's 1983 September laws and culminating in a series of public order laws enacted by military regime of Omar Al-Bashir in the early 1990s under the auspices of what the Islamists called the 'cultural project'. The establishment of an Islamic state in the Sudan entailed, among other things, the eradication of social and cultural practices deemed 'un-Islamic'. These laws were reinforced by a special unit of the police force. *Zar* was banned; dress codes were imposed; songs had to glorify religion and the war in the south. Women could not dance with men. Wedding parties required a permit. Singers were routinely beaten up, detained, and persecuted. Video and music cassettes of songs mentioning physical contact between men and women, or alcohol were confiscated and erased.

Sudanese music has also lost one of its most distinctive features, the large orchestras in which a wide range of instruments were used. The orchestra has gradually been replaced by the synthesizer and the organ, which depend on a single player. Sudanese media channels pay little attention these days to the advance of African music on the world stage, even from the neighbouring region of the Sahel. On Sudanese radio and TV it is rare to see or hear artists as Youssou

N'Dour, Baaba Maal, or Salif Keita. And in Sudan, in the past two decades, the production of original and high quality music has virtually disappeared. The majority of the singers of the golden era have passed away or retired. And the new generations have confined themselves to the reproduction of music of the earlier periods

Recommended Reading

Al Fatih, al-Tahir. *Ana Omdurman: Tarikh al-Musiqa fil Sudan*. Khartoum: al-Nashir al-Maktabi, 2003.
Ahmad, Ahmad Sidahmad. *Tarikh Madinat al-Khartum taht al-Hukm al-Misri, 1820-1885*. Cairo: al-Ha'yat al-Misriyya al-Amma li-l-kitab, 2000
Al-Tayyib, al-Tayyib Muhammad. *Al-Indaya*. Khartoum: Dar Azza, 2004.
Jum`a, Jabir. *al-Musiqa al-Sudaniya: Tarikh, Turath, Hawiyya, Naqad*. Khartoum: Sharikat al-Farabi, 1986.
Sikainga, Ahmad. 'Sudan: a musical history', *Afropop*, 2008
http://www.afropop.org/multi/interview/ID/126/Ahmad+Sikainga+on+Sudan,+A+Musical+History.
Verney, Peter. 'Does Allah like music?', *Index on Censorship*, 27, 6 (1998): 75-78.

15

Sudan's Regional Relations

GERARD PRUNIER

Sudan is both the largest country on the African continent and the one with most neighbours. Its regional relations are bewildering in their diversity. With the formal development of independent external relations on the part of the Government of Southern Sudan since 2005, this complexity has already increased further. In order to grasp the significance of these relations, Sudan's relationship with each neighbouring country needs to be considered separately.

Egypt

Cairo's main preoccupation has long been with the great Nile river. For Egypt, which receives 100 per cent of the Nile waters on which it depends from upstream, securing the valley in one form or another is a matter of life and death. Hence its cautious relationship with Sudan, its suspicion of southern secessionist tendencies and its extreme wariness of anything Ethiopia might want to do with the Blue Nile waters. Egypt's relationship with Sudan is also shaped by its own historical experience as a conquering power. Sudan as we know it today is in part a product of Egyptian imperial ambition; Turco-Egyptian conquest created 'the Sudan' as a political unit in the nineteenth century. Nominally at least, Sudan was ruled by Egypt jointly with Britain from 1898 to 1956. During the period of Sudan's negotiations for independence, Cairo's understanding was that, in accord with the then popular slogan of 'Unity of the Nile Valley', Sudan would slide out from under British domination straight into union with Egypt. This would have returned Sudan to the colonial situation of the nineteenth century, before the Mahdist revolt drove the Egyptian regime from the country.

The Unionist Party, which won the pre-independence elections in Sudan, derived its name from its programme of union with Egypt. But most Sudanese – including most Arab Sudanese – were not enthused by the idea of reunion with the former colonial master. The Unionist Party therefore found many excuses not to live up to its name and keep the new country independent. Gamal Abdel Nasser, the Egyptian president, reluctantly had to tolerate this manifestation of Sudanese nationalism, but the ambivalence of his attitude was evident in Egypt's role in southern Sudan. In the 1950s the Egyptians courted southern Sudanese politicians in an attempt to unsettle the government in Khartoum. However, much as the Egyptian government disliked an independent Sudan, they liked the idea of two independent Sudans even less. When discontent in the south turned to outright war in the 1960s, Egypt gave direct military support to Khartoum.

Sudanese views of Egypt, and of Egyptians, mirror this ambivalence. In northern Sudan, there are links created with Egypt through Islamic practice, Arab identity and certain shared customs, but suspicion of Egyptian ambitions and motives persists. In the south, Egypt is remembered not only as the former colonial master but also as the driver of the nineteenth-century slave trade. Sudanese views of Egypt may fall easily into stereotypes – themselves contradictory – running from 'our brother country' to 'those slave drivers', depending on who you talk to.

For some in Cairo, it is hard to shed the notion that Egypt must be prepared to intervene in Sudan. I remember being told in 1989 by the then Egyptian head of military intelligence that 'one day we will have to go back and re-conquer that country because these people are such a mess and they are incapable of governing themselves.' He was commenting on the possibility of a coup in Khartoum – which did occur three months later – and he felt disgusted by the confusion of Sudanese politics and by the war that was raging at the time.

But impatience and anxiety over the Nile on the part of Egypt is tempered with a pragmatic desire to avoid direct conflict. After 1989, Cairo was wary of the new Islamist regime in Khartoum, but nevertheless made it a priority to remain on good terms. It went to remarkable extremes not to break with Sudan: in 1995 when the Sudanese regime was implicated in an attempt to kill Egyptian president Hosni Mubarak during a visit to Addis Ababa, many expected an interruption of diplomatic relations at least. But this did not occur because of Egypt's deep reluctance to turn its back on a country that is vital to its survival. In recent years President Mubarak supported the Sudanese government's position on Darfur and used his good relations with the United States to intercede on behalf of Khartoum. It is likely that future leaders of Egypt will follow the same pattern. Khartoum's view of Cairo, likewise, regardless of who is in power in Sudan, will remain superficially friendly but guarded. Meanwhile, the long-running dispute over the Hala'ib Triangle on the Egypt–Sudan border is a continuing source of tension. The Triangle is now under effective Egyptian occupation, but Sudan continues to lay claim to it. In reality, though, the Khartoum government has little means to press its case.

Since the signing of the January 2005 Comprehensive Peace Agreement (CPA) in Nairobi, Egyptian diplomacy towards Sudan has had two aims. The first has been trying to prevent Southern Sudan's independence. As that aim came to seem increasingly unattainable, Cairo instead focused on a second strategy: establishing a good relationship with Juba in advance of secession. In November 2008 President Mubarak flew to Southern Sudan – the first visit there by an Egyptian head of state since Gamal Abdel Nasser's in 1963 – and made generous promises of economic aid. The issue is particularly pressing as Ethiopia has led a diplomatic revolt on the part of the upstream riparian states against the 1959 Treaty on the Nile Waters. This is a treaty that gives Egypt and Sudan the right to 90 per cent of the flow of the river. Cairo has increased its economic cooperation with the Provisional Regional Government in Juba. These attempts at retaining a good relationship with an independent South Sudan have been welcomed by the Juba authorities. Among the Arab League, however, they are less popular, being seen as support for the dismantling of a fellow Arab state.

Libya

Sudan's relationship with Libya is also largely conditioned by geography, though a very different kind. While the Nile Valley creates a strong, umbilical link between Sudan and Egypt, the Sahara desert has isolated Sudanese territory from the coasts of Tripolitania and Cyrenaica. Even the trans-Saharan caravan roads did not link Libyan space with today's Sudan but rather with what is now Chad, while the routes from Kordofan and Darfur followed the Wadi el Malik to the Nile. In the nineteenth century, the great religious and commercial Libyan Muslim brotherhood of the Senussiya had its trade routes oriented due south, not south-east.

No significant diplomatic relationship developed between Sudan and Libya before Colonel Gaddafi's coup in 1969. Following the coup, Libyan interest in Darfur became considerable as Gaddafi saw the area as essential for his wars of conquest in Chad. Libyan military involvement in Darfur started as early as 1977 when Gaddafi sided with the Gukuni Weddey wing of the Front de Libération Nationale du Tchad (FROLINAT) against the Hissène Habré wing in the Chadian civil war. Darfur was used as a back door to enter Chad. At the same time, several of the peoples of Darfur were also present in Chad, along the border and could be used in the Libyan recruitment drive.

The importance of Darfur for the Chadian situation was confirmed in 1982 when Gaddafi's enemy Hissène Habré launched a raid from Darfur across the country to N'Djamena and took power. Gaddafi remembered the lesson and in 1985, after the fall of Nimeiri in Khartoum, he made his move on Darfur. Nimeiri had become a close ally of the United States during the late 1970s and therefore supported the Hissène Habré camp in its confrontation with the Libyan regime, to the point where Washington had been able to implant a group of anti-Gaddafi rebels in training camps in Chad. Gaddafi used Nimeiri's fall to reverse that trend, taking advantage of the coming 1986 elections in Sudan. In supporting the Umma leader Sadiq al-Mahdi, who was in a good position to win the elections, he hoped to be given permission to use Darfur as a base in his own struggle with Hissène Habré. In December 1990 a rebel force under the pro-Libyan warlord Idriss Déby repeated Habré's 1982 *ghazzua* (desert commando raid), using Darfur as a springboard to take N'Djamena for the second time.

Such prolonged Libyan involvement in Darfur – in 1988 Gaddafi went so far as to ask Khartoum for its annexation through a Sudano–Libyan 'Treaty of Union' – has led to the development of new commercial routes through the desert. These are used by many people from western Sudan to migrate to Libya in search of work. The routes are extremely dangerous (people regularly die of thirst in the desert) but they continue to be travelled by labour migrants and by bandits and smugglers.

The extended Libyan presence in Darfur has left a damaging legacy: it was the Libyans who first armed local Arab tribes and used them in the so-called *Failaka al-Islamiyya* (Islamic Legion). Gaddafi had two aims behind this. He wanted to reinforce the Arab presence in Darfur against the non-Arabs, in order to increase his potential constituency for an eventual Libyan annexation, and he wanted to use Failaka al-Islamiyya as shock troops for the conquest of Chad. But once the Darfur Arabs were armed, nothing prevented them from using the guns for their own purposes – or for those of the government in Khartoum, as happened after 1989. A large part of the intractable situation in Darfur today finds its roots in the dangerous and confused policies once pursued there by Libya. Even though Libyan involvement in Darfur is no longer so significant, it is far from over and, as usual in the case of Libyan diplomacy, it remains contradictory. Tripoli pretends to support the Khartoum regime while frequently undermining it by giving assistance to the rebels, particularly the Justice and Equality Movement (JEM).

Chad

The relationship between Sudan and Chad is the mirror image of that between Sudan and Libya. Before the 1990s Khartoum had little interest in Chad, either diplomatically or commercially, as it bordered Sudan's most neglected region – Darfur. This changed in December 1990 when Khartoum, together with Paris, backed the Chadian rebel force led by Idriss Déby that took N'Djamena from the pro-American Hissène Habré. Through this coup, the Sudanese Islamist regime scored a major victory against the United States. The French government also saw it as victory: they had deposed Habré, who had become anti-French (despite the support that France had offered him against Gaddafi), annoyed the Americans, and improved their relationship with the pariah regime in Khartoum, which needed at least one major Western power on its side. The situation had the air of a long-delayed revenge for the Fashoda incident of 1898, the imperial dispute between Britain and France, when a French expeditionary force was compelled to withdraw from their bridgehead on the Nile near Malakal.

This power change in Chad started a honeymoon period between Khartoum and N'Djamena, during which the Sudanese regime, isolated internationally, felt it had acquired some solid support. It also enabled Khartoum discreetly to play N'Djamena off against Tripoli, since Idriss Déby, a former officer in Habré's army who had defeated the Libyans at the battle of Maa'ten es-Sarra, had little sympathy for Gaddafi. The Islamist regime in Khartoum, while wanting to keep superficially good relations with Gaddafi, had no real enthusiasm for a leader who was seen by Islamists everywhere as a potential heretic and as a competitor.

The honeymoon lasted until the Darfur revolt erupted in February 2003. At first, faithful to the Sudanese regime that had supported him, Déby tried to help Khartoum crush the insurrection, even loaning the Sudanese army several helicopters. But this position soon became untenable because of Chadian internal politics. Déby is a Zaghawa from the Biday group and many of the Sudanese insurgents were themselves Zaghawa. Thus, in supporting Khartoum he was supporting the destruction of fellow tribesmen. In May 2005 a number of Zaghawa Chadian Army officers carried out a quasi-coup in which they forced Déby to reverse his Darfur policy and start backing the rebels.

Khartoum answered in kind, assembling a full-size army of Chadian rebels and launching it against N'Djamena. In April 2006 the rebels set out from the Central African Republic and attempted to take the capital, but were defeated. Khartoum took the plan back to the drawing board and used the time-honoured practice of starting from Darfur in a second attack in February 2008. This one also failed because the French helped Déby by buying ammunition from Gadaffi for his Soviet era T-55 tanks. The tanks wiped out the rebels' Toyotas.

In return, Déby supported the JEM, the Darfur rebel group also led by a Zaghawa, Khalil Ibrahim, against the Sudanese regime. In May 2008 Khalil and his men attacked Khartoum in a daring raid from Darfur across the width of Sudan. Although the attack was repulsed it put the regime in Khartoum on the defensive; it provided further support to attacks by anti-Déby rebels in Chad. By early 2010, though, diplomatic engagement had improved. What finally – or perhaps only temporarily – brought these ongoing retaliations to a halt was the self-determination referendum in Southern Sudan. Feeling overwhelmed at the prospect of a possible conflict on two fronts, Khartoum decided to mend fences with Chad. President Déby cut off his support for the JEM while the Sudanese regime stopped helping the Chadian rebels. Khartoum used this window of opportunity to renew its attacks on the Darfur rebels. It is clear, though, that this improvement in relations between N'Djamena and Khartoum is mostly tactical and might not survive a more general conflagration in Sudan.

The Central African Republic

The Central African Republic (CAR) is the neighbouring country with which Sudan has had least relations. This is due both to its colonial history as a French possession, bordering the British colonial realm in Sudan and the fact that the border area between the two countries – arid, virtually unpopulated and a region of high tsetse fly infestation – is one of the most inhospitable areas in the African continent. This has turned it into a political wilderness where rebels of all kinds find easy shelter: the control of the Bangui government does not extend more than a few kilometres outside the capital. The scant local population in this border area is made up mainly of nomads, smugglers and bandits known locally as *zaraguina* or, in French, as *coupeurs de route* (road cutters). Recently these have come to include the notorious Lord's Resistance Army (LRA), which has migrated north west from Uganda and Sudan's border with the DRC.

Under President Ange-Félix Patassé (1993–2003) the CAR regime was on good terms with Libya (which had saved him several times from rebellions by his own army), and with Chad and the Sudan. But when Idriss Déby was forced to switch his support to the Darfur rebels he fell out with Patassé and backed a coup by General François Bozize, who chased Patassé out of the CAR and reversed alliances, becoming a friend of N'Djamena and an enemy of Khartoum and Tripoli.

President Bozize, as an ally of Déby, was considered an enemy by Khartoum, who started to push rebel forces against him, turning the CAR into a secondary theatre of operations in the Chad–Sudan conflict. Bozize convened a large meeting of all opposition forces in Bangui in December 2008, during which Patassé agreed to abandon his opposition and recognize Bozize as president. The largest and only organized rebel group in the CAR (others are mostly loose bands of armed men), the Armée Populaire pour la Restauration de la Démocratie (APRD) led by lawyer Jean-Jacques Demafouth, also agreed to enter a process of coalition, which was geared towards preparing general elections. This significantly reduced Khartoum's capacity to continue interfering in Central African affairs. But it did not stop the banditry that had developed along the Sudanese border and that still remains an obstacle to normal life in north-eastern CAR. Meanwhile the LRA, a predatory migrant group (its members were initially

Ugandan but today have between six and eight different nationalities among their ranks), continues to operate in the east of the country, probably with support from Khartoum.

The Democratic Republic of the Congo

As with the CAR, geography and history have combined to restrict relations between Sudan and the Democratic Republic of the Congo (DRC) to a minimum. Where relations have developed, they have mostly been linked to periods of civil strife. During the first Congolese civil war of 1960–65, Nasser's Egypt, then closely allied to the Soviet Union, gave support to the left wing pro-Lumumba anti-government rebels in Kisangani, using the Sudan as a conduit. General Abboud, then ruler of Sudan, rendered this service to Nasser to maintain good relations with Cairo. As a result, when Marshal Mobutu won the war on the government's side, very cold relations ensued between Sudan and the DRC.

Mobutu was unsympathetic towards the SPLA struggle against Khartoum, which he saw as Communist-inspired during the years when it was based in Mengistu's Ethiopia (1983–1991). Therefore neither the Sudanese government nor the southern rebels had much to do with Zaire during that time. The SPLA did, however, take advantage of the almost complete absence of administration in north-eastern Zaire to cross freely over the borders, both of the CAR and Zaire, in order to sidestep Sudanese Army operations and move troops between Western Equatoria and Bahr al-Ghazal.

After the fall of Mengistu's regime in 1991, the SPLA had to flee Ethiopia and depend much more heavily on its relationships with Kenya and Uganda. Mobutu had sustained a low-intensity conflict with Museveni's regime since the day he took power in Kampala, and as an extension of this strategy started to collaborate with Khartoum, creating links that were briefly interrupted when Museveni's ally Laurent-Désiré Kabila came to power in 1997. These were quickly resumed a year later when Kabila fell out with his former supporters, but by then the rebel SPLA was locked – if informally – in the general anti-Kabila alliance through its links with Kampala. This led to Khartoum entering the war in Congo unofficially by using its air force to help ferry troops and bomb the northern front along the Sudanese border where Jean-Pierre Bemba's rebel Mouvement pour la Libération du Congo (MLC) was operating. After Kabila's assassination in 2001, Khartoum's relationship with Kinshasa became distinctly distant when the former president's son Joseph Kabila entered into peace negotiations with the Rwandese–Ugandan alliance. Still, Sudan continued to use the DRC against its Great Lakes enemies in any way possible, and as late as September 2008 it was delivering weapons to the Forces Armées de la République Démocratique du Congo (FARDC) when fighting broke out between the government and the rebel General Laurent Nkunda.

Recently, the DRC has suffered from the depredations of the wild, omni-directional LRA insurgency. In the 1990s the LRA leader Joseph Kony was forced to flee northern Uganda to escape military pressure and took refuge in southern Sudan with the help of the Khartoum government. After the CPA, when the SPLA took over control of Juba from the Khartoum government, Kony and his followers crossed the Nile and walked to the DRC, and reestablished themselves in the Garamba National Park, close to the tri-border of Sudan, Uganda and the

DRC. On 14 December 2008 an offensive by the armies of these three countries tried to dislodge him. But the attack was poorly organized and the LRA managed to flee, causing massive havoc in the region. In the space of three weeks it killed nearly 500 civilians in the Congo and more than 40 in the southern Sudanese state of Western Equatoria. Since then it has continued to operate in northern DRC.

The question remains as to whether the Khartoum regime still provides the support for the LRA that it did in the past. There is no proof of current Sudanese government involvement, but its past record – following a pattern of denials by Khartoum, then contradicted by material evidence – creates a strong likelihood of complicity.

Uganda

Sudan's relationship with Uganda became stormy in the 1970s, after the overthrow of President Milton Obote by General Idi Amin Dada in a military coup. Idi Amin, who had been put in power with Israeli help, initially supported the anti-Khartoum Anyanya guerillas, which led Khartoum to provide Obote with a military base at Owinyi Kibul in southern Sudan from which to harass northern Uganda. But Amin did an about-turn, rallied to the 'progressive' Arab camp, and betrayed the Anyanya rebels. In return, Khartoum kicked out Obote. Amin nevertheless maintained his contacts with the former guerillas, and when the Addis Ababa Agreement ending the first Sudanese civil war was signed in Addis Ababa in 1972, he recruited many demobilized southern Sudanese to his army. After Amin was ousted in 1979 they retreated back to Sudan; Sudan then became an informal rear base for anti-Ugandan government guerillas.

West Nile province of Uganda, bordering Sudan, became an area of low-intensity guerilla fighting for the Sudanese-supported West Nile Bank Liberation Front (WNBLF), a distant and cautious ally of Yoweri Museveni's National Resistance Army. In 1986, when the post-Obote Military Commission disintegrated in Uganda and Museveni's guerillas took back Kampala, the survivors of the defeated regime fled to southern Sudan. In Khartoum, the government of Sadiq al-Mahdi, which made much of the fact that Museveni had known John Garang as a student at the University of Dar-es-Salaam, was convinced that Uganda was going to become a rear base for the SPLA. Khartoum therefore provided aid and support to 'the Okellos' (Tito and Bazilio Okello were the leaders of the Military Commission), who launched a guerilla war in northern Uganda. Their attempt failed in part because they were pre-empted by an unexpected new socio-religious phenomenon, the emergence of Alice Lakwena's Holy Spirit Mobile Battalion. Alice Lakwena was an *ajwaka* (an Acholi prophetess) who preached the moral regeneration of Uganda through her millenarian cult. She literally 'stole' the troops of the Okellos, who watched all their men desert to join her movement. The Sudanese government was bewildered by Alice's brand of prophetic politics and declined to support her. But after she was defeated in 1987 and fled to Kenya, her movement was picked up by her nephew Joseph Kony who turned it into the LRA.

Starting in 1993, Kony received full support from the Sudanese government, which used him as a weapon against Museveni and to try to disorganize the SPLA's rear echelons in Uganda. By the late 1990s the intensity of the fighting had resulted in nearly two million internally displaced persons (IDPs) in northern Uganda and the Ugandan Army regularly crossing the border in hot pursuit of LRA fighters. Since the CPA was signed in January 2005 Khartoum has made conciliatory noises and claims to have stopped supporting the LRA. But there is continued suspicion that the Sudanese Military Security has continued giving discreet support to Kony, including air drops of weapons, medicines and ammunition. If this is the case, the intention must be to increase confusion in the south and make the work of the new government in Juba harder. It may also be to keep an active means of political destabilization, in line with the political grand designs of the Sudanese Islamist movement for the eventual Islamization of the Great Lakes region.

Uganda has benefited economically from the CPA. Southern Sudan, which is oil-rich but unindustrialized, imports many goods from Uganda and also employs many Ugandan skilled workers. In economic terms, Southern Sudan, at the end of 2010, can be seen as a Kenyan/Ugandan colony, a state of affairs that has caused much resentment on the Sudanese side and has fed border tensions.

Kenya

In spite of having been used by the SPLM/A as a political rear base during most of the civil war, Kenya is one of the few countries bordering Sudan that has had a largely non-conflictual relationship with its government. There are several layers of explanation for this paradox. First and perhaps foremost, Kenya was an economic and refugee rear base for the struggling southern Sudanese movement but never a military rear base. Kenya provided administrative offices for the guerrillas, hosted a major humanitarian aid operation with large refugee camps, and provided accommodation for the SPLM leadership and diplomatic support. But it offered no guns. One reason for this demilitarization of Kenya's support was the massive presence of UN aid agencies and independent NGOs, which, particularly after the 1989 creation of the multi-agency Operation Lifeline Sudan (OLS), did not want their humanitarian action mixed up with any form of military support. At the time the military means of the SPLA were still concentrated in Ethiopia, so there was a kind of task-sharing: guns in Addis Ababa and humanitarian supplies in Nairobi. After the fall of the Mengistu regime in 1991, the guns switched to Kampala but were never kept in Kenya, even though Mombasa was used as a trans-shipment facility.

Another reason is perhaps the fact that Nairobi was a kind of 'Cairo South': a cultural and human conduit to the outside world for the black African communities of Sudan, in the same way Cairo was for the Sudanese Arabs. Throughout its stormy history, Sudan has been a place of limited freedoms and its people have always needed a route to the outside world. Ethiopia could not play that role, being as politically disturbed as Sudan, especially after the fall of Haile Selassie. The countries to the west were isolated and with poor communications, and both the Congo and Uganda suffered long periods of violence and/or misadministration. This left Kenya as the only stable and peaceful black African state neighbouring Sudan, just as Egypt was the one natural cultural outlet for the Arab community in the north. In Kenya, a Sudanese could open a foreign bank account, buy a house or send their children to school while still, in a way, feeling at home. Kenya was also seen as protected by the United Kingdom and

United States and therefore not to be tangled with by Khartoum. This resulted in a tacit consensus that the place should be kept as neutral ground and the various Kenyan regimes, whether of Kenyatta, Daniel arap Moi or Mwai Kibaki, have all appeared to know that there was an unspoken compact with Khartoum, which implied that 'you can help our enemies with everything but guns and we can always come there and talk.' Thus the long (2002–05) peace negotiations between the Islamist regime and John Garang were conducted entirely in Kenya and the chief African mediator, General Lazarus Sumbeiywo, was a Kenyan.

Today, without saying so openly, Nairobi is looking forward to the birth of an independent South Sudan, which it sees as a natural sphere of economic expansion for Kenyan goods and services. The south became a market for Kenyan entrepreneurship during the war, and there are many plans for the development of communications between the two areas. These include an oil pipeline for southern Sudanese crude, which would provide Juba with an alternative to the Port Sudan terminal, a railway line, and an entirely new deep-water harbour on the northern Kenyan coast, near Lamu. Before these grand designs even start to take shape, thousands of Kenyans are already moving to Southern Sudan to ply their various trades, ranging from plumbing and electrical work to transport and petty trade. They are useful but resented by much of the local population for monopolizing some of the economic opportunities brought by peace.

Ethiopia

Like Egypt, the area of Ethiopia had historical links with the Sudan region long before the birth of a Sudanese state. The relations go back to deep antiquity, between Meroe and Axum. They were often conflictual, particularly after Sudan became progressively Islamized between the eighth and sixteenth centuries while Abyssinia remained a bastion of Eastern Christianity. The rugged mountainous terrain protected Abyssinia from Islamization from the west, leaving the greatest threat of Islamic conquest coming from the east, from the Somali lowlands at the time of the sixteenth century invasion by Imam Ahmed Gragn. The tensions grew after the 1821 Egyptian conquest of Sudan, which led to progressive infiltrations from Cairo's forces in the north of Ethiopia and to an all-out attempt at military conquest in 1877. Egyptian forces were defeated by the Ethiopians but there were further Sudanese raids during the period of the Mahdiyya in the 1880s. In recent times the pattern of conflict and rivalry has roughly been a trade-off between periodic Sudanese help to the secessionist guerrillas after the beginning of the revolt in Eritrea in 1961, and varying degrees of support from the Ethiopians to the southern Sudanese insurgents between the mid-1950s and the end of the recent war in 2002.

The Ethiopian regime, which came to power in 1991, is the first to have tried seriously to develop trade links with Khartoum. This is probably because its leaders had long found shelter in Sudan during the war years and, contrary to their predecessors, tended to see it as a friend. Deprived of access to the sea by the 1998–2000 Ethio–Eritrean war, Addis Ababa has developed oil imports through Port Sudan and the Metemma road – long a neglected artery, now improved and busy with commercial traffic. There are also plans to link up the growing hydro-electric potential of Ethiopia with Sudan, whose electrical consumption has dramatically increased following the development brought by oil exploitation. This is, of course, contingent to some extent on the evolution of the diplomatic relations between Addis Ababa and Cairo. Egypt is extremely wary of Ethiopia undertaking any sort of Nile Basin water management, fearing loss of water through upstream irrigation; the 2010 decision by the riparian states led by Addis Ababa to reject the 1959 Nile Waters Treaty has only increased these fears. Khartoum used to be unbothered by such prospects but is now beginning to reconsider its previous unconditional support of the Egyptian position.

Eritrea

The Eritrean state is only seventeen years old at the time of writing, and so its relations with Sudan are a very modern phenomenon. Nevertheless, they precede the birth of the Eritrean state by some thirty years as Khartoum provided the main support and foreign backing for the Eritrean revolt from the beginning. The first Eritrean guerillas belonged to the Beni Amer tribe of the Beja who live on both sides of the border, many of whom could have been considered Sudanese. In spite of the strong left-wing orientation of the guerrillas, Sudanese support had no ideological political dimension. It was simply a modern extension of the age-old Muslim–Christian rivalry between the Sudanese lowlanders and the Abyssinian highlanders. The early rebels were almost uniformly western Eritrean Muslim lowlanders from Barka and Gash-Setit. The rebellion was even described as an Arab movement, a definite misnomer but one the rebels themselves were happy to let fly while it brought them support from the Arab world.

Eritrean independence was a victory for the Sudanese, if it is seen in the perspective of the ancient rivalries between the two opposing cultural and political spheres. But the Islamist regime in Khartoum, then still in its expansionist revolutionary phase, had plans to go further and supported a coalition of three Muslim fundamentalist movements that had united under the name of Jihad Eritrea back in 1988 – before independence. Jihad Eritrea immediately tried to overthrow the newly-born Eritrean regime through renewed guerrilla warfare. Initially, they were merely a peripheral nuisance in the Beja-populated provinces of Barka and Gash-Setit. When their importance grew as a result of Sudanese support, Asmara countered by backing the so-called Eastern Front, then fighting the Khartoum regime, leading Asmara into growing confrontation with Sudan.

The situation changed brutally when relations between Asmara and Addis Ababa, which had been good since the dual change of power in 1991, fell apart and the two countries went back to war in May 1998. Asmara immediately reconciled itself with Khartoum to bring Sudan on side in the renewed conflict with Ethiopia. Khartoum duly disbanded Jihad Eritrea while Asmara forced the Eastern Front into a hasty 'peace agreement' with the Sudanese regime. Since the end of the war with Ethiopia, Eritrea has deepened its relationship with Khartoum through blackmail.

The Asmara regime kept its channels of communications open with the Sudanese opposition even after distancing itself politically for the sake of improving relations with Khartoum. This allowed President Issayas Afeworqi to support the Darfur insurrection when it erupted in 2003. Playing on the widespread fragmentation of the Darfur guerrillas, the Eritrean regime has continued to blow hot or cold on the Darfur war, depending on the changing situation.

When the conflict dies down, Asmara fans the embers; when it seems to be getting out of control (and particularly when Chad appears on the verge of acquiring an overwhelming influence over it), Eritrea cools it down. Khartoum is aware of this game but cannot control it. In turn, Asmara uses this on/off switch to keep Khartoum on its side in its ongoing confrontational relationship with Ethiopia.

A new dimension of Sudanese–Eritrean relations has recently developed with the rapprochement between Asmara and Tehran. Iran has established a military foothold in the Eritrean harbour of Assab and used it to supply Hamas with weapons. These transited through eastern Sudan, leading to Israeli air raids on weapons convoys in 2009. Khartoum was annoyed with this new development but refrained from condemning either Eritrea or Iran for the shipments.

Conclusion

There is no clear, general pattern in Sudan's relationship with its neighbours, beyond a persistent inclination to meddle in each other's politics through hosting or actively supporting political exiles and rebels. For Khartoum, such meddling has been encouraged by one overriding concern: the north–south confrontation, now made worse by the existence of the oil reserves. Regime survival, interference in the next country's internal problems, commercial ties (or the lack thereof), diplomatic niceties and direct armed intervention have all been all determined by the north–south struggle. Now, with the Darfur conflict, the north–south confrontation has been incorporated into a wider centre–periphery contradiction, which represents the core problem of the Sudanese polity. Sudanese foreign policy has therefore been mostly conflictual because of its own domestic contradictions, not because of historical, in-built problems with its neighbours. As a result, it can be hoped that an eventual solution to Sudan's internal conflicts could translate into an easing of tensions with the surrounding region. To a certain degree this has already been the case with Ethiopia, Chad and Eritrea. But the 2011 self-determination referendum still casts a long shadow over diplomacy throughout the region.

Recommended Reading

Beshir, Mohamed Omer (ed.). *Sudan: Aid and External Relations*. Khartoum: University of Khartoum, 1984.

Prunier, Gérard. 'Rebel movements and proxy warfare: Uganda, Sudan and the Congo (1986-1999)', *African Affairs*. 103, 412 (2004): 359-383.

Prunier, Gérard. 'Chad, the CAR and Darfur: dynamics of a conflict', *Open Democracy*, April 17, 2007, http://www.opendemocracy.net/democracy-africa_democracy/chad_conflict_4538.jsp.

Prunier, Gérard. 'Chad : between Sudan's blitzkrieg and Darfur's war'. Open Democracy, February 19, 2008, http://www.opendemocracy.net/democracy-africa_democracy/chad_conflict_4538. jsp.

Warburg, Gabriel. *Historical Discord in the Nile Valley*. London: Northwestern University Press, 1992.

Waterbury, John. *The Nile Basin*. New Haven: Yale University Press, 2002.

16

The International Presence in Sudan

DANIEL LARGE

This chapter offers an overview of successive waves of international involvement in Sudan, outlining the evolution of the international presence since the nineteenth century and the context of Sudan's changing foreign relations. One theme is the continuing importance to the present day of external intervention in Sudan. Another is the manner by which different generations of Sudanese have been able to control or manage these external forces from a position of apparent weakness, appropriating resources provided from outside to consolidate and augment their own authority. A third, related theme is the way in which external assistance, including humanitarian relief and development aid, have had unintended consequences on political developments in Sudan. Finally, the chapter looks at the diversity of the international presence, the presence of countries that are not Sudan's neighbours on the continent. The meaning of 'international', formerly more or less confined to Europe and the United States, has more recently expanded to include Asian countries – Malaysia, India and, especially, China.

The Turkiyya

The territory that became Sudan had a long history of international connections prior to the Egyptian invasion of 1820–21 and the Turkiyya period that followed. The invasion inaugurated, however, a new kind of international presence, predicated on the growing global economic and political dominance of Europe, already apparent in Egypt itself. A number of European adventurers were involved in Egypt's territorial conquests. These included the British explorer Samuel Baker, who led an expedition to conquer the new province of Equatoria in 1869 and became its Governor-General on behalf of the Khedive Ismail. The era of the Turkiyya in Sudan saw the growth of a small community of Europeans, many of whom were based in Khartoum. They were a mixed group: alongside missionaries, a few engineers, geologists and medical officers, Khartoum's earliest expatriate European community included numerous self-employed male adventurers of modest social origins striving for the success they had not achieved at home. Profit was the motive. International pressure on Egypt to open Sudan up to trade increased commercial opportunities. In 1849, for example, the gum arabic trade was liberalized and international merchants travelled to

164

Kordofan to buy this prized commodity. In southern Sudan, meanwhile, the slave trade burgeoned: a barter system saw merchants exchanging cowrie shells, trinkets or Venetian glass beads for slaves and ivory.

From the mid-nineteenth century Sudan became the object of moral attention on the part of the European public, with a focus on the slave trade. Having played a role in developing the trade, Europeans now intervened to help suppress it. In 1848 a Maltese Catholic missionary established Khartoum's first modern Christian mission with the express aim of fighting slavery. By the 1870s, Sudan had become a key example of the rising disagreement over how best to suppress the trade. Those in Sudan who were engaged in attempting to curtail the trade became increasingly at odds with campaigners outside the country, who held militant views about ending both the trade and slavery itself as an institution.

The rise of the Mahdist movement in the late nineteenth century saw most Europeans and Egyptians leave Sudan and encouraged an outpouring of literature in Europe identifying the Sudanese as a people suffering under tyranny, desperate for foreign intervention to free them. Anti-slavery became a rallying cry for groups seeking to promote the cause of civilization in Africa; an alleged resurgence of slave-trading during the Mahdiyya was used as one of the justifications for invading Sudan in 1898.

The Condominium

Created through conquest, the new Anglo-Egyptian Condominium regime was imbued with a military character. The first soldier-administrators in charge of governing the Condominium used force to establish and then to maintain order. They were gradually superseded by the more professional, administrative elite of the Sudan Political Service (SPS), staffed predominantly by graduates of Oxford and Cambridge universities and driven by an imperialist blend of patriotism, desire for adventure, and moral purpose founded on a profound belief in the superiority of their own values. The way in which the SPS developed partly reflected broader changes in employment during the Condominium: a salaried civil service and more institutionalized opportunities for merchants. The social composition of the international presence in Sudan also became more diverse, and English became the main language of banking, commerce, science, and government.

The Condominium's economic policy was driven principally by the desire to generate revenue to support the state. This simple principle led to a focus on developing exports, most notably, the Gezira cotton scheme in the area between the Blue and White Niles. Inaugurated in 1925, by 1950 more than 1.1 million feddans (1.15 million acres or 450,000 hectares) was under irrigation in the Gezira. Cotton became the mainstay of Sudan's overseas trade. The possibility of wider economic development was only belatedly addressed in the late Condominium, and involved the employment of many Europeans to manage the Gezira scheme and plan other projects. In the face of the conservative paternalism of the SPS, there were no attempts at major economic development in southern Sudan until the Zande Scheme, which was planned and initiated in south-west Equatoria during the Second World War. This experiment sought to effect 'the complete social emergence and the social and economic stability' of the Zande through a comprehensive development project featuring education, cotton cultivation, light industrial development, and transport infrastructure. It was intended to demonstrate a new model of development that would not be reliant on exports, with cotton being grown and processed locally into clothes for a local market. The scheme brought in more European experts and advisors in a brief whirlwind of activity, but eventually failed at considerable human and financial cost.

Post-colonial Sudan

Following independence in January and admission to the United Nations in December 1956, the government of Sudan pursued a policy of formal non-alignment, under the influence of Nasser's Egypt. It initially received little external assistance. The aid it did receive was mostly technical, limited by domestic political sensitivities over accepting foreign help, particularly from the United States. State investment in infrastructure (for instance, railways linking the centre of the country to Darfur and southern Sudan) accompanied the intensification of the economic geography established by British rule. Irrigation schemes and rain-fed agriculture expanded.

During much of the first civil war in southern Sudan there was little international engagement and even less actual involvement. The conflict was little-known, closed off to the world's media till its last stages by a 'grass curtain'. (This phrase derived from the British policy of shielding southern Sudan from northern influence; it was later the title of a newspaper published by southerners and dedicated to southern Sudanese issues.) The war led to a steady reduction in the number of expatriates in Sudan; large numbers were expelled in 1963. The doctrine of sovereignty and non-interference in Sudan's internal affairs upheld by the UN and the Organization for African Unity meant that appeals for international intervention and investigations into war atrocities met with little response. Active concern was largely limited to the missionary Verona Fathers in Rome, one of the church bodies expelled by the government in Khartoum, and to assistance from the UN to Sudanese who had crossed international borders to become refugees in neighbouring countries. The civil war became more internationalized as a result of changing Cold War and Middle Eastern politics. Joseph Lagu secured Israeli military support for southern rebel fighters after the 1967 Arab–Israeli war.

Following the May 1969 coup in Khartoum, the government of Sudan briefly turned to the Soviet Union for support and drew on socialist inspiration to drive state-directed economic development. President Nimeiri, combining Arab nationalism and anti-Americanism, dreamed of Khartoum becoming the Havana of Africa. During a programme of extensive nationalization, Sudan saw thousands of Western expatriates leave and Soviet and East European technicians arrive. But Sudan's Soviet moment was short lasting. After the failure of the Sudan Communist Party's July 1971 coup attempt, and Moscow's botched response to it, the majority of Soviet personnel left Sudan and Nimeiri opened up to the West, switching to Western assistance and especially US aid. This Soviet period may have been brief, but it was a turning point in that control of commerce was taken into Sudanese hands; from then on, most expatriates going to Sudan were aid or development workers, or engineers in extractive industries.

Nimeiri sought political legitimacy through economic development, partly as a result of his new alliance with political forces in southern Sudan following the 1972 Addis Ababa peace agreement. International assistance was mounted to support reconstruction and refugee resettlement in the south; a Relief and Resettlement Conference on the Southern Region was held shortly afterwards. Three months after an official Appeal for Assistance to the Government of Sudan in July 1972, US$12.5 million was sent or pledged to Khartoum, including US$7.8 from the United States. Assistance also came from Eastern Europe and China. The United Nations High Commissioner for Refugees (UNHCR) initially played a coordinating role, sub-contracting most of the projects it supported to international non-governmental agencies such as the Lutheran World Federation, which built schools, for example, in Upper Nile. During this period an international presence became active in southern Sudan: Juba, the region's new capital, became second to Khartoum as a centre for international development operations. It was home to at least six UN agencies, four bilateral development agencies and 22 international NGOs, all involved in post-war refugee repatriation, construction and development activities.

The central state was a comparatively effective actor at this point in Sudan's post-colonial history. It was able to respond effectively to such problems as drought (1972–74) and refugee influxes (1975–78) without significant international assistance in a manner that is hard to conceive today. There were functioning governing structures that demonstrated a practical commitment to public welfare and a degree of service provision. But the ability to manage the country's internal social crises proved to be a passing phase as the state was undone by its own ambition.

Development Drive

The acceleration of Sudan's development drive in the 1970s was underpinned by ambitious state-directed initiatives to drive economic productivity through generating export revenue, and an open door policy to attract external investment. Sudan's stated aim was to become the breadbasket – initially of the world but then, more modestly, of the Middle East. Agricultural development aimed to increase crop and livestock production substantially by combining Sudanese natural resources (land, labour and water), with western technology and finance from the Middle East. As well as an expansion of mechanized agriculture, there was increasing oil exploration led by the US company Chevron, which struck oil in 1978. International agencies also ran a plethora of development schemes during this period: USAID, for example, operated some 25 projects such as the Abyei Integrated Rural Development Program, and the Blue Nile Agricultural Development Program.

The state's development dreams crystallized into more ambitious schemes, notably infrastructure projects intended to improve agricultural exports. In 1979 work began on the Jonglei Canal, a 360 km-long waterway designed to reduce transpiration from the White Nile by bypassing the Sudd, thereby making more water available for irrigating export agriculture in northern Sudan and Egypt. The project was abandoned in 1983 at the start of the second civil war in the south. Its completion would have irrevocably changed the environment, affecting the livelihood of tens of thousands of people living along its path. The scheme may yet be revived.

Development was central to Nimeiri's attempt to spearhead Sudan's modernization and national renewal. But the foreign assistance it provided, however, coupled with Khartoum's manipulation of Sudan's strategic advantages in the Cold War, instead became critical to his regime's survival. Rather than a breadbasket, the reality that emerged was a story of wasted resources, mismanagement and corruption. In the phrase of the time, not a breadbasket but a basket-case. Skilled northern Sudanese left the country to earn their living in the Arab world, contributing to a growing remittance economy in Sudan itself.

Nimeiri is said to have boasted that Sudan could soak up development finance like a sponge. This proved true, with far-reaching consequences: debt built up on the back of reckless, unchecked borrowing, and much aid was diverted into private consumption or to maintain Nimeiri's increasingly corrupt patrimonial rule. Sudan was unable pay its debts when these fell due in 1977–78. Economic crisis necessitated tactical domestic political changes for Nimeiri and closer relations with the US government, whose support for Khartoum was especially important at the IMF. Sudan's unrealistic Six Year Plan of Economic and Social Development (from 1977-8 to 1982-3) was replaced by a more modest IMF-inspired plan, which froze new development projects and attempted to address the chronic balance of payments deficit. The ensuing cycle of economic crisis, concurrent as it was with the growth of a private remittance economy of Sudanese working in the Middle East, defied all known rules of economic gravity.

Support for Sudan from the United States became critical to Nimeiri's survival. By the early 1980s, Sudan was an important regional actor in the confrontation between the West and the Soviet bloc. Relations with America had improved after the 1974 coup in Ethiopia that brought a pro-Soviet regime to power. Khartoum's support for the 1978 Camp David agreement, cooperation in the CIA's covert war against Libya in Chad, and Iran's 1979 Islamist coup also strengthened ties. Valuing Nimeiri's hostility towards Libya, and regarding Islam as a useful proxy against world communism, the Reagan administration markedly increased economic, military and humanitarian aid. Within Sudan, however, Nimeiri's pro-US policy was unpopular, as America was seen by many Sudanese as complicit in prolonging a repressive regime. Nimeiri's domestic position therefore deteriorated as US support for him surged.

In the 1980s, the external orientation and international dependence of the Sudanese regime became more pronounced as Nimeiri's domestic legitimacy eroded. One target of popular protest was Operation Moses, the US-assisted airlift of Ethiopian Jews or Falashas to Israel via Sudan in 1984, which took place with Nimeiri's approval. Khartoum was becoming progressively delinked from domestic accountability: it was insulated from without by international patronage, and from within by the gradual privatization of government welfare provision. The role of international agencies in this process was influential. During the 1970s, Sudan's National Commission for Refugees worked through the Sudan Council of Churches, as well as refugee organizations. But following a conference on refugees in Khartoum in 1980, the privatization of relief started, initially with refugee programmes in eastern Sudan. The state relinquished control as donors channelled increasing assistance to refugees through UNHCR and international NGOs. In southern Sudan, during the 1970s, well-resourced international NGOs that provided welfare services and undertook development projects became a functioning substitute for the under-resourced regional government in Juba. In so doing they undermined its legitimacy. The upshot was the consolidation – mirrored in Sudan as a whole – of welfare privatization and externalized government accountability.

The outbreak and spread of renewed civil war in southern Sudan interrupted oil exploration and other development projects, halting foreign investment. The SPLA targeted prominent international projects in 1984. Three expatriate oil workers were killed in an attack on Chevron's Rubkona base near Bentiu on 3 February. France's Total suspended its oil operations after the SPLA attacked the Sobat camp of the French company digging the Jonglei Canal on 10 February. Following the time-honoured European example in Sudan, the company quickly evacuated its staff by river steamer to Malakal and, after carrying out 166 miles of work, the giant Jonglei digger was abandoned to rest and rust.

International Responses to Famine

The first major international response to famine was the Western Relief Operation in 1984–85. Drought and famine in western Sudan set in after 1983. The government in Khartoum was slow to respond amidst a cover-up and denial campaign by President Nimeiri, who was concerned not to jeopardize his image and further investment in the breadbasket strategy. Darfur had not previously experienced a major food aid programme. Responsibility for relief work in this area, according to the geographical division of Sudan agreed by major donors and agencies, fell to the US, with food distribution carried out mainly by Save the Children Fund (UK). As part of its leading role in the famine relief response, USAID sent two consignments of sorghum, which became known as 'Reagan durra'. The words of a song by displaced Darfuris symbolize how the US president and not the Sudanese state came to their rescue: 'If Reagan had not come we would have died of hunger.' Under strong pressure, Nimeiri finally admitted the famine a year after drought became evident, but, according to Alex de Waal, his delayed response caused an 'entirely preventable tragedy [that] cost an estimated 250,000 lives'.

Humanitarian relief to war-affected southern Sudan became a more pressing issue after the popular overthrow of Nimeiri on 6 April 1985, and as the civil war spread and intensified under Sadiq al-Mahdi's new government, elected in 1986. Attempts were made to refocus attention from western to southern Sudan at this time. Operation Rainbow, a publicity stunt seeking to use global media attention to highlight the denial of relief to southern Sudan, failed to galvanize international pressure for humanitarian access. Donors argued that Sudan's sovereignty precluded such operations. The Sudanese regime asserted its authority by expelling the UN special representative in late 1986 and disrupting attempts to secure greater access for aid organizations to southern Sudan. The SPLA also opposed international relief to government territory, including Juba, its main garrison town. In 1985 it formed the Southern Relief and Rehabilitation Association (SRRA) with the aim of making it the SPLA's humanitarian wing; this also served as a mechanism to support the armed struggle.

The next, more severe, famine occurred in Bahr al-Ghazal in 1988. Khartoum's counter-insurgency strategy against the SPLA depended upon arming and mobilizing proxy militias and depopulating rebel-held areas. At this point international relief was mostly flowing to Khartoum, to government garrison towns in southern Sudan, and to refugee camps in Ethiopia, with the inadvertent effect of assisting the Sudan government's efforts to depopulate parts of the south. In 1988, relief to SPLA-held areas remained a sensitive subject in UN and donor discussions. This was influenced by fears of possible government retaliation against international development operations in northern Sudan, a prevailing deference towards government priorities, and an unwillingness to question Khartoum's definition of the problem. Moreover, the UN's legal mandate for working with war-affected displaced civilians was confined to a definition of refugees as those crossing international borders. This resulted in the lack of clear responsibility for assisting famine victims and those displaced within Sudan, including large numbers of southerners who had moved to the north in and around Khartoum.

Nevertheless, efforts were made to access the south during the famine. UNICEF made small-scale attempts to facilitate relief to SPLA territory. It opened a Coordinating Office in Nairobi in June 1988 to assist private relief agencies wanting to work in SPLA-held areas, but this closed in October following criticism by the Sudanese government. With certain exceptions, including ICRC operations and relief flights by the Lutheran World Federation starting in 1988, no significant relief was provided to rebel-held areas in southern Sudan until 1989 – after the worst of the 1988 Bahr al-Ghazal famine was over. The defining aspect of international responses in this period was the lack of a concerted donor reaction to famine as a political phenomenon: famine was largely defined as a nutritional crisis, disconnected from its political origins and designs.

The year 1989 saw the creation of two important and very different aid projects that came to exercise influential roles in Sudan. Following a conference in Khartoum in March, Sadiq al-Mahdi's government agreed to establish Operation Lifeline Sudan (OLS), a unique working arrangement for the international humanitarian presence, enabling its expansion and deepening role. After 1989 the number of international agencies and expatriate staff grew significantly, vast resources were directed into humanitarian relief, and there was greater access to remote villages throughout Sudan via air relief operations. Thanks to its airfields, wartime rural southern Sudan had more contact with the outside world than at any period in its history.

Operation Lifeline Sudan

OLS was a tripartite agreement between the Government of Sudan (GoS), the SPLA and the UN in 1989 to allow humanitarian relief to be delivered to both government and rebel-held territory. Premised on the right to humanitarian assistance by civilians in need, OLS was the world's first humanitarian pro-gramme to assist civilians on both sides of an ongoing war within a sovereign state. OLS aimed to avert an anticipated famine through nutritional interventions (grain distribution and feeding centres). It was produced by a conjunction of circumstances: flooding in Khartoum in August 1988 that led to media coverage of the autumn famine in that year, moves by the GoS and SPLA towards peace, and political developments outside Sudan, including a new US administration. OLS was organized into a Khartoum-based Northern Sector led at first by the United Nations Development Programme (UNDP), and a Nairobi-based Southern Sector coordinated by UNICEF, with the help of a new logistical base in Lokichoggio, northern Kenya. The UN provided coordination and support to an NGO consortium on the basis of agreed principles, including the neutrality of humanitarian relief. Some NGOs (including Norwegian People's Aid, otherwise known as the NPLA, the Norwegian People's Liberation Aid) preferred to retain their ideological and operational independence, and did not sign up for UN coordination.

OLS began as a time-bound 'crash relief programme' but grew on an *ad hoc* basis. It slowly institutionalized and lasted until the UN transition following the signing of the CPA. The 1989 NIF coup disrupted the agreement, but it was eventually renewed. Because OLS gave control over relief flight locations to the GoS through a system of negotiated access, there were regular flight bans. Certain areas – Abyei, the Nuba Mountains or the Funj region – were excluded from assistance, despite being badly affected by the war. One broad impact of OLS was the shift away from using starvation as a military tactic towards increased efforts to manipulate external assistance for strategic gains. OLS was providing assets into a war zone and the diversion of aid was a constant risk for humanitarians and opportunity for combatants. Having to rely to a great extent on pre-existing formal or informal power structures, humanitarian agencies unsurprisingly found their operations incorporated into the strategies of armed groups. Following its break from the SPLA mainstream, the Nasir faction, for example, while using a language of human rights and democracy in an effort to present a respectable face to external audiences, was accused of appropriating aid intended for civilians for its own military purposes.

The northern and southern sectors of OLS worked under different operating circumstances and developed different cultures, producing a north–south divide within the consortium. OLS–Northern Sector operated according to government priorities, including programmes for the new, internationally-ascribed category of 'internally displaced' southerners in camps around Khartoum; other operations were premised on and supported Khartoum's 'development' objectives. OLS–Southern Sector, by contrast, developed a distinctive system of working with the SPLM/A. A catalyzing factor behind this was the callous execution of three aid workers and a journalist in September 1992, which spurred efforts to regulate the terms of relations between OLS and its rebel counterparts. This was codified after 1994 into a Ground Rules agreement attempting to provide a more secure, clearly defined basis for humanitarian aid. OLS similarly worked with the other main southern rebel factions and their own humanitarian relief wings after the 1991 SPLA split. It was also active in disseminating humanitarian principles and human rights in southern Sudan through a series of workshops.

The politics of Sudan's sovereignty dogged humanitarian operations for the duration of OLS. When negotiated, OLS was widely thought to be heralding a 'post-sovereign' age as part of a widespread questioning of state sovereignty and arguments that it could not protect violators of human rights. Sovereignty was no abstraction, but a practice routinely used as Khartoum's card to trump international relief by invoking a sovereign right to declare 'no go' areas to aid. As international humanitarianism grew, so did a central state bureaucracy, replicated at lower levels, that was dedicated to controlling and managing it. OLS–Southern Sector was a symbol of Sudan's fractured sovereignty and de facto partition. Khartoum regularly accused the UN and NGOs of violating Sudan's sovereignty. From the other side, however, the UN was accused of not violating this sovereignty enough; rebel groups and particularly the SPLA, which enjoyed quasi-sovereign relations with the UN, criticized the agency's respect for the sovereignty of a GoS-governed Sudan and lack of greater military intervention.

The OLS period as a whole saw the evolution of international relief responses and a more multifaceted operation, from emergency assistance and service delivery, to institutional development of its humanitarian counterparts and southern Sudanese civil society. In its later stages it also promoted interest in development-oriented activities and civilian protection, and verified and monitored ceasefires or preparations for peace. The evolution in the profile of international humanitarian personnel during the OLS period was a reflection of wider changes in the global aid industry, notably the expansion of humanitarianism as a professional career and the growing numbers of young, often unattached, university educated aid workers able to work in conflict zones. Having been the norm under the SPS, it became rare for careers be devoted just to Sudan, though many aid workers found themselves returning to the country after rotations in other crisis zones. Central to the Sudan operations of international humanitarian agencies were also employees from Kenya, Ethiopia and other African countries.

OLS undoubtedly saved many lives and saw a vast, if unquantifiable, financial, logistical and human effort. Questions about impact and the accountability of international agencies ran throughout its duration. Controversy was omnipresent: aid fuelling conflict or creating dependency, besides persistent northern accusations of neo-crusading Western charity. The conspicuous distance between the stated intentions of international interveners, and the willingness and capacity to adapt these ideals in practice, was a recurring source of discontent. The idea of humanitarian protection, for instance, was widely held to refer to protecting relief agency assets rather than civilians, and the incongruence between the promotion of human rights by OLS and its inability to make such notions material realities was criticized during workshops disseminating humanitarian principles. At times these also became forums of critique against international agencies and saw supposed beneficiaries measuring the lack of fit between humanitarian or human rights aspirations and the reality of their wartime predicaments.

The world woke up very late to the human devastation of the wars in southern Sudan. Given the nature and duration of these conflicts, the region received very little attention compared with that which Darfur would attract after April 2004. Nonetheless, as outside involvement in Sudan broadened from the 1990s, it was accompanied by a growing global concern with human rights issues. Prominent in these were campaigns about slavery and abduction, including internationally-sponsored slave redemption schemes sponsored by evangelical groups such as Christian Solidarity International. Sudan's oil development was initially upstaged by attention to continuing humanitarian crises. The 1998 Bahr al-Ghazal famine, for example, which eventually produced a huge airdrop operation by the World Food Programme, occurred just as the construction of Sudan's oil infrastructure was launched, and as Chinese and other companies rushed to build the pipeline and Khartoum refinery to send and sell oil overseas.

Another area of human rights advocacy has focused on the wartime operations of oil companies, which increased following the creation of the Greater Nile Petroleum Operating Company (GNPOC) in 1997 by China's National Petroleum Corporation (CNPC), Malaysia's Petronas, and the Canadian company Talisman. There was a correlation between forced civilian displacement, fighting, and the expansion of oil field activity. Oil infrastructure, like airstrips or all-weather roads, also served military purposes. The GoS terrorized civilian populations in the oil regions through proxy militias, Antonov bombers, helicopter gunships and arms imported from outside. The surge in revenue from oil exports after 1999 saw an increase in military spending and the development of a military–industrial arms manufacturing complex in northern Sudan, built with the assistance of foreign experts, including many from China.

Campaigning on oil gathered momentum in the late 1990s as human rights, religious and anti-slavery NGOs drew attention to the links between oil development and war. High-profile divestment campaigns were directed towards Western oil companies, notably Talisman, which tried fighting a public relations war of its own. Its CEO claimed that the company was good for Sudan, but it eventually retreated. The unintended result, however, was to open up Sudan to the overseas branch of India's national Oil and Natural Gas Corporation, ONGC Videsh, whose employees ceremonially raised the Indian flag in the GNPOC camp in Heglig on 18 May 2003. Like its Chinese and Malaysian counterparts, ONGC has proved to be largely impervious to divestment advocacy.

Khartoum looks East

Following Chevron's exit in 1992, Sudan's oil sector became dominated by Chinese, Malaysian and later Indian national oil companies. The Chinese oil engagement was particularly significant for the NIF. Strategic necessity and international political isolation compelled President Omar al-Bashir to request Chinese assistance with oil development in 1995. Relations were based on pragmatic necessity but became mutually beneficial for the both parties. China proved a willing alternative partner for Khartoum, and Sudan became a notable overseas success for China's fledgling oil sector. CNPC and other Chinese companies made a substantial contribution towards building Sudan's oil export industry amidst war. Khartoum appreciated Beijing's policy of non-interference in Sudan's internal affairs. However, just as the principle of neutrality upheld by international humanitarian agencies was easier to express in words than put into effect, so too China's claims not to be involved in Sudan's internal affairs was hard to accept in reality, especially for southern Sudanese during the war.

Acting as the regime's main international patron, Beijing provided multi-stranded economic, military, and political support to Khartoum. China sponsored and helped implement a range of energy and transport infrastructure projects in northern Sudan, and the oil boom, which Chinese companies helped to produce, was conducive to Chinese business expansion. If international aid and development organizations emphasized the importance of process, or doing no harm, and did not always deliver lasting outcomes, then the Chinese approach emphasized practical results and was not overly concerned with the human impact of how they were achieved. In some cases, projects that China has helped to fund and construct were schemes first mooted in the Condominium, such as the Meroe dam, at the Fourth Cataract of the Nile River. Khartoum is now reviving the rhetoric of Sudan as an agricultural breadbasket and looking to work with China, India and South Korea, as well as a number of other investors from the Middle East, to ensure agriculture can replace oil as Sudan's economic future.

By the time the CPA was signed in January 2005, the international presence in Sudan operated according to a de facto division of labour. With Sudan subject to economic sanctions, commerce was the preserve of a range of Asian and Middle Eastern businesses (with only a minority of exceptions, notably in the oil sector where Total had kept but not developed its old concession). A predominantly Western international presence largely assumed responsibility for aid and development interventions. Western states also paid most of the bill and made important contributions to the multinational UN peacekeeping mission established by the CPA.

During the CPA negotiations, preparing for peace was a popular phrase and a large exercise known as the Joint Assessment Mission (JAM) produced a thick report. Following the CPA, a scramble by a multitude of international agencies and investors followed John Garang's declaration that Juba would again be the capital of a semi-autonomous Southern Sudan. Some of the houses built for international organizations in Juba in the 1970s were reoccupied. New camps sprung up along the Nile bank, a military front-line transformed into a new Riviera complete with upmarket restaurants.

After deploying across Southern Sudan, the United Nations Mission in Sudan (UNMIS) became, as the saying in Juba went, 'UNMISsable'. By July 2010 it had 9,445 troops from 55 countries, and 665 police officers from 40 different countries, and a budget of US$938,000,000. UNMIS had a Chapter VII mandate from the Security Council to protect civilians, but what this meant in practice, on the ground, was far from obvious. Following the CPA, the role of the international presence in Southern Sudan's economy became more visible, mostly in the more urban centres, led by Juba. As well as the UN and international development organizations, a host of private investors and entrepreneurs became active, and consulates from the United States, United Kingdom, China, India and a number of African states set up their diplomatic shops ahead of the referendum. Egypt has also shown greater interest in engaging with Southern Sudan, with Cairo apparently doing more than Khartoum to make unity attractive, and organizing conferences by the League of Arab States on development in the south. Meanwhile, in contrast to the impact of the oil-boom on Khartoum, the importance of the 'peace dividend' in Southern Sudan, so widely talked about before the CPA, has been slow to materialize, despite extravagant international pledges.

Darfur and Sudan in the Global Political Imagination

In April 2004, the tenth anniversary of the Rwandan genocide coincided with mounting concern about conflict in western Sudan. The war in Darfur had been delinked from the CPA negotiations in Naivasha, but a massive mobilization of international interest and involvement followed. There was a rapid scaling up of emergency responses and the international presence in Darfur increased significantly. In April 2004, 11 international NGOs, seven UN agencies and the ICRC employed some 37 international staff between them. By May 2005, there were around 79 international NGOs and 13 UN agencies employing some 964 internationals (out of a total of 11,219 humanitarian staff) operating in Darfur. And the African Union mission in Darfur was expanded to become the African Union/United Nations Hybrid Operation in Darfur (UNAMID).

Humanitarian action in Sudan has historically been led by Western charitable organizations. The most recent Darfur crisis was no different, with Middle Eastern and Asian donors reluctant to participate in Western-dominated relief efforts. There was, however, support for Darfur from these quarters, most of it channelled through Khartoum, with Gulf states providing funds; the Saudi Arabian Red Crescent sending food, shelter and medicines; Egyptian and Turkish medical teams setting up field hospitals and clinics in El-Fasher and Nyala, and the Chinese government sending humanitarian assistance.

Darfur elevated Sudan in the global political imagination to an unprecedented level, through the advocacy of Darfur campaign groups, extensive media attention and the role of celebrity Hollywood activists. The 'Genocide Olympics' campaign mounted by US advocacy groups further raised the global profile of China's association with northern Sudan, and of the NCP's association with China; some of these advocacy groups also pursued corporate divestment campaigns targeting corporate exposure to Sudan. Under scrutiny, and widely criticized before the August 2008 Beijing Games, the Chinese government became more engaged and pressured the NCP to accept UN peacekeepers in Darfur. Beijing was motivated – like certain Hollywood actors – by international reputational concerns, as well as by the need to protect its investments in Sudan. UNAMID was established in July 2007 partly as a result, with a peacekeeping mandate amidst ongoing conflict.

The pariah image of the Government of Sudan was reinforced by Darfur. From the early days of the NIF Sudan had been associated with terrorism. Hassan al-Turabi's internationalist Islamist ambitions and the attempted assassination of the Egyptian president in Addis Ababa in June 1995 had brought about a range of international sanctions. The United States and the European Union pursued contrasting policies on Sudan, the former more confrontational and the latter tending more towards constructive engagement. But the public position of the US Government obscured an area where the GoS was cooperating with the United States – sharing intelligence for Washington's post 9/11 counter-terrorism efforts. The NCP sought international political rehabilitation and normalization of relations with the United States; the United States sought intelligence information for its 'war on terror'.

Darfur put Sudan and Africa on the map for a new American generation and, in different ways, for the Chinese. The indictment of President Omar al-Bashir on war crimes and crimes against humanity by the International Criminal Court attracted further international scrutiny. By July 2010 UNAMID had 19,555 military personnel from 36 countries, and 6,432 police from 35 countries and a budget of nearly US$2 billion (US$1,808,127,500) for the year. Many questioned its impact, however, as the conflict in Darfur continued. The international attention that Darfur attracted gave way to the belated realization that sustained, high profile interest in Darfur had resulted in neglect of the north-south peace process and the future of the CPA.

Conclusion

The past of the international presence in Sudan has a clear bearing on the present day. For Sudanese – both those in marginalized rural areas and those at the centre of power – historical memories play an important role in reactions to foreign interventions. These interventions have been characterized by waves of influence in which British, US and more recently Chinese involvement have made their distinctive marks. The streets of Khartoum – laid out on a ground plan that reflects the Union Jack – continues to attest to the formative influence of the British administration in shaping modern Sudan. The bombed ruins of Al Shifa factory symbolize the change in America's position following its former influence and support for Sudan amidst the shifting geopolitics of the Cold War and the Middle East. Khartoum's Chinese-built oil refinery, meanwhile, symbolizes the benefits of new relations with China and the growth of a Chinese business presence in Sudan.

Contemporary international interventions are better resourced than at any point in Sudan's previous history, but the aims and intentions of the international humanitarian and development presence are uncertain and their application inconsistent. The lesson drawn by many from direct experience of international involvement in Sudan's wars of the 1990s has been: address the causes, not just the effects, of violence. In practice this has meant political engagement, but of an uncertain nature.

In the wake of the vote for separation in the 2011 referendum on self-determination for the south, the international presence in Sudan has prepared for the prospect of a separate north and south. This could presage a new era of international involvement, with popular speculation about a Sudan that is separated into new spheres of influence: a north left to China, the Gulf States and Egypt, and the south to Western countries and East Africa. The immense needs and challenges of state-building in the south make the continuation of a significant international role likely. The NCP-state in Khartoum, with investments from the Middle East, China, Malaysia and India, is more established and resistant to political influence.

Recommended Reading

de Waal, Alex. *Famine Crimes: Politics and the Disaster Industry in Africa*. Oxford: James Currey, 1997.

Duffield, Mark. *Global Governance and the New Wars: The Merging of Development and Security*. London: Zed Books, 2001.

Keen, David. *The Benefits of Famine*. 2nd ed. Oxford: James Currey, 2008.

Karadawi, Ahmed. *Refugee Policy in Sudan: 1967-1984*. Oxford: Berghahn Books, 1999.

Karim, Ataul, et al. 'Operation Lifeline Sudan: A Review'. Geneva: UN Department for Humanitarian Affairs, July 1996, http://www.sudanarchive.net/ cgi-bin/sudan'a=d&d=Dl1d2.

Paul Santi and Richard Hill (eds), *The Europeans in the Sudan, 1834-1878*. Oxford: Clarendon Press, 1980.

Kirk-Greene, Anthony. 'The Sudan Political Service: a profile in the sociology of imperialism', *The International Journal of African Historical Studies* 15, 1 (1982): 21-48.

17

The Past & Future of Peace
EDWARD THOMAS

The recent history of Sudan is, in general, one of erratic and coercive attempts at modernization that have become entangled in highly destructive wars. It is also a history of attempts to end conflict, to resolve the national question, and establish a form of government that can satisfy the aspirations of all Sudanese, rather than those of the members of a regionally and ethnically-defined elite that controls the state.

The country currently faces unprecedented political change. Can its historical experience of interrupted political projects, economic schemes and armed conflict offer clues to the future? What did Sudanese political leaders want when they started wars, or wrote constitutions, or took out huge development loans? Did their forgotten manifestos and five-year-plans set out anything that looks like the Sudan of today? Did the strategic embrace of unity by southerners conceal a vision for the future of southern Sudan that goes beyond independence?

Sudan's exposure to international forces has imposed equivocation and ambiguity on political leaders seeking to articulate visions for the country. The SPLM, equivocal between southern separatism and a national idea of a new Sudan, were not the first to adapt their goals to the requirements of foreign allies. Colonial-era urban nationalists had to negotiate between two colonial powers, Egypt and Britain. Egypt was dominated by Britain, a junior partner necessary for the legal propriety of the Condominium, according to the international law of that era. Nationalists and proto-nationalists knew that if they aligned with Egypt, that could bring pressure on the British for political change.

Sudan's first nationalist movement, the White Flag League, suppressed after a mutiny in 1924, was influenced by the anti-colonial struggle in Egypt. Its supporters were mainly drawn from Nuba and southern Sudanese living in northern Sudan. Although the League was clearly experimenting with national ideas, its formal aim was union with Egypt. Tactical use of Egyptian-inspired political objectives was a characteristic of radical nationalism over the next three decades. Challenges to British power were articulated as support for union with Egypt, but this idea had no real support – union was rejected unanimously by Sudan's first parliament.

Another problem for Sudanese politicians seeking to articulate visions for the future of their country is the disjunction between the experiences of educated elites and ordinary people. Many Sudanese leaders rejected the White Flag

League's attempt to deploy the dislocated peoples of the periphery in order to articulate a Sudanese identity. A newspaper editorial of the day (quoted by Fatima Babiker Mahmoud in *The Sudanese Bourgeoisie*) dismissed them as 'the scum of society' who 'disturbed people of status, merchants, businessmen and men of good origin'. Instead, the elites sought inspiration for Sudanese nationalism in the cities of Egypt and the Arabian peninsula, which were unintelligible places to many Sudanese.

'People of status' were benefiting from the small but powerful export economy that the British set up to finance their administration, based overwhelmingly on cotton. The British concentrated investment in the irrigable areas of the Nile valley, creating sharp regional imbalances and entrenching the distinction between the centre and the periphery. The first Sudanese cabinet was dominated by the beneficiaries of this British development policy, and it ruled out any redistribution of wealth and power. Government intervention was restricted to land grants for a few wealthy clients of the elite. Sudan's rulers preferred the inherited order, even though it exposed them to the uncertainties of the world economy. Just as the nationalists were taking over, the Korean war ended, bringing an end to the considerable profits for Sudanese cotton on which Sudan depended for its foreign currency. The price shift generated by competition from East Asia set the scene for the fall of the first parliamentary regime a few years after independence.

The dictatorship that took over fell in 1964, and the second parliamentary regime that followed it saw the emergence of political movements in the periphery – such as the Darfur Development Front – which regarded modernization and development as a way to mitigate the economic marginalization of the region. It was also the heyday of Sudan's Communist Party. Since 1948 the Communist party had established its bases among workers in railways and factories – bringing a familiar Marxist vision and strategy for future transformation, one that had wide influence on Sudanese political life. In the 1960s, some party members briefly experimented with Maoism – a revolutionary strategy starting in the countryside rather than the town. All these movements sought to shift the country's centre of economic gravity to the periphery.

Modernization and development were international fashions, and they were adopted in Sudan after another coup. In 1969, the military regime of Jaafar Nimeiri took over with the support of the Communist Party. Nimeiri's government hoped that development could rework the contradictions inherited from the colonial era. It was a time of optimism and the government attracted foreign capital to a network of agricultural schemes which it proposed would make Sudan a breadbasket of the world. But the late 1970s combinations of energy price rises and stagnation hit Sudan hard. The country borrowed more to keep its mismanaged development plans afloat just as world interest rates soared, leaving it with a legacy of debts that still exposes it to the force of financial markets today

War in the South

Self-determination has been the political objective of many southerners since it was first mooted by southern political leaders in 1954. Their experience as subjects of a state has been, in historical terms, brief, and usually coercive. Most southern Sudanese societies existed outside any state until the nineteenth century. And resistance to colonial rule continued until the 1930s, well after the conquest of Sudan by the British. The Mahdi had mobilized people in many areas of northern and western Sudan against the Turco-Egyptian regime. But the Mahdist state did not resolve the unequal relationship between the centre and the periphery, and nor did the Anglo-Egyptian colonial regime that followed. As the colonial period drew to its end in 1955, the conflict between southern Sudan and the Khartoum government began. In the 1960s this developed into a fully-fledged bush war.

The Addis Ababa Agreement of 1972 gave southern Sudan a considerable degree of regional autonomy, but not self-determination. It established a regional government run by southerners, and the arrangement was incorporated into the 1973 Permanent Constitution. But the ten-year peace came to an end in 1983 after President Jaafar Nimeiri abolished the Southern Regional government. The SPLA was formed the same year. Khartoum's repudiation of the peace deal was part of a reshuffling of domestic alliances in response to a global economic crisis. One of the beneficiaries was the modern Islamist movement.

In the late 1970s, the Islamists invested in urban commerce, anticipating the shift away from national development to globalized trade before anyone else in Sudan. Good fortune attended them: the Islamists were able to attract funds from Arabian oil-exporting states, which had benefited from enormous oil price inflation; they extended private credit to potential supporters working in trade and services at the centre of Sudan, building a constituency for a radical change. Islamists sometimes organized in peripheral areas, but aimed for transformation, beginning in the capital. After Nimeiri was deposed in 1985, and after a short parliamentary interlude, Islamists took control of the country. Some argue that the timing of their coup was set to forestall peace between the southern rebels and the parliamentary regime that succeeded Nimeiri. Once in power, the Islamists set out to reshape northern culture around their own version of Islam, and in 1992, in response to continued insurgency by the SPLA, they declared *jihad* on the south, a term they interpreted as meaning religious war.

The Second Civil War

The right of peoples to self-determination has been recognized in international law since the 1960s. But for thirty years, African states refused to acknowledge the claims of minority populations within colonially-defined states to enjoy this right. During the Cold War, African states collectively rejected any change to colonial borders. This posed an obstacle to southern Sudanese calls for independence from the north. But in 1994, a regional group of countries, now known as the Inter-Governmental Authority on Development (IGAD) acknowledged the right of self-determination of the peoples of Sudan. IGAD's Declaration of Principles was a remarkable and concise statement of the Sudanese political problem from an African standpoint. Sudan's diversity must be affirmed, it said, through a restructuring of the state around the principles of secularism, democracy and fair sharing of national wealth. If that were not possible, Sudan's constituent peoples would have the 'the option to determine their future including independence through a referendum'.

IGAD's diagnosis and prescription for Sudan's problems echoed those of the SPLM, the political wing of the SPLA, and isolated the Islamist leadership in Khartoum. Islamists claimed that the secularism of the Declaration of Principles was a stumbling block, and broke off the negotiations with a statement that declared that their government's mission was to Islamize the whole of Africa. Yet within three years, Khartoum had accepted the right of southern Sudanese to self-determination. This was a slightly different formulation from IGAD's. IGAD had presented self-determination as a right conditional on the failure to create an inclusive state. But the 1997 Khartoum Peace Agreement (KPA) between the government and a number of dissident factions of the SPLM/A presented the people of the south with self-determination as an unconditional right.

The mainstream SPLM/A, like IGAD, called not for independence, but for a new, inclusive Sudanese state, a new Sudan. This was an innovation in Sudanese politics: a southern party with a national vision. But the factions that signed the Khartoum Peace Agreement called explicitly for Southern self-determination, for a potentially separate south. Although the agreement was denounced by the mainstream SPLM/A it set important precedents for the southern movements. First, it recognized *sharia* law as the basis for Sudan's political order. Second, it gave one group of Sudanese citizens – the mainly non-Muslim southern population – the right to opt out of that political order. The formulation proved durable, and also palatable to the United States, which played an increasingly dominant role in the peace process after 2001. The US accepted the NCP's claim to represent and articulate a unified Muslim identity on behalf of the peoples of northern Sudan. The south, seen as non-Muslim, had a right to secede from this *sharia*-inspired political order, (though the US position did not initially favour self-determination leading to independence), but the political order itself was not in question. This was to have long-term implications for the prospect of secular politics in northern Sudan.

US involvement came shortly after the split in the ranks of the NCP, which led to the defection of its chief ideologue, Hassan al-Turabi. The ruling party perpetuated its hold on power by exploring, with US support, an audaciously pragmatic deal with its enemy – the SPLM – in the process that culminated in the CPA.

The agreement marked not just the end of the war, but the culmination of decades of friction between central governments and political forces in southern Sudan and the borderlands. On paper – and to some extent in reality – the CPA radically restructured the institutions of government. It created an autonomous Government of Southern Sudan and provided mechanisms that offered previously marginalized areas of central Sudan a say in determining their future. The Interim Period provided for in the CPA explicitly enjoined the parties to make the continued unity of Sudan attractive. And, it gave one group of Sudanese – the people of Southern Sudan – a vote on the issue in the form of a referendum on self-determination.

The CPA offered a new system of sharing wealth and power between north and south; and it promised a new political dispensation in the whole country. But it followed the Khartoum Peace agreement rather than the original IGAD declaration in tacitly accepting the cultural dominance of Islam in northern Sudanese politics. In signing the CPA, the SPLM and IGAD accepted the NCP's vision of the state. The price paid for southern self-determination, it turned out, was the effective abandonment of the SPLM's earlier vision of a new, secular

Sudan. Faced with this choice, the SPLM began to move away from its allies in the north, secular parties that rejected the use of Islam as an organizing principle of politics.

The CPA was an elite agreement between two parties who, at that point, had no clear elected mandate. It was bilateral, rather than comprehensive. It forced northern opponents of the NCP to seek their own agreements with the Khartoum government. Between 2005 and 2006 the NCP-led government signed the Cairo Agreement with political parties from the parliamentary regimes of the past and the Eastern Sudan Peace Agreement (ESPA) with SPLM allies in the east of the country, drawn mostly from pastoralist groups in the area. In Darfur, where the signing of the CPA had been one of the factors in the rebellion, the Khartoum government signed the Darfur Peace Agreement (DPA), but with only one of the rebel factions.

The mutinies in the northern peripheries – in the east and in Darfur - had not existed before the Islamists took power. These regions had little investment and little representation in the central state. They were managed through patronage systems organized by Sudan's traditional parties, the Umma party and the DUP, which were linked to Islamic sects established throughout the north. But the security apparatus of the new government undermined the role of the traditional parties and fragmented tribal leadership. This strategy allowed the NCP to assert control of the periphery, but it divided societies in many parts of rural Sudan.

The peace agreements for eastern Sudan and Darfur use the language and structures of the CPA – central government posts, regional investment, regional political structures. But there were two important differences: first, the CPA allowed the SPLA to keep its own army. And second, the CPA had a single short clause on the question of national reconciliation, and set up no institutional framework for reconciliation. The Darfur Peace Agreement, in contrast, required the incorporation of rebel armies into national commands, and refers to reconciliation throughout the text, setting up councils and programmes to achieve it. (Signed by only one significant rebel group, the DPA may have contributed to deepening the divisions amongst Darfur's rebels.)

On paper, these peace deals offer insights into Sudan's future: a peace based on unified military command and reconciliation in the north, and a peace based on a balance of forces between the north and the south. But that vision is far from realization. One of the main reasons is limited progress on security structures. Sudan is still a country of militias, in north and south. Militias in the remote peripheries can pressure Khartoum with small insurgencies, and if they survive the counter-insurgency that follows, they can make peace agreements where they exchange their weapons for government posts and regional invest-ment. These agreements are not necessarily implemented in practice, but can help to maintain an exhausting temporary peace. This is the story of many of the myriad former rebel factions in Darfur.

The elections of 2010 were supposed to help address the fragmentation of the country. Neither the SPLM nor the NCP had ever faced a competitive electoral test, and electoral politics might have allowed regional or other constituencies to articulate their interests. Voter turnout in the elections was high, but hopes of increased representativeness were disappointed. The SPLM and other major parties boycotted the polls in the north, leaving small parties to stand up to the enormous and wealthy NCP electoral machine. The NCP factionalized these small parties, and in most constituencies opposition parties only won if there was no

NCP candidate standing against them. With only two real choices, the election delivered overwhelming victories for the ruling NCP in the north and for the SPLM in the south, revealing little of the real political interests of ordinary voters. If those divisions are to be overcome, both parties will need to develop mechanisms to mediate them, or insurgencies may continue. Sudan's latest interim constitution was an ambitious one, and achieved some of its many objectives: a ceasefire, a government in the south, and an election. But it does not seem to have made good its central goal, which was to make the unity of Sudan attractive, and to limit the possibility of fragmentation.

Articulating the Future

There are many reasons why the CPA's interim period has failed to convince southern Sudanese of the benefits of a unified Sudan. One reason for this is that many – perhaps most – in the SPLM were aiming all along at a different target. But for strategic reasons did not publicly articulate the future that they really wanted. In his account of the war, *The Politics of Liberation in South Sudan*, Peter Adwok Nyaba, a former SPLA commander, described southern reserve thus:

> There is a marked tendency on the part of the south Sudanese political elite to shy away from clearly naming what they and the people wanted. There is always a tendency to hide behind a facade suggestive of some degree of lack [of] self-confidence in the cause being undertaken. More attention was paid to what others will say about us than what we want ourselves.

Many southern leaders, dismayed by Nimeiri's abrogation of the Addis peace deal, wanted independence for the Southern region, but the movement was not well-placed to call for secession. At the time, it was militarily dependent on Ethiopia, a Marxist state that could not encourage secession in Sudan while rejecting similar aspirations at home. During the first civil war, secessionist diplomacy failed to move the Organization of African Unity (the regional inter-governmental body of that era) from its stand against any change to colonial borders. These lessons from the past were one of the factors that led the SPLM leadership to reframe the problem of the south in a way that might be more palatable to its allies. Instead of taking the south as the starting point for analysis, John Garang presented south, west and east as a periphery with a shared economic experience: reservoirs of labour and sites of primitive accumulation, the process by which self-sufficient societies are deprived of their resources. The elite of the centre, they argued, used their control of the economy, their dominant culture, and the coercive apparatus of the state to subordinate the majority. The SPLM manifesto, and subsequent speeches and publications by John Garang, called for a new, inclusive state, which Garang called the New Sudan.

This analysis did not necessarily represent the views of others in the SPLM/A, as Garang sometimes implicitly acknowledged. Many southerners were fighting for an independent south, but they went along with a movement that aimed publicly for liberation of all Sudan. The idea of a new Sudan, and the analysis of the Sudanese political economy that went with it, has been influential. Within a decade, a similar set of ideas became a kind of orthodoxy for IGAD; and its influence is clear in the Interim Constitution. But John Garang's vision of a 'New Sudan' failed to convince most southerners, including most of today's leadership of the SPLM. Still, they had to equivocate because they needed the CPA, and its international sponsors, in order to reach their goal.

A Return to the Past

In 1989, when Sudan's Islamists took control of the state, they planned to change the country from the centre. Ironically, one of their techniques was to reorganize rural Sudan around the political systems of the past, the system of indirect rule through local leaders that the British called native administration. Both the NCP and the SPLM appear to believe that this is the way forward for administration of rural Sudan. The NCP adopted a law in 1993 that helped to reinstitute Native Administration, whose powers had been weakened since the 1960s. The state gave itself new powers in the selection of tribal leaders, aiming to destroy links between tribal leaders and sectarian parties, and used some tribes as recruiting grounds for militias, to reduce the financial burden of running a war in the south. The Islamists returned to the British system of managing the periphery without investment and using ethnicity to isolate the periphery from national political movements. Local militias were deployed as proxy counter-insurgency forces, funded from the spoils of war. The regime's Salvation Pro-gramme (1992-2002) had envisaged a Sudan that was self-reliant and financially stable. It was the local populations at the margins that paid the cost. With the support of international financial institutions, the regime transferred the cost of the previous decade's financial failure to the periphery, simultaneously making them responsible for funding social services and cutting their budgets. Almost a decade after the programme ended, Sudan's health and education expenditures are still the lowest in the region.

During the first outbreak of conflict in Darfur, the government used tribal con-flict to depopulate agrarian Darfur, arming landless pastoralist tribes against farmers. When the depopulation was more or less complete, the landless tribes then fought each other for the spoils, creating further social divisions in the region. It suits the government to present these rural political formations as primordial, while constantly reworking them for the shifting aims of its military strategy. And in the DPA, the government sees this system as a means to resolve the problems of the future in Darfur, providing the troubled region with a system of transitional justice and war compensations for the 2003-2005 war that led to the ethnic cleansing of millions of its people. Few Darfurian political leaders advocate an independent Darfur – and this makes the search for reconciliation within Darfur, and between Darfur and the centre an urgent one. The Native Administration often gets tasked to deliver reconciliation, because its customary law is based on mediation rather than punishment. It is not, however, a system that can deal easily with mass killings and state violations of human rights.

Tribal authorities also appear to be a part of the future of South Sudan. The Interim Constitution of Southern Sudan gives a key role to traditional authorities (the term more commonly used in the south for Native Administration) in the shaping of the Southern state system. The customary laws of these authorities are one of the constitutionally-recognized sources of law.

Southern traditional authorities did not serve as a link between local const-ituencies and sects or political movements at the centre, as their counterparts did in the north. They mediated between local people and armed forces, trading taxes, supplies and manpower for protection. The lineage system of southern tribes survived the many displacements of the war, providing connections between rural areas, cities and a foreign diaspora. These human connections meant that traditional leadership emerged after the civil war with more legitimacy than most other southern political institutions. For some involved in drafting the Southern constitution, this – perhaps idealized – memory of a form of leadership based on consensus and self-sacrifice offered a template for a future political order preferable to the authoritarian system developing in Juba and southern towns after the establishment of GoSS.

The experience of Darfur shows the enormous risks that can arise when tribes are used as the basis of rural order. In Darfur tribal conflict fed on decades of impoverishing economic policy and conflict over land. And in 2009, ethnic conflicts in Southern Sudan gave rise to more fatalities than in Darfur. The conflicts in the south are linked to land and livestock, but also to the lack of investment in rural areas. Southern Sudan's parliamentary system gives politicians few resources to address the problems of rural areas, but leads them to involve themselves in local conflicts for electoral purposes, and this aggravates tendencies towards intercommunal strife. Meanwhile the practice of putting traditional authorities on state payrolls is liable to lead to the gradual abandonment of self-sacrifice and consensus and their replacement by more tangible rewards.

In supporting Native Administration or traditional authority, both the NCP and the SPLM have chosen a system that organizes the people of rural Sudan around ethnicity. This may keep costs down, but it has many implications for rural peace.

The Role of Youth

The future of Sudan, whatever the future holds, will be shaped by new generations. As in other African countries, young people are a majority. According to the 2008 census over 40 per cent of Sudanese are under 15, and over 60 per cent under 25. In the peripheral areas of the country the proportion is even greater: in some states, such as Gedaref, Warrap and South Darfur, almost half the population is under fifteen.

Despite its oil wealth, Sudan spends less than half as much on health and education than most of its neighbours in the region. In 2006, a little less than a third of Sudanese children joined primary school on reaching primary age. Once again, there are huge regional variations. Northern Bahr al-Ghazal state recorded a net intake of just one per cent. In River Nile state it was 70 per cent. In Darfur the conflict may, paradoxically, have increased school intake: the ethnic cleansing campaigns were also, effectively, urbanization campaigns, since they drove huge numbers of Darfur population into displacement camps on the edges of cities where access to schooling became easier. In the south, gender disparities in education are starker than elsewhere. One in eight girls get married before they are 15; a third are married by 18. It is in the area of mother and child welfare that the starkest difference between the periphery and the centre lies, in the statistics for maternal mortality. The figures for mothers dying in childbirth in southern Sudan are among the worst in the world, reaching one in every fifty births. Rates of orphanhood in Jonglei are twice the national average – one fifth of children in Jonglei have lost a parent.

War and poverty have not slowed Sudan's birth rate, which remains about three per cent per annum. The ranks of youth are still swelling. In the boom-towns where wealth is concentrated, the richest youth can tune in to global culture and high-end global consumption patterns. But most youngsters will have a different set of choices – as migrant workers, young soldiers, living on the peripheries of urban areas, seeking their livelihoods and identities in an undefined space between the kinship networks they are born into, the unrealized optimism of peace deals, and the hectic change of Sudan's globally exposed economy. It would be rash not to expect that the youth growing up in these peripheries will find new forms of resistance.

Recommended Reading

Nyaba, Peter Adwok, *Politics of Liberation in South Sudan: An Insider's View*. Kampala: Fountain, 1997 & 2000.

Mahmoud, Fatima Babiker, *The Sudanese Bourgeoisie: Vanguard of Development*. London: C. Hurst and Co., 1984.

World Bank, *Sudan Stabilization and Reconstruction: Country Economic Memorandum*. Washington DC: World Bank, 2003.

18

Epilogue: The Next Sudan

JOK MADUT JOK
& JOHN RYLE

In Sudan one civil war is barely over; another is yet to end. Millions of Sudanese have died as a result of these wars. In half a century of independence from colonial rule the country has seen barely a decade of peace. Despite new wealth from oil, most citizens of Sudan still live in poverty. And the country is now poised to split into two new states, each heir to this heritage of failure.

As the country divides, Sudan stares its history in the face: a seemingly unending story of exploitation and accumulation at the heart of the state and conflict and dispossession elsewhere. Why is it that successive governments have failed the people of Sudan so consistently' What are the prospects for improvement under the new political dispensation made possible by the Comprehensive Peace Agreement (CPA)' Could this have a permanent effect' Can two new states devise complementary notions of Sudanese nationhood that will enable them to coexist' The essays in this book have looked at the realities of past and present-day life in Sudan from many different perspectives. In conclusion, this epilogue examines some of Sudan's possible futures

The South

Following the end of the interim period in July 2011, responsibility for governing the south, albeit with its borders still undetermined, will fall on a newly sovereign government of South Sudan. Since the peace agreement in 2005 and the establishment of a government in Juba there has been only sporadic criticism of the failure of the Government of Southern Sudan (GoSS) to expedite a peace dividend. After many decades of war, the people of Southern Sudan have learned patience. They seem willing to give GoSS the benefit of the doubt, blaming the Government in Khartoum both for the effects of the war and for the deficiencies of the peace – for lack of transparency in wealth-sharing arrangements, and delays in implementation of other aspects of the CPA.

With a sovereign government in South Sudan this is liable to change. The currently muted criticism of maladministration and corruption in the southern government will intensify. A youth leader from a southern advocacy organization put it like this: 'Right now we do not strongly condemn government failure because we have to get our freedom first ... if we succeed, many of our people

186

will quickly turn their criticism away from Khartoum and focus it squarely on Juba.'

The new government in South Sudan and the main government party, the Sudan People's Liberation Movement (SPLM), face a historic choice. One path they can take is to turn away from the authoritarian habits developed during the civil war and embrace the principles of an open society. It is an idea of government that has parallels in the culture of many of the societies of pre-colonial southern Sudan. This would entail a commitment to accountability, respect for free speech and promotion of human rights. The other path would be to adhere to the repressive and autocratic style of politics established by earlier governments in Sudan, allowing predatory administrative practices and short-term pursuit of financial gain to entrench themselves, while social welfare and the conservation of natural resources are neglected, leading to the establishment of another security state on the Nile. Which path is taken will determine the fate of the new nation.

The South also needs to beware the growing involvement of western countries in its political and economic development. The prospect of independence opens the gates to outside investors, mainly in the oil industry. Few countries in Africa have benefited from sudden oil wealth and the sudden, misshapen development it brings in its train. An independent south will need to learn from their mistakes. Southern Sudan is seen, moreover, by some western interests as a buffer zone between sub-Saharan Africa and the Islamic world – even as the front-line in a global conflict between Islam and the west. Yet one of the positive features of Sudanese history is a tradition of religious tolerance. Even at the height of state-sponsored Islamism, with multiple local conflicts between north and south, conflict on religious grounds has been strikingly absent. The coexistence of two world faiths and a multitude of indigenous belief systems in Sudan is a valuable heritage.

The North

After 2011 the north will be another country too. In the new north, the historic challenges to the authority of the central state that have emerged progressively from the periphery will be reconfigured. The country will still include at least three marginalized areas: Nubia, the west and the east. Even without the South this future Sudan will be scarcely less diverse in terms of culture, economic development and ways of life than the greater Sudan of old.

With more than twenty years in power the current government in Khartoum carries a heavy responsibility for the ills of the country, greater than any other institution in Sudan's recent history. The Khartoum government, like the government in Juba, has blamed the burden of fighting civil wars for the many enduring deficiencies in government services – for the grim statistics in the areas of physical security, infant mortality, sexual violence and life expectancy that have put Sudan near the bottom of the global human development index. The end of the war in the South and the advent of oil wealth leave them with no excuse. In 2010 the rule of the NCP gained an endorsement through a national election, but the election was flawed, and followed by renewed constraints on political freedoms. The new shape of the northern polity could be an opportunity to transform the relation between government and governed, but the government in Khartoum has yet to show that it can become accountable to its own people.

The West and the East

The first task of any government in Khartoum is to find a solution to the conflict in Darfur. Most of Sudan's peace processes, and the agreements that resulted from them, have been lengthy, costly and disappointing, undermined by broken ceasefires and the fomentation of division among opposition forces. This was the case in the south before the CPA; it is the case currently in Darfur. The rebel movements in Darfur, unlike those in the south, have not embraced, either explicitly or tacitly, a secessionist agenda, and thus have not threatened the territorial integrity of the country. So a settlement there is possible without the major political reordering made likely by the CPA in the south. At present it is possible that a kind of peace will come in Darfur through the progressive cooption of rebel leaders and the granting of some degree of regional autonomy, as foreshadowed in the original, failed Darfur Peace Agreement. Yet Darfur is not the only part of Sudan where regional insurgencies are present. In Kordofan and eastern Sudan there are long-term discontents that are liable to reignite. Unless the government in Khartoum can address the enduring structural inequalities of all the regions of the new north, such mutinies will not cease.

The North-South Borderlands

Sudan may become two countries, but their fate will remain intertwined for the foreseeable future. Of all the uncertainties in the era following the CPA, the fate of the peoples of the north-south borderlands is the most uncertain. The border is one of the longest in Eastern Africa. Here, local rivalries, intimacies and enmities have been progressively militarized as a result of conflict at the wider, national level. Indigenous patterns of cooperation and conflict have been affected by the politics of Sudan's ruling political-military elites. These border areas have become the testing ground for the peace process.

   In the course of the war, military forces on both sides systematically exploited the competition between border peoples over productive resources such as water and grazing, already sharpened by environmental pressures. As a result of the CPA and, in some places, a lengthy series of parallel local negotiations, an intermittent peace came to prevail in most of the north-south frontier area. But the CPA has ushered in a new phase of clandestine proxy military activity and ongoing manipulation of local political rivalries. And these are now further complicated by electoral politics. In the meantime the mineral wealth in parts of the borderlands is being exploited at a growing rate, to the benefit of the National Government in Khartoum and the Government of Southern Sudan. These authorities have been simultaneously engaged in negotiations on re-demarcation of the north-south borderline. And both have made preparations for a possible return to war.

   Addressing local interests and aspirations on both sides of the frontier – and the extent to which they do or do not reflect the interests of the governing powers – is vital to keeping the wider peace process in Sudan on track. The failure of peace negotiations in Darfur illustrates the difficulty of ending a civil war without taking into account the rival interests of particular communities that inhabit a specific zone of conflict and that share its resources, and understanding the patterns of leadership in those communities. And the case of Abyei has shown, specifically, that detailed elucidation of the history of rival local claims to resources is necessary for there to be a chance of resolving conflicts that may arise.

Along the north-south border there are many other Abyeis. That is to say, other communities in long-standing relationships of cooperation and confrontation, each with a particular sense of their claims over local resources and with a particular, historically-defined relation to the government and other powers in the land. On the northern side, the popular consultations provided for Blue Nile and South Kordofan in the CPA fall short of the right to self-determination as accorded to the people of Southern Sudan. And the prospect of an independent South Sudan has created a feeling of abandonment among inhabitants of these areas, a perception that they have no political or military backup in challenging the Khartoum government on their political future; these are likely flashpoints for future conflict

The peoples of the borderlands are of fundamental importance to the success or failure of the national peace process. They have a particularly acute awareness of the historical failure of the state to represent them, to resolve their disputes with their neighbours or to protect them from wider patterns of violence. Some of them are liable, for this reason, to take matters into their own hands. The western part of these north-south borderlands is also, tellingly, where the emerging polity of South Sudan is most exposed to the open violence in Darfur and the still-building social and political tensions in South Kordofan. Historically, this is where Sudan's two wars converged. And where the peace will be tested.

The Three Towns

The fate of the border peoples is the most immediate issue of the new era in Sudan. A further issue, potentially most difficult of all, is the situation of southerners in the north. Greater Khartoum itself is a kind of border area, with a huge population of displaced southerners, westerners and Nuba from South Kordofan, victims of misgovernment who have fled from war and famine over the past three decades. During this time the labour of these migrants has fuelled the development of the centre. And they have maintained the historic heterogeneity of Khartoum, a city that will be of enduring cultural and economic significance to South Sudan even when it is no longer its national capital.

Khartoum reproduces the social geography of the country, with migrants living in camps and shanty towns on the edge of the city, while the central areas house the institutions of government and the dwelling places of the wealthy and politically privileged. It will continue to do so, to a greater or lesser extent, whatever happens in South Sudan. Upholding the right of southerners, as well as other Sudanese, to work, live, own property and move freely in the north is another political challenge the northern government will face. Its attitude to the great displaced of Khartoum will be a test of its goodwill in adapting to the new political dispensation, where governments and citizens of the Sudans must find a way to live together in peace.

Chronology

From the early states on the Nile to the Condominium (2600 BCE-1898 BCE)

2600-2400 BCE	Emergence of Kingdom of Kush with its capital at Kerma.
1750-1650 BCE	Kingdom of Kush extends its borders northwards up to the First Cataract and raids with impunity deep into Egypt.
1500-1070 BCE	Egyptian Pharaoh Thutmose I vanquishes the Kushite king in a battle at the Third Cataract and occupies Nubia.
850-750 BCE	Kushite King Kashta takes control of southern Egypt; his successor, Piankhi, conquers the whole of Egypt. Piankhi's four successors rule until a resurgent Egypt forces a retreat south.
300-400 CE	The gradual impoverishment of the Roman Empire and the rise of a different trade route outside Kushite control deprives Kush of a vital source of revenue, and weakens the kingdom which eventually collapses.
500-600	Christian missionaries from Byzantine Egypt and Constantinople convert Nobadia, Makuria and Alwa – three successor states to the Kushite Kingdom – to Christianity.
642-652	An Arab army from Egypt, led by Abdullahi bin el-Sarh, invades Nubia in 642 but is defeated. A decade later, Abdullahi, by then Governor of Egypt, again leads an army south against the Christian kingdoms of Nubia, but suffers heavy losses. Hostilities end with the signing of a peace accord, the *Baqt*, guaranteeing the territorial integrity of Nubia.
1504-5	Creation of the Funj Sultanate with its capital at Sennar.
1523	The Sennar monarchy officially converts to Islam.
1620-1640	Foundation of the Fur Sultanate.
1820-1	Muhammad Ali, the Egyptian Viceroy of the Ottoman Sultanate in Istanbul, sends an army to conquer Sudan in the quest for slaves and gold. The last Funj Sultan, Badi IV, surrenders without resistance.
1825	Uthman Bey, the Turco-Egyptian Governor-General of Sudan, founds Khartoum at the confluence of the Blue and White Niles.
1839-1841	Muhammad Ali sends an expedition to find the source of the Nile. On the second attempt, the expedition successfully navigates through the Sudd.

190

1854	Viceroy Said Pasha orders an end to the slave-trade in Sudan. A post at Fashoda, the southern limit of Turco-Egyptian rule, is established to stop the transport of slaves down the White Nile, but with little success.
1869-73	Turco-Egyptian boundaries extend to include new provinces of Equatoria, annexed by Samuel Baker, and Bahr al-Ghazal, formally annexed by the appointment of Zubayr Rahma Mansur as Governor, in recognition of his control over an extensive slave-trading empire in western Bahr al-Ghazal.
1874	Zubayr Rahma Mansur, as Governor of Bahr al-Ghazal, invades Darfur, overthrowing the Fur Sultanate.
1881	Muhammad Ahmad publicly proclaims in Aba Island that he is the Mahdi. Government troops are sent to Aba Island to apprehend him but are repulsed by his followers.
1882	Political and financial instability in Egypt. Britain occupies Egypt to safeguard its imperial interests.
1883	The Mahdi and his followers attack El-Obeid. After a four-month siege, the city's garrison surrenders. The Mahdist revolt continues to spread. An Egyptian expeditionary force of 10,000 soldiers led by Colonel William Hicks, a British officer, is sent to destroy the Mahdi but is massacred at Shaykan, south of El-Obeid.
1884	General Charles Gordon travels to Khartoum to organize the evacuation of Egyptian residents but, contrary to orders, stays to defend the city.
1885	Mahdists capture Khartoum, beheading General Gordon, and conquer Darfur. The Mahdi dies of illness and is succeeded by Khalifa Abdullahi who rules from Omdurman.
1889	Mahdists defeat Ethiopians at Gallabat. Egypt defeats a Mahdist attack.
1889-1890	Successive droughts in northern Sudan lead to poor harvests and widespread famine.
1896	Anglo-Egyptian 'reconquest' of Sudan begins under General Horatio Kitchener, Sirdar of the Egyptian Army.
1898	Mahdists defeated at the battle of Omdurman/Kerreri, but Khalifa escapes to Kordofan. Collapse of the Mahdist state. Darfur regains independence and Fur Sultanate is restored under the rule of Ali Dinar.

Condominium period (1899-1956)

1899	Britain and Egypt sign the Anglo-Egyptian Agreement, restoring Egyptian rule of Sudan but as part of a British-dominated condominium. The new government recognizes Ali Dinar as Sultan of Darfur. An army is dispatched to Kordofan to crush the Khalifa who dies at the battle of Umm Diway-karat.
1902	Gordon Memorial College opens to educate sons of prominent families to meet the government's growing need for educated Sudanese bureaucrats.
1910	Reginald Wingate, Governor-General of Sudan, begins the

withdrawal of northern Sudanese and Egyptian officers and soldiers from southern Sudan, replacing them with a locally-recruited Equatoria Corps.

1916   Britain sends an expedition to overthrow Sultan Ali Dinar and conquer Darfur, which is annexed to Condominium Sudan.

1922   The government promulgates the Powers of Nomad Sheikhs Ordinance, granting greater powers to nomadic tribal Sheikhs and leaders in pursuit of Indirect Rule. In southern Sudan, the Passports and Permits Ordinance restricts the access of northern traders to the south. The government begins to establish chiefs' courts there. Egypt gains formal independence from Britain but remains under British occupation.

1923   Dar Masalit incorporated into Sudan.

1924   Anti-British demonstrations gather strength. The White Flag League, founded a year earlier by Ali Abdel Latif, organizes demonstrations in support of the unity of the Nile Valley; the British repress the '1924 revolt' by force and expel Egyptian officers and officials from Sudan. Increasingly hostile to the *effendiya*, the British rely more heavily on tribal leaders and traditional authorities to govern the country.

1925-6   Sennar Dam on the Blue Nile is completed and the Gezira Cotton Scheme inaugurated.

1927   Promulgation of the Powers of Sheikhs Ordinance bestows the same powers that were earlier granted to nomadic sheikhs and tribal leaders on their sedentary counterparts in a shift towards administration based on ethnic groups rather than territorial units.

1930   Southern Policy, designed to limit the spread of Islam and the Arabic language in the south, is introduced.

1936   Signing of the Anglo-Egyptian Treaty of 1936, which allows for the return of Egyptian forces and personnel to Sudan and helps formalize and secure Britain's strategic interests in the Suez Canal at a time of Italian aggression in north-east Africa.

1938   1,080 graduates of intermediate school gather in Omdurman and establish the Graduates Congress, appointing Ismail al-Azhari as its Secretary-General, to represent and promote the interests of educated Sudanese.

1942   The Ashiqqa faction in the Graduates' Congress send a memorandum to the government containing twelve demands, which includes the right to self-determination for post-war Sudan. The government rejects the memorandum.

1943   The government establishes the Advisory Council for northern Sudan to divert attention from the Graduates' Congress; the Ashiqqa, which by then has gained control of the Graduates' Congress, boycotts the Council. The council is disbanded in 1948.

1945   Supporters of Sayyid Abd al-Rahman al-Mahdi form the Umma Party, under the Sayyid's patronage, which calls for Sudan's complete independence. Sectarian divisions in the Graduates' Congress lead to its disintegration.

1946	Negotiations between Egypt and Britain over the revision of the Anglo-Egyptian Treaty of 1936, break down over Egyptian assertion of sovereignty over Sudan; the Governor-General forms an Administration Conference tasked with recommending how Sudanese could play a more significant role in the administration of the country.
1947	The first report of the Administration Conference recommends the creation of a legislative assembly to represent the whole country, including the south. At the Juba Conference, seventeen southern and three northern representatives agree to send representatives to the legislative assembly of a united Sudan.
1948	Elections for the first Legislative Assembly are held; pro-Egyptian groups boycott it and the Umma Party wins an overwhelming majority of the seats.
1950	The Umma majority force a resolution through the Assembly calling for self-government by the end of 1951.
1951	Anglo-Egyptian relations deteriorate. Egypt abrogates the Anglo-Egyptian treaties of 1899 and 1936 and presents a new constitution for Sudan declaring a unified Egypt and Sudan. The government and all Sudanese parties, except the Ashiqqa, reject outright the new constitution. Britain accelerates constitutional steps to self-government in Sudan.
1952	The Free Officers' coup, led by General Muhammad Neguib, overthrows King Farouq in Egypt and renounces claim to sovereignty over Sudan. Pro-Egyptian Sudanese groups join a united National Unionist Party led by Ismail al-Azhari.
1953	In January, Egypt signs an agreement with all Sudanese parties for self-determination within three years. Britain signs a new Anglo-Egyptian agreement a month later stipulating a three-year transition period to self-determination and a plebiscite to choose between full independence or union with Egypt. The NUP wins a landslide victory in national elections held in November.
1954	Ismail al-Azhari forms a new government in January and Sudan's first Parliament opens in March. Rapid sudanization of government; but only a handful of southerners are appointed to junior administrative posts in the south, all other posts allotted to northern Sudanese with little or no knowledge of southern Sudan.
1955	Al-Azhari and the NUP abandon support for union with Egypt in favour of full independence. Soldiers of the Equatorial Corps mutiny in Torit; eight other mutinies break out across southern Sudan. Al-Azhari's government, urged by Britain, circumvents the self-determination plebiscite and opts for a declaration of independence from Parliament, persuading southern members to vote for independence on the promise that a federal constitution would be considered.
1956	Sudan becomes independent (1 January). Ismail al-Azhari becomes Sudan's first prime minister.

From Independence to the present (1956-2011)

1956	Twenty-one members of the NUP defect and form the People's Democratic Party, forcing al-Azhari to resign. Umma Party leader Abdullah Khalil becomes Prime Minister in an Umma-PDP coalition.
1958	The Umma Party wins the general election but, failing to secure a strong majority, again forms a fractious coalition with the PDP. Of southerners elected, the majority campaign on a pro-federalist platform. Amid growing political confusion and sectarian quarrels, General Ibrahim Abboud leads a coup; he declares a state of emergency and dissolves all political parties and trade unions.
1959	Egypt and Sudan sign the Nile Waters Agreement, which paves the way for Egypt to begin constructing the Aswan dam.
1961	Abboud government announces the resettlement of Nubians to make way for the Aswan Dam, sparking violent demonstrations in Nubia.
1962	Widespread school strikes take place in the south in opposition to Abboud's policy of building national unity through Arabization and Islamization. First southern Sudanese political movement in exile formed, the Sudan African Closed Districts National Union (later the Sudan African National Union). The first civil war begins.
1963	Anyanya emerges as an organized guerrilla force in the south.
1964	The government expels all foreign missionaries working in the south. Demonstrations and riots against Abboud's military government erupt across Khartoum. Abboud overthrown in 'October Revolution'. Sirr al-Khatim al-Khalifa becomes Prime Minister.
1965	The Round Table Conference between government and southerners in Khartoum is held to solve the 'Southern Problem' but fails to reach any agreement on the constitutional status of the south. The Umma party wins Sudan's second election since independence and Muhammed Ahmed Mahjoub becomes Prime Minister of a four-party coalition government. The army carries out massacres in Juba and Wau.
1966-68	A succession of three coalition governments in the space of three years.
1967	Following the Six Day Arab-Israeli war Sudan breaks off diplomatic relations with the US.
1969	Jaafar Nimeiri, leading the socialist-leaning Free Officers, seizes power in a military coup and establishes a Revolutionary Command Council, which has close ties to the Sudanese Communist Party.
1970	The Ansar, led by Imam al-Mahdi, stage a revolt from Aba Island, which is crushed by the army. In the south Joseph Lagu unites the Anyanya under his command and supplants the exiled politicians as leader of the movement, now renamed the Southern Sudanese Liberation Movement, with Israeli and Ugandan support. Nimeiri nationalizes banks and a number of businesses.

1971	Tensions rise between Nimeiri and the SCP, prompting Hashem al-Atta to stage a communist-backed coup; the coup is quashed and its leaders executed. Nimeiri abolishes the multi-party system and makes the Sudan Socialist Union the sole permitted political organization in Sudan. Native Administration is formally abolished with the introduction of the People's Local Government Act.
1972	Addis Ababa Agreement signed, ending the first civil war. The south becomes the semi-autonomous Southern Region, with Juba as its capital. Diplomatic relations with US resume.
1973	New Permanent Constitution enshrined creating executive presidency with sweeping powers, incorporating regional settlement in the south and new local government system. The Islamic Legion, created a year earlier by Libyan leader Muammar Gaddafi, begins operating in Darfur.
1974	French construction company signs contract to begin work on the Jonglei Canal.
1975	Akobo Mutiny and emergence of ex-Anyanya forces opposed to Addis Ababa Agreement. Following an attempted military coup, Nimeiri further centralizes power in his own hands.
1976	Mutiny of ex-Anyanya in Wau. Supporters of Sadiq al-Mahdi, armed and trained in Libya, infiltrate Khartoum aiming to attack Nimeiri at airport; southern troops play significant role in defeating attempted coup.
1977	Nimeiri embarks on 'National Reconciliation', bringing strongest northern opponents, Sadiq al-Mahdi and Hassan al-Turabi, into government.
1978	Former Anyanya leader Joseph Lagu is elected president of the Southern Regional Government.
1979	Chevron confirms the discovery of oil in Upper Nile and southern Kordofan. Work begins on Jonglei Canal. Sudan agrees to IMF loan terms.
1980	Nimeiri dissolves Southern Regional Assembly and calls new elections; Abel Alier wins a second presidential term. Hassan al-Turabi, then Attorney-General, fails to pressure the National Assembly to redraw the North-South border to include southern oil fields in the north. Anyanya II, with bases in Ethiopia, begins guerrilla operations in south. Regional governments introduced throughout northern Sudan.
1981	Nimeiri introduces stringent economic measures on recommendation of IMF. Railway-workers strike in Atbara; riots in Khartoum.
1983	Southern troops in Bor mutiny when ordered to transfer north. Nimeiri abrogates the Addis Ababa Agreement, abolishes Southern Regional government, redividing south into three sub-regions. Sudan People's Liberation Movement/Army is formed in Ethiopia under the leadership of John Garang. Second civil war begins. Nimeiri introduces *sharia* criminal law.
1984	Chevron leaves Bentiu and work on Jonglei Canal ceases, following SPLA attacks. Fighting in Upper Nile and Bahr al-

Ghazal. Nimeiri declares state of emergency. Drought leads to famine in Darfur prompting mass migration east to Khartoum and other urban centres.

1985   Nimeiri executes Mahmoud Mohamed Taha, leader of the Republican Brothers, on the charge of apostasy. Popular demonstrations and general strike. Senior army officers overthrow Nimeiri's government and form Transitional Military Council, led by General Abdel Rahman Siwar al-Dahab, which pledges a return to civilian rule within one year. The SPLA expands the war out of the south with first incursions in southern Blue Nile and the Nuba Mountains. Chevron suspends operations.

1986   Following elections, Sadiq al-Mahdi becomes prime minister of an Umma-DUP coalition, restoring parliamentary government; the SPLM/A and most southern parties boycott the elections.

1987   Displaced Dinka in Ed Daein, in South Darfur, killed by Rizeigat civilians. Army massacres civilians in Wau. Fur-Zaghawa conflict escalates in Darfur. Truce between SPLA and Anyanya II.

1988   Most of Anyanya II incorporated into the SPLA. Famine in Bahr al-Ghazal.

1989   SPLA makes major advances in the south and Nuba Mountains, seizing and holding several towns. Operation Lifeline Sudan begins. Government of Sadiq al-Mahdi agrees to negotiate with the SPLM/A, but negotiations are brought to a halt by a military coup led by Omar al-Bashir who becomes the Chairman of the newly formed Revolutionary Command Council. Northern opposition parties, now in exile, form the National Democratic Alliance. The Popular Defence Force is formally established by decree.

1990   SPLA and NDA agree to work together. United States cuts all aid to Sudan. Twenty-eight army officers accused of planning an anti-NIF coup are executed; Bashir declares a state of emergency and dissolves parliament. Idriss Déby becomes president of Chad in military takeover.

1991   Fall of Mengistu, the SPLA's main supporter, forces the SPLA to evacuate its bases in Ethiopia. SPLA splits after Riek Machar and Lam Akol, based in Nasir, announce the overthrow of Garang and make clandestine contact with Khartoum. SPLA mount an incursion, led by Daud Bolad, into Darfur; Bolad captured and killed.

1992   *Jihad* is declared against Nuba supporters of the SPLM/A at a meeting of regional governors in Southern Kordofan, intensifying the war in the Nuba Mountains. Khartoum mounts a successful offensive in the South retaking several towns. William Nyuon splits from Garang and joins the Nasir faction.

1993   SPLA-United is formed as anti-Garang coalition. After appointing Omar al-Bashir president, the Revolutionary Command Council is disbanded. The Inter-Governmental Authority on Development initiates a peace process.

1994	Fighting among its Nuer supporters splits SPLA-United. Riek Machar forms South Sudan Independence Movement/Army. IGAD brings together rival factions of SPLA who accept the Declaration of Principles and agree on the separation of religion and the state, and self-determination for the south. The SPLM holds its first National Convention in Chukudum. Agreement between SPLA and Umma Party recognizes the south's right of self-determination.
1995	SSIM/A fragments; many commanders rejoin SPLA. Sudanese government is implicated in assassination attempt on Egyptian president Hosni Mubarak in Addis Ababa. Bashir visits Beijing and secures Chinese support for oil development.
1996	Presidential elections, criticized as effectively single-party, are held. Omar al-Bashir is elected for a term of five years. Hassan al-Turabi becomes Speaker of the National Assembly. Sudan's nine regions are divided into twenty-six states. Riek Machar signs a Peace Charter with Khartoum.
1997	The government signs the Khartoum Agreement with Riek Machar and a number of other anti-Garang commanders. The South Sudan Defence Force is formed. New national constitution. Government declares a state of emergency in Darfur. United States imposes a trade embargo on Sudan and freezes government assets.
1998	Fighting between units of the SSDF in the western Upper Nile oil fields. Kerubino Kwanyin Bol rejoins SPLA and attacks Wau but is repulsed; later rejoins pro-government militia of Paulino Matip. Khartoum is implicated in the bombings of the US embassies in Nairobi and Dar es Salaam. United States launches cruise missile attack on the Shifa pharmaceutical plant in Khartoum North, claiming it is making components of chemical weapons.
1999	New Sudan Council of Churches organizes peace meeting between Dinka of Bahr al-Ghazal and Nuer of western Upper Nile at Wunlit, in Warrap State. Pipeline to Port Sudan completed and oil exports begin. Kerubino Kuanyin Bol is killed in internecine strife. Omar al-Bashir declares a state of emergency and dissolves parliament, sidelining Hassan al-Turabi.
2000	Riek Machar resigns from government in Khartoum. *The Black Book*, written by disaffected Darfurians alleging regional discrimination by successive governments, circulates in Khartoum. The NDA launches an offensive against the Khartoum government in the Kassala and Hamesh Koreib areas of eastern Sudan.
2002	Riek Machar rejoins the SPLM. US support renews the IGAD peace process. Warring parties agree to a ceasefire in the Nuba Mountains. GoS and SPLM/A agree the Machakos Protocol, which establishes overall framework for a peace agreement and provides for a referendum on self-determination for the south.
2003	Heavy fighting occurs in oil field areas of western Upper Nile as GoS shifts troops from the Nuba Mountains. Lam Akol

rejoins the SPLA. In Darfur, the war escalates: Sudan Liberation Army and Justice and Equality Movement are formed; rebels attack El-Fasher airport, marking the beginning of current conflict in Darfur; government-sponsored *janjawid* counter-offensive begins.

2004   After a major government offensive, President Omar al-Bashir declares law and order restored in Darfur. UN Coordinator calls Darfur 'the world's worst humanitarian crisis'. The first Darfur ceasefire, agreed in N'Djamena, is immediately broken. African Union military observers arrive in Darfur and large-scale humanitarian intervention begins. In August, Darfur peace talks begin in Abuja. Government forces go on the offensive in Shilluk Kingdom, despite agreement on cessation of hostilities. GoS and SPLM/A reach agreement on peace protocols in Naivasha.

2005   The CPA is signed in Nairobi on 9 January, bringing an end to the second civil war. Garang is sworn in as First Vice-President on 9 July but dies three weeks later in a helicopter crash. His death leads to violent street protests by southerners in Khartoum. The Abyei Boundaries Commission (ABC) submits its report to the presidency, which Khartoum rejects. The Government of National Unity and the Government of Southern Sudan are formed. Civil war in Chad when Sudanese-backed rebels launch attacks in eastern Chad; Chad declares a state of war with Sudan.

2006   The Chadian President Idriss Déby, the Libyan leader Muammar Gaddafi and Sudanese President Omar al-Bashir sign the Tripoli Agreement, briefly ending hostilities between Chad and Sudan. Chad accuses Sudan of backing rebel assault on N'Djamena. Mini Menawi's faction of SLM/A is the only Darfur rebel group to sign the Darfur Peace Agreement with Khartoum; non-signatories to the agreement create the National Redemption Front in Asmara. The Eastern Front, a coalition of rebel groups in the east, signs the Eastern Sudan Peace Agreement with Khartoum.

2007   The International Criminal Court issues arrest warrants for government minister Ahmed Haroun and militia leader Ali Kushayb. Rebels go on the offensive in eastern Darfur and Kordofan and attack the AU base at Haskanita. GoNU and SPLM reach a deadlock in the implementation of the CPA, prompting the SPLM to briefly suspend its participation in GoNU.

2008   UNAMID takes over from AMIS in Darfur. Sudanese-backed rebels attack N'Djamena, Chad. Sudan conducts its fifth national population and housing census. JEM launches an attack on Omdurman. SPLM holds its second National Convention in Juba. SPLA and SAF clash violently in Abyei, much of the town is razed and many of its residents displaced; the Abyei road map is agreed.

2009   The NCP and JEM sign a goodwill agreement and Qatar backs negotiations between the two parties in Doha. ICC issues an arrest warrant for President Bashir. Lam Akol splits from the SPLM to form SPLM-Democratic Change. NCP and SPLM publicly accept the ruling of the arbitration court in The Hague on disputed Abyei region.

2010   A new Darfur coalition, the Liberation and Justice Movement, is formed; JEM signs a peace accord with the government, but it quickly falls apart. Following national elections in April, Omar al-Bashir gains a new term as President of Sudan, winning 68 per cent of votes, and Salva Kiir is elected President of Southern Sudan with 93 per cent.

2011   In referendum on self-determination for southern Sudan 98 per cent of southerners vote for separation from the north.

Key Figures in Sudanese History, Culture & Politics

Abdallahi al-Taisha (1846-1899). The Khalifa. Muhammad Ahmad al-Mahdi's successor (*khalifa*) as leader of the Mahdist movement. Born in Darfur, he was one of Muhammad Ahmad's earliest followers and became the leader of the 'Black Flag' division of the Mahdist army. He ruled Sudan from al-Mahdi's death in 1885 until the Anglo-Egyptian defeat of the Mahdist army at the Battle of Omdurman at Kerreri in 1898. As ruler of the Mahdist state, he consolidated his position by bringing Baggara, especially his Taisha kinsmen, from Darfur to resettle in Omdurman and by awarding the most important offices of state to his relatives. He established a centralized administration but spent most of his thirteen-year reign struggling to suppress insurrections, especially in the west, and to see off challenges to his position as *Khalifa* from members of the Mahdi family. He continued to pursue the Mahdi's *jihad* beyond the borders of Sudan with mixed success: in 1889 he defeated the Abyssinian monarch but his ill-conceived invasion of Egypt was defeated the same year. He fled from Omdurman after the Battle of Omdurman in 1898 and was killed a year later at the battle of Umm Diwaykarat, near the present-day town of Kosti.

Abdel Khaliq Mahgoub (1927-1971). Marxist theorist and Secretary-General of the Sudanese Communist Party until his death. Born in Omdurman, he was introduced to communism while completing his studies at Fouad University in Egypt. After being dismissed from the university for his political activities in 1948, he returned to Sudan and became the Secretary-General of the Sudanese Communist Party. As leader of the SCP he was arrested under Ibrahim Abboud's military regime. A longtime advocate of democracy and broad-based political mobilization, he reluctantly joined the May Revolution that brought Nimeiri as the leader of the communist-affiliated Free Officers group to power in 1969. In 1971, Abdel Khaliq Mahgoub was alleged to have been involved in a failed communist-backed coup against Nimeiri; he was arrested and executed.

Abdel Wahid Mohamed Ahmed al-Nur (b.1968). Lawyer and Chairman of the Sudan Liberation Movement/Army, a Darfur rebel group. Born in 1968 in Zalingei, west Darfur, he founded the SLM while studying law at the University of Khartoum. As the conflict in Darfur escalated in 2001, the SLM created a military wing, the Sudan Liberation Army, with its forces concentrated around

Jebel Marra. Abdel Wahid's SLM/A declined to sign the Darfur Peace Agreement in 2006 and has since remained outside various peace processes. In recent years, the SLA has fractured and many of its more senior figures have either formed their own rebel factions or defected to other rebel groups. Living in exile in Paris, Abdel Wahid's influence has waned, but he is said to remain popular in IDP camps in Darfur and Chad.

Abd al-Rahman Muhammad Ahmad al-Mahdi (1885-1959). A dominant figure in Sudanese politics from the time of the First World War until his death in 1959. The posthumous son of Muhammad Ahmad al-Mahdi, he assumed his father's spiritual mantle, becoming the leader of the Ansar following the death of the Khalifa Abdallahi. The authorities of the Anglo-Egyptian Condominium treated him circumspectly because of his lineage and influence. To allay their suspicions, he denounced neo-Mahdist uprisings and convinced his followers to support Britain against Turkey during the First World War. In return for his support, the government allowed him to regroup his Mahdist followers into a religious order and to develop his family's estate on Aba Island, on the White Nile. In 1945 his supporters founded the Umma Party under his patronage. In the decade leading up to independence in 1956, he was strongly opposed to union with Egypt (as advocated by the Nationalist Unionist Party, the other major political party at that time) and campaigned for the full independence of the Sudan.

Abd al-Rahman Siwar al-Dahab (b.1930). Born in El-Obeid graduated from the Sudanese Military Academy and was Minister of Defence and Commander-in Chief under President Jaafar Nimeiri. He seized power after Nimeiri was ousted by the popular uprisings, the *intifada*, of 1985. He became chairman of the Transitional Military Council, which ruled along with a civilian Council of Ministers, and made a public commitment to restore democracy within twelve months. He duly handed the presidency over to Sadiq al-Mahdi and his elected government in 1986. A year later he became chairman of the Islamic Call organization, *al-Dawa al Islamiyya*. He lives in Qatar.

Abdullah el-Tayeb (1921-2003). Academic from Ed-Damer, known as the 'dean' of Arabic literature in Sudan. A graduate of Gordon Memorial College, he obtained his PhD from the School of Oriental and African Studies, University of London, in 1950 before being appointed as a Professor of Arabic at Khartoum University in 1956. He became the Dean of the Faculty of Arts, and Vice Chancellor of the University. He was also the founding Director of Juba University. In 1990 he became President of the Arabic Language Council at the University of Khartoum. He wrote poetry, plays and literary studies, and produced the first collection of northern folk stories. He is remembered for his colloquial Sudanese Arabic interpretation of the Quran on a radio programme running from 1985 to 1993; for series of radio and television lectures on classical Arabic literature and history; and for his canonical work, *The Guide to the Making and Understanding of Arab Poetry*.

Abel Alier Kwai (b.1933). Southern Sudanese politician, lawyer and judge from Bor. He studied Law in Khartoum and London, and become Sudan's first southern judge. He did not join the first southern rebellion, but was a prominent leader of the Southern Front, the largest southern party at the time. He was elected to the national parliament in 1968 and held various ministerial positions in President Nimeiri's government. As Minister for Southern Affairs he played a key role negotiating the Addis Ababa Peace Agreement in 1972. He was the first Vice-President of Sudan from 1972 to 1981 and President of the Southern High Executive Council between 1972 and 1977 and again from 1980 to 1981. He is the author of *Southern Sudan: Too Many Agreements Dishonoured* (1990). He is a member of the International Court of Justice at The Hague and served as the Chairman of the National Election Commission, the official body responsible for organizing the 2010 elections.

Ahmad Muhammad Haroun (b. 1964). Politician. Born and educated in North Kordofan, he studied Law at the University of Cairo and worked as a judge for a few years before joining the government. In the early 1990s he was involved in the mobilization of the government's Popular Defence Forces in South Kordofan and, later, the forcible relocation of many Nuba to government 'peace camps'. Between 2003 and 2005, he was Minister of State for the Interior, during which time he headed the Darfur security desk. In 2006 he was appointed Minister of State for Humanitarian Affairs in the Government of National Unity and UNAMID liaison. In May 2007 he was indicted by the International Criminal Court for war crimes and crimes against humanity in Darfur. He was appointed governor of South Kordofan state in 2009.

Ahmed Ibrahim Diraige (b.1935). Son of a Fur Paramount Chief and founder of the Darfur Development Front in 1963. He became an Independent Member of Parliament in 1965 and was appointed Minister of Labour and Cooperatives between 1966 and 1967. He was appointed Governor of Darfur by Nimeiri in 1981. During a severe drought in 1983, Diraige warned of impending famine in Darfur while Nimeiri continued to promote Sudan as a future 'breadbasket of the Arab World'. As the 1984-85 famine took hold, he was forced into exile. He later created the Sudan Federal Democratic Alliance and joined the umbrella opposition movement, the National Democratic Alliance. In 2006 he was appointed head of the short-lived National Redemption Front, a coalition of Darfur rebel groups that declined to sign the 2006 Darfur Peace Agreement.

Ali Abd al-Latif (*c*.1892-1948). Born in Wadi Halfa to Nuba and Dinka parents, former slaves. A graduate of Gordon Memorial College who served as an officer in the Egyptian army and fought in the punitive campaigns of the Anglo-Egyptian government in the south. He rose to national prominence as the leader of the White Flag League, promoting a form of Sudanese nationalism that transcended ethnic and class distinctions. He was scorned by Abd al-Rahman al-Mahdi and Ali al-Mirghani, the two most prominent sectarian leaders of that period, as well as many other members of the elite, who viewed him as an upstart. The White Flag League was suppressed by Britain in 1924 and quickly fell apart. Abd al-Latif died many years later in confinement in Cairo. Today, he is widely remembered in Sudan as a hero of the anti-colonial struggle.

Ali al-Mirghani (1878-1968). Political leader, a member of the Mirghani family and the head of the Khatmiyya Sufi order. His family worked with the authorities of the Turkiyya and were strongly opposed to the Mahdi and his movement. He lived in Cairo throughout the Mahdiyya era, and subsequently cooperated in the Anglo-Egyptian 'reconquest' of Sudan. From the 1930s until Independence in 1956, he was the patron of the nominally pro-Egyptian party, the NUP, a position determined more by his longtime rivalry with the Mahdi's son Abd al-Rahman, who supported independence, than by a genuine desire for union with Egypt. He remained influential in the era of civilian government after independence.

Ali Osman Mohamed Taha (b. 1944). Politician and prominent member of Sudan's Islamist movement. The son of a railway worker, Ali Osman Taha joined the Islamist movement while still a student at secondary school. He began his political career in parliament as an outspoken critic of Sadiq al-Mahdi's administration in the latter half of 1980s. He was Turabi's heir to the leadership of the Islamist movement. Appointed Minister of Social Affairs in the NIF government, he oversaw the Islamist project to reorient state and society along Islamist lines in the early 1990s. When the movement split in 1999, he sided with Omar al-Bashir and distanced himself from his former mentor. He negotiated the final terms of the Comprehensive Peace Agreement with John Garang and in January 2005 signed the agreement, as Vice-President of Sudan, on behalf of the Government. Despite rumours that he has been sidelined in the NCP, Taha was reappointed as Second Vice President of Sudan in 2010, a post he has held since 2005.

Babikr Bedri (1861-1954). Educationalist and pioneer of education for women. He was born in Atbara and grew up in Rufaa, in Blue Nile. He joined the Mahdist army and took part in the siege of Khartoum and the later unsuccessful invasion of Egypt. After the defeat of the Mahdists in 1898, he left Omdurman and returned to Rufaa. In 1903 he founded a primary school there and in 1906 he overcame opposition from conservative religious and traditional leaders to found Sudan's first girls' school. He continued to promote education until his death in 1954. His efforts helped paved the way for the first women's university college, al-Ahfad, built in 1966.

Al-Balabil (Ar. the nightingales). Musical trio. Nubian teenage sisters – Hadia, Amal and Hayat – transformed the Khartoum music scene in the 1970s, challenging conservative social attitudes to women's involvement in the performing arts. The group parted company after the three sisters married, but they sang together again in Eritrea in 1997 and at the 2008 Sudanese Festival of Music and Dance in Chicago and Detroit.

Bona Malwal Madut Ring (b. 1935). Politician and journalist. Born in Gogrial County, son of a prominent Twic Dinka chief, Madut Ring, he was the editor of the Southern Front's newspaper, *The Vigilant* (1965-9), until parties were banned and the paper closed after Nimeiri's coup. After the 1972 Addis Ababa Agreement he joined the national Ministry of Information and later became Minister of Information in Khartoum. He was also Minister of Energy and Mining and later Minister of Finance in the Southern Regional government of Abel Alier (dissolved by Nimeiri in 1981). An opponent of the redivision of the south he was detained by Nimeiri (1983-4), then went into exile in the UK. After Nimeiri's overthrow in 1985 he returned to Khartoum as editor of the independent *Sudan*

Times, going into exile again after the 1989 NIF coup and editing the independent monthly *Sudan Democratic Gazette*. He wrote in support of the SPLM/A but broke with Garang over the slave redemption programmes (buying back of southerners abducted by northern militias) in which he was involved. After the CPA in 2005 he was appointed advisor to President al-Bashir. He leads the South Sudan Democratic Forum, one of the southern parties in opposition to the SPLM.

Gadalla Gubara al-Faki (1920-2008). Sudan's first professional film-maker and a pioneer of African cinema. Born in Khartoum and educated at Gordon Memorial College, he was first exposed to film making while serving in the British Army Signal Corps in North Africa during the Second World War. After the war, he was employed by the Anglo-Egyptian government to produce educational documentaries on Sudan's agricultural schemes. He later became the Director of the film section of the Ministry of Information. In 1974 he left government service and established his own film studio, 'Gad Studio', in Khartoum. In 1979 he made the prize-winning *Tajuj*, an epic love story set in eastern Sudan and the first feature film produced in Sudan. In a career spanning over sixty years, he produced a total of 31 documentaries and four feature films.

Ghazi Salah al-Din Attabani (b. 1951). Prominent politician in the ruling National Congress Party. Born in Omdurman, he studied medicine at the University of Khartoum, where he returned to teach after obtaining a PhD in Clinical Biochemistry from the University of Surrey, UK. A long-time member of the Islamist movement, he has held numerous official positions since the Islamist military coup in 1989, including Minister of Culture and Information, Secretary-General of the National Assembly, and leader of the Government of Sudan negotiating team at Machakos. In February 2010 he signed the short-lived preliminary framework agreement in Ndjamena, Chad, with the Justice and Equality Movement, the largest rebel group in Darfur.

Gordon Muortat Mayen (1922-2006). Politician. Born in Karagok village near Rumbek, in 1951 he graduated from Sudan Police College and in 1957 became an Assistant District Commissioner. In 1965 he was appointed leader of the Southern Front delegation at the Round Table Conference between northern and southern Sudan. In the same year he was appointed as Minister of Works and Mineral Resources in the post-Abboud transitional government. In 1967 he left the country and joined the Anyanya guerrilla movement. He was an outspoken critic of the 1972 Addis Ababa agreement and lived in the United Kingdom until the CPA. In 1994 he was appointed an Advisor to John Garang. He represented his Rumbek constituency in the Southern Sudan Legislative Assembly from 2006 until his death in 2008.

Hassan Abdullah al-Turabi (b.1936). Ideological and political architect of the post-independence Islamist movement in Sudan. The son of an Islamic Judge, al-Turabi was born in Kassala in 1932. He joined the Muslim Brotherhood while studying law at the University of Khartoum in the 1950s and obtained his doctorate from the Sorbonne, Paris. He emerged as the leader of Sudan's Islamist movement in the mid 1960s with the creation of the Islamic Charter Front (later renamed the National Islamic Front then the National Congress Party). As

President Nimeiri's reliance on the support of Islamists grew from the late 1970s, al-Turabi was able to increase his influence in government, where he served as Attorney-General and Adviser on Foreign Affairs. From within the government, he laid the groundwork for his party's military coup in 1989. Al-Turabi reached the height of his power in the years following the military coup. However, his decision to back Iraq in the first Gulf War and his support for radical Islamist causes beyond Sudan's borders in the early 1990s, condemned Sudan to a decade of international isolation. In 1999, he attempted to extend his power within the regime, but was preempted by Omar al-Bashir who dissolved parliament and placed al-Turabi under arrest. Al-Turabi's power has been considerably curtailed since the 1999 split. He has founded his own Islamist party, the Popular Congress Party, and on a number of occasions has publicly criticized Omar al-Bashir and the National Congress Party.

Ibrahim Abboud (1900-1983). Sudan's first post-independence military dictator. Born near the town of Suakin on the Red Sea, Ibrahim Abboud graduated in engineering at Gordon Memorial College and then attended Military College in Khartoum. A career soldier, he fought in Eritrea and Ethiopia during the Second World War. He became Commander of the Sudan Defence Force in 1949 and then Commander-in-Chief of the Armed Forces when Sudan gained its independence in 1956. He overthrew the government of Abdullah Khalil in a bloodless military coup in 1958. While he had some limited success in improving the economic situation of the country, his aggressive pursuit of Arabization and Islamization in the south provoked civil unrest, which, by 1963, escalated into civil war. His popularity gradually plummeted and in October 1964 popular riots and demonstrations forced General Abboud to hand over power to a civilian government. He died in Khartoum in 1983.

Ibrahim el-Salahi (b.1930). Artist. Born in Omdurman, he studied art at the School of Design at Gordon Memorial College (now the University of Khartoum). He received a scholarship from the Slade School of Fine Art in London. On returning to Sudan, he taught at the Khartoum School of Fine and Applied Art. Considered a pioneer of modernist Sudanese art, he developed a distinctive style, characterized by abstract forms and the use of lines, and was one of the first artists to incorporate Arabic calligraphy into his work. He has also worked for UNESCO and held posts in various government ministries. He was imprisoned for six months in 1975, accused of conspiring against Nimeiri's government, and on his release he went into exile abroad.

Ismail al-Azhari (1900-1969). A leading figure in Sudan's nationalist movement. He was one of the founders of the Graduates' Congress in 1938. He became the leader of the Congress's younger, more radical members, known as the Ashiqqa, who by 1943 had transformed themselves into a political group calling for the unity of the Nile Valley. He became Sudan's first Prime Minister in 1954 and, in a reversal of his earlier support for union with Egypt, led the country to independence in January 1956. He was forced to resign as Prime Minister when 21 members of his National Union Party defected to form a new party. In 1965, a year after the collapse of General Abboud's military regime, al-Azhari was appointed to the largely symbolic position of President of Sudan, but was overthrown by Nimeiri's coup in 1969. He died later that year.

Jaafar Nimeiri (1930-2009). Politician, born in Omdurman, the son of a postman. After graduating from military college in 1952, Jaafar Nimeiri joined a group of officers committed to socialism and pan-Arabism. As leader of the Free Officers who seized power in a military coup in 1969, Nimeiri ruled Sudan for the next 16 years. He won acclaim in 1972 when he signed the Addis Ababa Agreement, which ended the first civil war and granted semi-autonomy to a new Southern Region. But Nimeiri is also remembered for his increasingly authoritarian rule and unscrupulous political pragmatism. At first affiliated to the communist party and a proponent of secular government, by the early 1980s he had become increasingly isolated and unpopular and shifted towards the Islamist movement. In 1983 he passed the 'September Laws', which introduced *sharia* criminal law. He was deposed in 1985 following popular protests against rising fuel and food prices and a general strike that paralyzed the country. In 1999, Nimeiri returned to Sudan, from exile in Egypt, at the invitation of President Omar al-Bashir. He died ten years later.

John Garang de Mabior (1945-2005). Leader of the Sudan People's Liberation Army and Movement, principal rebel group in Sudan's second civil war. A Dinka, born in Kongor County, he completed his secondary school education in Tanzania, from where he won a scholarship to Grinnell College in Iowa to study economics. When he returned to Sudan, he joined the Anyanya guerrilla movement not long before the end of the first civil war. After the 1972 Addis Ababa Agreement he was integrated into the Sudanese Army. He returned to Iowa to complete a PhD in Agricultural Economics. In 1983 he became leader of the SPLM/A, with the stated aim of creating a democratic, secular and united 'New Sudan'. He was a charismatic and strong leader, but his often authoritarian suppression of dissent earned him many opponents in the south. He died in a helicopter crash three weeks after being sworn in as First Vice-President of Sudan, following the Comprehensive Peace Agreement of 2005. News of his death sparked violent protests by southerners in Khartoum.

Josephine Bakhita (d.1947). Roman Catholic saint. Born in the second half of the nineteenth century in Darfur, Josephine Bakhita was kidnapped as a child by slave traders, taken east to El-Obeid and sold, eventually, to an Italian diplomat who brought her to Italy and left her in the custody of the Canossian Sisters in Venice. In 1890 she was baptized. Following a dispute with the diplomat, an Italian court ruled that she was no longer a slave and in 1896 she chose to join the order of the Canossian Sisters. She died in 1947. In October 2000, she was declared a saint by the Catholic Church. After the outbreak of conflict in Darfur in 2003 her fame began to spread through Sudan's Catholic community. In 2006, Bakhita Radio Station was established by the Catholic Archdiocese of Juba.

Joseph Lagu (b.1931). Politician. Born in Moli, in the Madi area eighty miles south of Juba, he was admitted to Sudan Military College in 1958 and posted to the 10th Battalion of the Northern Command. In June 1963 he left the army and joined other southern exiles in Kampala, Uganda. With backing from Israel, he was able to unite the various units of the southern rebel movement, Anyanya, under his command. In 1972 he signed the Addis Ababa Agreement. After retiring from the Army, he occupied a number of high-ranking political positions including President of the High Executive Council of the Southern Regional

Assembly, Second Vice-President of Sudan under President Nimeiri, and Sudanese Ambassador to the UN.

Khalil Ibrahim Mohamed. Chairman of the Justice and Equality Movement (JEM). A Kobe Zaghawa from western Darfur, as a member of the National Islamic Front, he held a number of regional government posts including Minister of Health and Minister of Education, before breaking away from the government in the late 1990s after the split between Hassan al-Turabi and Omar al-Bashir.

Lam Akol Ajawin (b.1950). Politician. Before joining the SPLM/A in 1986, a lecturer in chemical engineering at the University of Khartoum. In 1991, together with Riek Machar, he formed a rival SPLA faction to John Garang, whom they had unsuccessfully attempted to overthrow. In 1994 he split from Riek Machar and formed his own SPLA–United faction based in Tonga, Upper Nile. In 2003 he rejoined the SPLA in the south. After the 2005 Comprehensive Peace Agreement he served as the Minister of Foreign Affairs in the Government of National Unity for two years. In June 2009, he launched his own political party, SPLM for Democratic Change, criticizing the SPLM for its poor democratic credentials. He is widely seen as being close to the ruling National Congress Party.

Mahjoub Mohamed Salih (b.1928). Journalist. Together with Mahjoub Osman and Bashir Mohamed Saeed he founded *al-Ayaam*, Sudan's oldest independent daily newspaper, in 1953. Closed twice by Abboud's military government in the 1960s, and nationalized by Nimeiri's military regime in 1970, it was returned to its owners in 1986. The paper was again shut down by the government from 1989 to 1999, re-opening in 2000. Mahjoub Mohamed Salih gained prominence with his shrewd observations of developments in southern Sudan. He was awarded the 2005 Golden Pen International journalism award in recognition of his contribution to the defence and promotion of press freedom. He writes the daily column 'Aswat wa Asdaa' (Voices and Echoes) in *al-Ayaam*.

Mahmud Mohamed Taha (c.1909-1985). Religious and political leader. Born to a farming family in Rufaa, two hundred miles south of Khartoum, he studied engineering at Gordon Memorial College and worked briefly for Sudan railways before starting his own engineering business. In 1945 he founded, with a small group of like-minded friends, the Republican Party, a nationalist party that opposed colonial rule and published a series of inflammatory pamphlets which led to his arrest and brief imprisonment in 1946. Later that year he was again imprisoned after organizing a public demonstration in Rufaa. During this second period in prison, he underwent a spiritual transformation and developed a new, mystical interpretation of Islam. The Republican Party was transformed from a political party into an organization known as the Republican Brothers to promulgate this new concept of Islam, which they did throughout the 1970s and 1980s through public lectures and the distribution of their publications. In the latter days of the Nimeiri government, he published a leaflet demanding the repeal of Nimeiri's 'September laws' that introduced *sharia*. He was charged with apostasy and publicly hanged in the courtyard of Kober Prison in Khartoum on 18 January 1985.

Malik Agar Lyre. Soldier and politician. An Ingessana (Gamk), he was educated at the University of Khartoum. He joined the SPLM/A in 1986. After the 2005 Comprehensive Peace Agreement he became Minister of Investment in the Government of National Unity. In July 2007 he gave up this position to become the Governor of Blue Nile state. He won the governorship in the April 2010 elections. He is an outspoken advocate of increased autonomy for Blue Nile. He was selected as the first Chairman of the new party in northern Sudan to replace SPLM Northern Sector on 8 July 2011, immediately prior to South Sudan's independence.

Mek Nimr (1745-1846). Traditional leader of the Jaaliyin tribe at Shendi, then one of the kingdoms under the Funj Sultanate, in the early nineteenth century. In 1821 he submitted without resistance to the invading army of Ismail Pasha, the son of Muhammad Ali, the Egyptian ruler. But returning north a year later, Ismail is said to have slighted Mek Nimr, striking him across the face with a pipe. Mek Nimr invited Ismail and his soldiers to camp that night at Shendi, and when they were asleep he set fire to their camp, burning them all alive. Muhammad Ali sent an army to avenge the death of his son, but Mek Nimr fled to the borderlands of present-day Ethiopia where he continued to harass the Turco-Egyptian army.

Mini Arkoy Menawi (b. 1968). Leader of the Sudan Liberation Movement/Army-Mini Menawi faction. Born in North Darfur, a former teacher, he was a founder and former Secretary-General of the SLM/A. He split from the group in 2005, forming his own SLA-Mini Menawi faction, which, under his leadership, was the only major Darfur rebel group to sign the Darfur Peace Agreement in 2006. He was appointed Senior Presidential Assistant and head of the Darfur Transitional Authority as part of the agreement but was not reappointed after the April 2010 elections. He has since formally renounced the DPA and called for the overthrow of the Khartoum government.

Mohammed el-Amin (b.1943). Musician. Born in Wad Medani in central Sudan, he learned the *oud* (a lute) at the age of 11. He became honorary president of the Sudanese Artists' and Composers' Society. Jailed by Nimeiri in the 1970s, he left for Cairo in 1989 but returned quietly to Khartoum in 1994.

Mohamed Osman al-Mirghani. Hereditary leader of the Khatmiyya order who became the leader of the Democratic Unionist Party after the death of his father, Ali al-Mirghani, in 1968. He was a founding member and president of the National Democratic Alliance, a coalition of Sudanese opposition parties in exile formed in 1989 to restore national democracy and to oppose the NIF/NCP regime. In the last decade, however, the DUP has formed closer ties to the ruling National Congress party.

Mohamed Wardi (b.1932). Musician, known as 'The Golden Throat'. A Nubian, born near old Wadi Halfa, he went to school in Egypt and returned as an elementary school teacher. He moved to Khartoum in 1957 and became a professional singer two years later. He sings both in Arabic and in his native Nubian language and has done much throughout his professional career of more than five decades to promote Nubian culture and language. Not shy of mixing politics with music, he was arrested under Nimeiri's government and in 1989 went into voluntary exile, only returning to Sudan in 2002. In 1992, Wardi famously performed a concert for southern Sudanese displaced by the war at Itang refugee camp in south-west Ethiopia.

Muhammad Ahmad al-Mahdi (1844-1885). Religious leader who defeated the Turco-Egyptian forces and conquered Khartoum. Muhammad Ahmad was born on the Island of Labab, ten miles south of Dongola. Attracted to a life of religious asceticism and worship from a young age, he sought instruction from various sheikhs of the Sammaniya Sufi order. On becoming a Sheikh of the order himself, he spent several years in seclusion. In March 1881 on Aba Island, in what is now White Nile State, he experienced a number of visions in which the Prophet Muhammad appointed him the Mahdi, 'the Expected One', the religious redeemer who would prepare the way for the second coming of the Prophet Isa (Jesus) shortly before the Day of Judgement. Three months later, on Aba Island, he publicly declared himself to be the Mahdi and called for religious revival and *jihad* against the unpopular Turco-Egyptian regime. His revolt gathered strength and spread following a succession of military victories – most prominently, the conquest of El-Obeid and the defeat of 10,000 Egyptian troops at Shaykan, both in 1881. In 1885, the Mahdist army captured Khartoum, defeating General Charles Gordon and his forces. He died six months later in Omdurman, aged 41.

Musa Hilal (b.1961). The most prominent of the leaders of the government-supported militias in Darfur known as *janjawid*, appointed an adviser to the Khartoum government in 2008. He is the son of Sheikh Hilal Abdalla of the Um Jalul clan of the Mahamid section of Abbala Rizeigat in North Darfur. He is accused of leading the *janjawid*, from his base in Mistiriha, on a platform of Arab supremacism. In 2006 the UN Security Council adopted resolution 1672 that imposed travel restrictions and financial sanctions on Musa Hilal and three other Sudanese suspected of committing war crimes in Darfur.

Mustafa Said Ahmed (d.1996). Created a distinctive genre of Sudanese music introducing sophisticated, politically charged modern lyrics to Sudanese listeners. He enjoyed huge popularity in student and intellectual circles in the 1980s and 1990s. In 1989, after the military coup, he was forced into exile, first in Russia, then in Egypt and finally in Qatar where he died of kidney failure in 1996. His body was received by thousands at Khartoum airport.

Nafie Ali Nafie. Deputy leader of the ruling National Congress Party and Assistant to the President. Nafie Ali Nafie grew up in al-Nafab, a village not far from from Shendi, and studied agriculture at Khartoum University, where he taught until 1989. He was in charge of the state security apparatus in the early years of the Islamist Ingaz ('Salvation') government that came to power in a military coup in 1989. Named by Egypt and Ethiopia in connection with the assassination attempt on Egyptian President Hosni Mubarak in Addis Ababa in 1995, Nafie was officially transferred from security to the Ministry of Agriculture. In recent years he has re-emerged as one of the most powerful figures in the ruling National Congress Party.

Ngundeng Bong (*c.* 1830-1906). Nuer Prophet. Born at the end of the 1830s to a family of Gaaleak earth-masters, Ngundeng is generally considered to have been the most famous of the Nuer prophets. His prophecies and messages spread widely through hymns and praise-songs, which he presented in this form so that they could be easily remembered and transmitted. The Anglo-Egyptian adminis-tration, fearful of religious leaders who might, like the Mahdi, incite rebellion, perceived Ngundeng to be a dangerous threat and launched a number of punitive campaigns against him, and other southern prophets. In 1928, more than two decades after his death, government forces destroyed Ngundeng's last and largest shrine, a 60-foot mound, and killed his son Guek, also a prophet. In southern Sudan, Ngundeng is remembered for his peacemaking abilities and for his foretelling of the coming of war and foreign aggression.

Omar Hassan Ahmed al-Bashir (b.1944). Rose to power in the military coup that ousted Sadiq al-Mahdi's elected government in June 1989. He has been the head of the party, the NIF/NCP, that has ruled Sudan ever since. A Jaali, born in the village of Hosh Bannaga, between Shendi and the capital, Khartoum, he joined the army at 16 and studied at military academies in Cairo, Khartoum and Malaysia. He was appointed commander of the Eighth Brigade in southern Sudan in 1988. Following the NIF coup a year later, al-Bashir became the Chairman of the Revolutionary Command Council, the executive body of the new regime, and assumed the title of President in 1993. He was elected for further terms in 1996, 2000 and 2010 in flawed elections. In 1999 he consolidated his internal position within the NIF/NCP by briefly imprisoning Hassan al-Turabi, the ideological architect of the Islamist movement, and thereafter sidelining him from power. In March 2009, the International Criminal Court issued an arrest warrant for al-Bashir for war crimes and crimes against humanity, and in 2010, for genocide committed in Darfur.

Pagan Amum Okiech. Soldier and politician. An early recruit from the Shilluk area to the SPLM/A, he was trained in Cuba and became an SPLA Commander, later working closely with the National Democratic Alliance, a coalition of Sudanese opposition parties formed in 1989 to oppose the ruling Islamist government. He was closely associated with the New Sudan policy of the SPLM both before and after Garang's death. He was elected Secretary-General of the SPLM and, following the 2010 elections, was appointed Minster for Peace and CPA Implementation in GoSS, with primary responsibility for overseeing the negotiations for the final separation of the south.

Paulino Matip Nhial. Leader of Anyanya II, a southern rebel movement that became a pro-Khartoum militia. A Bul Nuer from Upper Nile, he allied with Riek Machar following the 1997 Khartoum Peace Agreement. From 2001, he was the Overall Commander-in-Chief of the primarily Nuer South Sudan Defence Force. He later formed the South Sudan Unity Movement/Army, a Bentiu-based militia supported by the government in Khartoum that was involved in forcibly displacing citizens from around the oil fields. However, a year after the 2005 Comprehensive Peace Agreement, he signed the Juba Declaration with Salva Kiir Mayardit, merged his forces with the SPLA and became the SPLA Deputy Commander-in-Chief.

Riek Machar Teny Dhurgon (b.1952). Became Vice-President of the Govern-ment of Southern Sudan in 2005. A Dok Nuer from Upper Nile, he gained a PhD in Engineering in the UK and joined John Garang's SPLA shortly after it was formed and became one its most senior commanders. In 1991 Riek Machar, alongside Lam Akol and Gordon Kong, attempted to overthrow John Garang as leader of the SPLA, forming SPLA Nasir faction, later renamed SPLA-United, with self-determination for southern Sudan as its declared aim. In 1996 he signed a Peace Charter with the northern government and then the Khartoum Peace Agreement a year later. In 2000 he left the government and returned to the south to rejoin the war against Khartoum. He rejoined the SPLM/A in 2002. He became Vice-President of Southern Sudan after John Garang's death in 2005 and was reappointed for a second term in 2010.

Sadiq Siddiq al-Mahdi (b.1935). Politician, great-grandson of the Mahdi and the current leader of the Umma Party. Born in Omdurman, he attended university in Khartoum and Oxford. In 1965, aged thirty, he won a seat in Parliament. The following year he became Sudan's youngest Prime Minister. However, within ten months his government collapsed. In 1976, when he was out of the country, his supporters staged, with Libyan backing, an unsuccessful coup attempt against Nimeiri's government. He was tried in absentia and sentenced to death. He remained in exile until invited back to Sudan again as part of Nimeiri's 'national reconciliation' in the late 1970s. He was elected Prime Minister for a second time following the return to civilian rule in 1986. Between then and 1989, he headed a series of weak coalitions, doing little, his critics argue, to prevent the NIF coup in 1989 that ended his premiership.

Salva Kiir Mayardit (b.1951). Soldier and politician. Joined the Anyanya rebel movement in the late 1960s, reaching the rank of Major by the end of the civil war in 1972. A Rek Dinka from Northern Bahr al-Ghazal, Salva Kiir was one of the founders of the SPLM/A and in 1999, became the Chief of Staff and deputy to its leader John Garang. He played a decisive role in the reunification of the SPLA, negotiating with Riek Machar and later with Lam Akol. After John Garang's death in July 2005, Salva Kiir became the President of Southern Sudan and First Vice-President of Sudan and formed a government that incorporated many of the movement's former opponents and rival factions. He was elected President of Southern Sudan in April 2010.

Tayeb Salih (1929-2009). Writer. He published his first work in Beirut in 1966, a collection of short stories in Arabic, *The Doum Tree of Wad Hamid*, and gained international acclaim when his novel *Mawsim al-Hijra ila al-Shamal* (1968) was published in English in 1970 as *Season of Migration to the North*. This was followed by another, *The Wedding of Zain* which was made into a film, but many of his other works remain untranslated. Born in Karkmakol, northern Sudan, Tayeb Salih spent most of his life in Europe and the Gulf, dying in London, aged 80, in 2009.

Yasir Said Arman. Senior northern Sudanese member of SPLM/A. A Cairo University graduate and former member of the Sudanese Communist Party, he joined the SPLM/A in 1986 becoming a commander and official spokesman of the SPLM. After the 2005 Comprehensive Peace Agreement he was appointed leader of the SPLM parliamentary group in the National Assembly, member of the SPLM Political Bureau and Executive Committee, and Deputy Secretary-General of SPLM Northern Sector. He was the SPLM's presidential candidate in the April 2010 elections, and gained 21.69 per cent of votes despite the withdrawal of his candidacy by the SPLM on the eve of voting. After the January 2011 referendum on self-determination for the south it was announced that the SPLM Northern Sector would form a new political party in the north on 8 July 2011, immediately prior to the formal secession of the South, with Yasir Arman as its Secretary General.

Yousif Kuwa Mekki (1945-2001) was a member of the SPLA High Command and SPLM governor of the Nuba Mountains during the north-south civil war. A Nuba from Miri, he attended Khartoum University and worked as a teacher in Darfur and the Nuba Mountains before being elected to the Kordofan Regional Assembly in 1981. He joined the SPLA in 1984 and went for training in Ethiopia and Cuba. He created a civil administration in the Nuba Mountains with high standards of accountability and struggled, with limited success, to bring international attention to the plight of its inhabitants. He died of cancer in 2001, aged 55, in Norwich, England.

Zubeir Rahma Mansur (1830-1913). Slave-trader. He left Khartoum in 1856 with a small army and travelled south, establishing zaribas – armed camps for trading slaves and ivory – as he went. By 1869, he controlled an extensive slave-trading empire in western Bahr al-Ghazal and was appointed Governor of the region by the Turco-Egyptian authorities. In 1874 he invaded Darfur and overthrew the Fur Sultanate, in return for which he was awarded the titles Bey and Pasha by the Egyptian Khedive Ismail Pasha. When General Gordon, who was appointed Governor General of Sudan in 1877, tried to suppress the slave trade, Zubeir Rahma Mansur travelled to Cairo to protest the fact that the Khedive had appointed an Egyptian as governor of Darfur and to make his claim for the position of governor of Darfur. When he tried to return to Sudan, he was refused permission to leave Egypt and settled in Cairo. He was permitted to return to his native country after the Anglo-Egyptian reconquest of Sudan in 1898.

Index